"They just found a baby in the walls of the Delta House," said B.J.

There was a shocked silence in the beauty parlor. "But that's impossible," said Sandy. "What on earth are you talking about?"

"Well, not a live baby," B.J. said. "It's a skeleton. In the airshaft—the one in that back bathroom."

Edyth looked thoughtful. "The airshaft . . . ?" Mary Alice asked, a blank look on her face.

"That airshaft was closed, wasn't it?" B.J. said.

"They had it open when they put in that bathroom." Sandy smiled grimly. "They closed it again after they finished . . . that summer. The summer all of us were there."

Friendships, Secrets and Lies

(former title: THE WALLS CAME TUMBLING DOWN)

BABS H. DEAL

FAWCETT CREST • NEW YORK

FRIENDSHIPS, SECRETS AND LIES
(former title: *THE WALLS CAME TUMBLING DOWN*)

THIS BOOK CONTAINS THE COMPLETE TEXT OF THE
ORIGINAL HARDCOVER EDITION.

Published by Fawcett Crest Books, a unit of CBS Publications,
the Consumer Publishing Division of CBS Inc., by arrangement
with Doubleday & Company.

ISBN: 0-449-24253-6

First Fawcett Crest printing: August 1969

New Edition: November 1979

Printed in the United States of America

11   10   9   8   7   6   5   4   3   2

For Borden—again

My grateful appreciation to The MacDowell Colony, Peterborough, New Hampshire, and especially to its director, Mr. George Kendall, for the time and space in which to finish this novel.

∞

Part
One

∞

Miley Innes left his brick house in Westwood at six o'clock on a mild late February morning. He carried a lunchpail containing two roast beef sandwiches, three hard-boiled eggs, and a thermos of coffee. He carried a jacket because sometimes the wind picked up in the afternoon. There was little traffic on University Road although occasionally a car passed him on the way to take workers out to the Finch Paper Mill. A slight mist, mixed with industrial fumes, lay groundward, but the sun was clearing it off. As he passed Hatter's Lake he could see the glint on the water and he thought that when this job was over he would have to go fishing again. He hadn't had a chance to go fishing in a long time. It had been a good year for the building trade.

There had been a lot of work from the university since the new president had come in. Dr. Edwards liked to see new buildings going up and old ones coming down. That was what Miley was going to do today, work at taking an old one down. It was a sorority house on the corner of University and Oak Lane. The street was still called that even though there weren't many oaks anymore. The new president liked to cut down trees, too. It was easy work because the building wasn't really old. The really old ones were hell; they had built them to stay up. But the Delta House had been put up sometime in the late thirties when builders were already getting the idea of obsolescence. The job was going well. They ought to have the lot cleared by the end of the week. Then Oscar Ridley could start to build his new concrete-block box for the Deltas. This was the first sorority house to be rebuilt; all the fraternity houses had been. There had been a fire in the Sigma Chi House and they'd had to rebuild. Within five years there wasn't an old house left on fraternity row, except for the Dekes, and they remodeled. Though from what Miley had heard Oscar hadn't done too well on that job. There were too many people persuading him to cut costs.

When they finished this job there was the new country club coming up. That would keep them busy up till the next summer. It was going to look like an airline terminal, but that wasn't any of his business. He was a carpenter, not an architect. Oscar Ridley wasn't an architect either, but nobody except Miley Innes knew that.

Oscar and Miley had started out together at the old River Lumber Company during the depression. They used to saw boards. Sometimes, if Old Man Finch was in a good mood, they got to look at a blueprint; but not often. Then World War II came along and Miley spent a spell of time in Pacific invasions and loading rice for the Japanese on the docks at Manila, trying to dodge the bombs the Americans were dumping on them. When he got back to Druid City, Oscar Ridley was the bright young man who had bought up the Hatter's Lake land and was going to fill it with low-cost housing for the influx the postwar years were going to bring to Druid City. By 1950 Oscar was designing houses for the doctors and lawyers on Cherokee Drive. By 1960 he was designing them all new houses at Warrior Shores.

Miley didn't have anything special against Oscar. He was even fond of him. But he wouldn't have done business with

10

him. He just worked and took his pay check on Friday and let the union make sure he got it.

He stopped at the traffic light on the edge of the campus and waved at Mary Alice Cross, who was getting out of her car in front of her dress shop. She was an awfully good-looking woman to have just become a grandma. She went into her shop next door to his wife's beauty parlor and he wondered if Edyth would be able to get her car started. It wasn't much of a second car, but he came in too early for her to have to haul out with him and it was better than nothing.

At the next corner he saw the pickup truck that belonged to the company and knew the first crew were already in. But not working, he'd bet. They'd sit around smoking and drinking coffee till he showed up. Which was the reason Oscar kept him as foreman even if he'd like to forget sometime about all that lumber sawing.

He parked around the corner on Oak Lane and got out of the car. It was going to be a warm day. He could feel it in the sun on his back. February was a good time of year in Druid City, Alabama. The cold days and the one snow ended with January. They might get a snap or two—Black-berry Winter, Easter Sunday Winter—but the really cold days were gone. He walked across the rubble on the green lawn.

The remains of the house stood forlornly against the blue of sky. Roofing was scattered around the lot and the doors and windows had already been hauled off. There was only a small area toward the back that hadn't come down. It contained a bathroom and an airshaft coming down to the kitchen. They'd left it Friday afternoon so as to get a good start on it this Monday morning. Miley ran a hand through his sparse gray hair, squinted at the sun, and started climbing. The two Negro workmen and the new boy, who'd gotten there early for once, followed him up the scaffolding.

From where he paused against the sky he could see into the stadium bowl. It looked grand and empty and beautiful. Miley admired the stadium. It was clean, functional, and

11

well built. It was going to last awhile, too, because even Oscar and the new college president couldn't persuade anybody that it needed to be replaced. Beyond it were the old streets with the old houses become boarding houses. He wondered how long they had. Closer to hand was the campus, new buildings intermixed with old. Far away in the other direction were the suburbs, and farther away, to the left, downtown. All the lumber and brick and concrete of Druid City. He couldn't help seeing it that way, a collection of building materials. As he often did, he thought about what one bomb could do to it, and he looked at what one small crew of men could do to one building like this one, and he sighed.

The upper bathroom was evidently an addition to the house. It was built out over the kitchen and after the inner walls came down Miley could see it had been built into an older part of the building, probably a storeroom. The inner walls which contained the old airshaft that had led down to meet the kitchen vent were much more solidly constructed than the beaverboard and plaster inner walls. He went to work on them himself.

By eleven o'clock Miley was sweaty, dirty, and choked with plaster, but the inner walls were down and the shaft was open. He started throwing brick out behind him. At 11:30 A.M. he found the skeleton of the baby in the wall.

1944

The world turned from Gemini through Leo, Sirius and the long hot dusty days of summer. World War II went on in the Pacific; World War II went on in Germany. In America the days were long and hot and still and in a time between.

There were nine of them in the Delta House that summer, nine girls and an old woman to look after them and a woman in the kitchen who loved them. Nine girls in a tower that wasn't—as towers never are—inviolate.

The Delta House was tall and wide and white with columns across the front and french doors on three sides. There was a fan light over the wide front door and the bricks of the porch, unlike the white-painted ones of the walls, were old and red and worn and had been given a patina by feet. The house rode the empty sea of the campus like a ship lost in the horse latitudes. There was no V-12 program at Druid City U. and the few men left on campus had gone home for summer jobs to help keep their draft deferments in. The girls had gone home to lie in hammocks and write V-mail letters. Only a few stayed for the summer session, fewer still for the long vacation of late-summer early-fall.

The nine of them in the Delta House stayed because they had nothing better to do, and because when they had discussed it in the spring it had seemed an adventure. If as many as nine would stay they'd keep the house open for them.

Dolly Cowan hadn't wanted to take the job as temporary housemother for the Delta Sorority for the summer session. She'd wanted to spend the summer with her daughter and grandchild in California, where her daughter had gone to be near port in case her husband, who commanded an LST, got into port for repairs. But she'd needed the money—and she hadn't been sure Katie had needed her. She'd consoled herself by saying she'd get a lot of sewing done. There wouldn't be many girls in the house and they wouldn't be dating much. There weren't many young men to date. Mrs. Jason, the regular housemother, had told her she'd managed to engage Clarissa Johnson, the regular cook, for the summer and Clarissa worked magic with ration books. There wouldn't be any formal functions at all, and they'd decided to have only one wing open so the housekeeping problems were minimized.

It was only after she'd accepted the job and written her daughter that the administration had informed her they were going to use the summer term to do repair work on the house. That was an annoyance and it was unfair of them not to tell her, but she'd just have to make the best of it. She did see the sense of it. They could begin the work with only the few girls in the house and finish it during the long

13

vacation. Besides, as they'd told her, they'd been lucky to get the priority at all.

She considered her position as she waited for the nine girls assigned to her care to come to her rooms for the getting-to-know-you tea she'd arranged. She was comfortable. Her predecessor's quarters were spacious and cheerful. The pay, while small, would certainly augment her small insurance money. The girls, from what she had seen of them as they settled in, were bright, well-brought-up young ladies. They were all from good homes, good families. Dolly Cowan believed in the verities of the American way of life. She was a terrific snob.

She arranged the tea service again, and settled her new cameo pin on her bosom. When the first knock came on the door she said, "Come in," in her affected, insecure voice.

She was glad to see that the first arrival was B.J. B.J. put her at her ease as none of the other girls did. She was big, rawboned, gawky, but with a clear blue gaze as innocent as a teddy bear. In fact she looked like a teddy bear, Dolly thought. Big, blond, warm, and huggable.

Dolly had decided to learn all the first names very firmly, then add the last ones as she went along. But B.J.'s last name she knew automatically, B.J. was a Lowe of Mobile, Alabama. And the Lowes were the Lowes. Her real name was Barbara Jean, but nobody called her that. She even signed her checks B.J., so Mrs. Cowan had bowed to custom.

"Come in, dear," she said. "Just have a seat anywhere. As soon as we're all here we'll have a little tea together."

"Yessum," B.J. said. She pushed her blond hair back with a brown hand and smiled.

"I should have thought you girls would have liked a vacation," Mrs. Cowan said. "I can't imagine why you want to come to summer school."

B.J. smiled. "Have you ever spent a summer in Mobile?" she said.

"I should think it would be pleasant," Dolly said. "It's a lovely city."

"It's the end of the earth," B.J. said.

There was another knock on the door. Two girls came in

14

this time, both looking a little disheveled but dressed nicely in print dresses and white sandals. "Sandy and Meredith," she said.

They both murmured yessum and sat down.

She contemplated the two of them, thinking that they were probably her two problems, if problems she had. They were both always in a hurry, always having been somewhere or going somewhere; both small, tense girls . . . girls she thought of as "attractive to boys." She couldn't have brought herself to say what she really thought which was "sexy."

They didn't look alike. Sandy was redheaded, with green eyes and a small, intricately shaped mouth. She was not really pretty, but vital. And she had absolutely astonishing legs. Meredith had good legs too but they didn't actually startle you the way Sandy's did. She was brown-haired and brown-eyed with a faint dusting of freckles on her nose. She had lovely hands, but Mrs. Cowan couldn't help noticing that her fingernails were bitten to the quick . . . another bad sign. Still, they were both nice girls. And both from right here in Druid City. Most of the girls here in the house this summer were. Delta was the local sorority and always had a preponderance of local girls.

"What a simply wonderful tea set," Sandy said.

"Thank you, dear. It belongs to Mrs. Jason," she said.

"Well, she never uses it," Sandy said. "I think it's nice of you to ask us to tea."

"I thought it would be a good way for us all to get a little better acquainted," Mrs. Cowan said. "There are so few of us here together. We must all be friends."

Meredith looked at her solemnly. So did Sandy. B.J. got up and went to look out the window. "Here comes Martha," she said. "Right on the dot. We were all afraid we'd be late and were therefore early. But not Martha. Here she is, right on time."

A knock on the door and all three girls exchanged amused glances.

Mrs. Cowan was annoyed. Martha was the steadiest of all her girls. She knew she would never cause trouble. But she had to admit she couldn't feel the warmth for her she did for B.J., or even that she did for those two scalawags sitting on her sofa.

Martha was wearing a neat navy blue suit and high-heeled shoes. She smiled impersonally at everybody and sat in a straight chair. "It's a very lovely afternoon," she said.

"Oh, come on, Martha," B.J. said. "Mrs. Cowan doesn't want us to feel formal. It's not like rush week."

Martha just looked at her.

Sandy smiled and fidgeted. Mrs. Cowan knew she wanted a cigarette, but she didn't tell them they could smoke. It wasn't that she was being cruel—they would eventually anyway. She just didn't think she should endorse it.

The small silence was broken by Joan Holmes's entrance. It was an entrance. Joan always made one. She was pretty, almost movie-star pretty, but with none of the vitality or whatever that Sandy and Meredith had. It was candy-box pretty, fluffy blond hair held back by an aqua halo of twisted silk, wide blue eyes, white skin, pink cheeks. She had on an aqua dress and shoes to match. She paused in the doorway. "Well . . . hi," she said.

Two girls entered behind her.

"We've been trying to catch you all the way across the campus, Joan," one of them said.

"You looked like you were strolling," the other said. "But you must have been running."

Joan bestowed a smile on each of them.

Mrs. Cowan watched the tableau. The two girls behind Joan were obviously her stooges. Neither of them seemed to be particularly friendly with any of the other girls. One of them, Dolores Powell, was a painfully ugly girl. She had bad skin and a thin face with too many teeth for her mouth. She was scrawny and unprepossessing. She came from Memphis. Why, the housemother wondered, do the ugly ones always pick the prettiest ones to run around with. She wasn't subtle enough to realize it was generally the other way around. The other girl, Kathryn Hodges, was from Newcastle, as Joan was, and they had been in high school

16

together. She was older and had sponsored Joan for the sorority.

The other girls watched Joan and her satellites in affectionate amusement.

"Been to play practice, Joanie?" Sandy said.

"No," Joan said. "I had to see one of my professors about my schedule."

"The brain," Sandy said.

"Oh, Sandy," Meredith said.

"Well, who's missing?" Mrs. Cowan said.

"Mary Alice and Edyth," Martha said. "They're probably trying to catch the last mail."

Mrs. Cowan glanced at her watch. "I think I'll tell Clarissa to bring the tea," she said.

"I'll tell her," Sandy said. She jumped up, paused, added, "If you like . . ."

"Fine, dear," Mrs. Cowan said. She watched Sandy go out the door, then turned to the other girls. "Well, is everyone getting settled into classes?" she said. They all murmured back at her. Then Sandy came back with Clarissa, the tea, and the two missing girls.

Mary Alice was a pretty thing too, Mrs. Cowan thought. There certainly wasn't any dearth of looks around this house. She was tall and brunette with blue eyes and a quiet smile. But there was a controlled energy about her that made Mrs. Cowan put her on the Meredith-Sandy-B.J. side of the register rather than the Martha-Joan. She wasn't sure what she meant by that, but she divided them that way in her mind. There was an acceptance of femininity in Joan and staid Martha that the others didn't have. That was as close as she could come to it.

Edyth she couldn't figure out at all. There was a certain placidity of appearance about Edyth that her eyes completely denied. She had the look of a very competent little airline stewardess, Mrs. Cowan thought. Except for those eyes. They were far too intelligent, far too aware and interested to go with the rest of the rather aseptic little face and body. She shook hands with Mrs. Cowan, taking her aback, and sat down on a footstool.

17

"B.J., would you help serve the tea?" Mrs. Cowan said.

B.J. blushed. "I'll probably break something," she said. "But O.K."

"You pour, Joan, please."

"Yes, m'am," Joan said, arranging her skirts and sitting up straight behind the teapot.

"You look just like Alice, Joanie," Sandy said. "I'll be the Mad Hatter and Meredith can be the March Hare and Edyth can be the dormouse."

"Everybody move down, please," Meredith said.

Sandy lit a cigarette. So did Meredith. Martha frowned at them.

"One lump or two, Mrs. Cowan?" Joan said.

B.J. laughed. "You know we don't have any real sugar," she said.

"But it sounds right," Joan said. "I can't say, How much substitute?" She poured daintily into the thin cups and B.J. took them from her and passed them around.

"Are your rooms all right?" Mrs. Cowan said, stirring her tea.

"Great," B.J. said. "Everybody having one to themselves is the best part."

"They're going to start the work tomorrow," Mrs. Cowan said. "I hope it won't inconvenience you too much."

"We're fine," Sandy said. "There is honeysuckle blooming and the campus is as empty as space. It's . . . I don't know . . . different. But fun."

Mrs. Cowan smiled on them all. "I think we're all going to get along beautifully," she said.

On the way to their rooms Sandy stopped and stuck her head in the kitchen door. "Clarissa, Clarissa," she said to the tall Negress sitting at the table. "The honeysuckle's blooming."

"It do be, honey," Clarissa said.

"Come on, Sandy," Meredith said. "You promised to play me a hand of gin before supper."

"I owe you nine thousand eight hundred and fifty dollars and sixteen cents," Sandy said.

18

"You can pay me when you become a famous ballerina," Meredith said.

Sandy pirouetted across the oak floor, fetching up against B.J., who was leaning on the staircase. They collapsed against each other, giggling.

"Oh, my Lord," Martha said, walking up behind them. "When are you all ever going to grow up?"

"Martha," Sandy said. "Growing up is loving what you can afford to. I doubt I'll ever make it."

"What's that supposed to mean?" Martha said.

"Nothing, Martha," Sandy said. "Nothing at all. Come on, Meredith. Cut for deal."

They had made their rooms their own, luxuriating in each having a double one all to themselves. In Sandy's there was a painting of a wild blue-haired nymph with a body suspiciously like Sandy's, flaunting nakedness to a blue forest. Underneath it was a bottle with varicolored candle drippings. Inside the closet door a picture of Oscar Wilde hung opposite one of Lord Alfred Douglas, so that poor Oscar seemed to gaze in impossible longing at Alfred every time Sandy wanted to change her clothes. She and Meredith sat on the bed to play gin. After a couple of hands Edyth wandered in.

"This room looks like Greenwich Village," she said.

Sandy laughed. "What would you rather I had around?" she said. "Van Johnson in that sweater? Or Robert Walker, gazing in anguish?"

"Oh, nuts," Edyth said.

"Hey," Sandy said. "What's all this about remodeling the house? How'd they get a priority?"

"Oh, I wrote Miley about it," Edyth said. "He said there wouldn't be any trouble about it if the alumni money was right." Miley was Edyth's boy friend who had been in the building trade and was now in the South Pacific.

"You and Miley are cynics," Sandy said.

"Well, somebody has to offset Martha and B.J.," Edyth said.

"B.J.'s an optimist all right," Sandy said. "But Martha? I wonder. I wonder if she isn't the cynic of us all."

19

"I heard that," Martha said from the doorway. "You'd better hurry. You haven't got but about fifteen minutes to lose another hundred to Meredith before supper." She went on down the hall to her own room.

Martha's room was, oddly enough, cluttered. It was antiseptically clean; she scrubbed the floor herself in between the maid's half-hearted cleanings, and she changed her sheets every two days. But she let clutter accumulate. She could never seem to put her mind to the task of clearing it all away and putting it in the appropriate place. Martha's mind moved slowly. She knew this, but it didn't bother her. She thought it was a sign of stability. Quick minds, like Sandy's and Meredith's, were too emotional. Edyth and Mary Alice she thought of as more stable. But she had to admit their rooms were as neat as monks' cells. They both had a sort of efficiency she lacked. Once they'd both come in and tried to tell her how to go about getting rid of the clutter. Edyth would say, "Martha, take all those books on the desk and line them up one beside the other." Then Mary Alice would say, "Martha, take all those little doodads on the dresser and put them inside a drawer." They'd ended up laughing and going for Cokes when she'd said, "But I need them where I can find them." She went to the dresser and picked up her lipstick, which was right where it should be on top of the dresser, and fixed her face for supper. Down the hall she could hear B.J. talking to Joan, B.J.'s room, of course, looked like a gym: tennis shoes, tennis rackets, sweaters, suntan oil, and even bottles of liniment. Martha laughed and shook her head. "We're a real crew," she told her image in the mirror. "A real weird crew, as Sandy would say."

Joan's room was full of bottles and jars and boxes. She had a white-framed mirror on her bureau and stuffed dogs and cats on her bed and a fluffy pink rug on her floor.

"I always feel like I'll knock something over," B.J. said, sitting in the one comfortable chair and throwing her leg over the arm.

"Silly," Joan said.

"You got a date tonight?" B.J. said.

"Yes," Joan said. "What shall I wear? It's so hot. I think my yellow thing." She opened her closet door.

"Try a sweet smile," B.J. said.

"Oh, you," Joan said. "You going out?"

"Maybe." She yawned and stretched. "I need to practice my backhand. My God, I wish the supper bell would ring. I'm starved."

Supper was a cozy meal at one long table in the empty dining room. The french doors stood open on the twilight, the smell of honeysuckle drifting into the room, the last sunrays striping the carpet.

"Remember the old fairy tale, 'The Snow Queen'?" Sandy said. "It was always my favorite. The last line said, 'And it was summer, glorious summer.' That's just how this time of day makes me feel."

"Sandy," Martha said, "you're a romantic."

"And you're a pragmatist," Edyth said.

"What are you, Edyth?" Meredith said.

"Something in between," Edyth said. "What're you?"

"I don't know," Meredith said. "I never thought about it."

"You're a romantic," Edyth said. "And B.J.'s a romantic. Joan's a pragmatist. Mary Alice is a pragmatist. And Dolores and Dot are romantics."

"Just like that?" B.J. said.

"No, nothing's ever just like that," Edyth said. "But approximately."

"Well, we've got peaches for dessert," B.J. said, "and I intend to feel romantically pragmatic about them."

"Let's take them out on the porch to eat," Sandy said.

"You see?" Edyth said.

They all went outside and sat on the steps to eat peaches and cream and watch the slow late twilight come over the empty campus. A new moon was visible over the Kappa House down the row, a thin sliver of silver on a darkening sky.

"Make a wish," B.J. said.

They were all silent, gazing at the frail bow against the blue.

21

"It's turning blue," Sandy said. "Once in a blue moon. That means the wishes will all come true."

"That means you all wishes too much," Clarissa said from the door. "Bring me them dishes back to the kitchen. Gonna be midnight before I get washed up."

"What do you wish, Clarissa?" Sandy said.

"Wish wishes grew on trees," Clarissa said.

They sat on in the coming dark for a while, smoking, watching the stars come out, reluctant to go about plans for the night. The heavy scent of honeysuckle was around them, the night sky over them, and a long way away the future was being forged for them on the world's battlefields. It didn't really touch them. They were all young, all immortal, and all—whether they knew it or not—beautiful.

Behind them the white brick of the Delta House was bathed in starlight. It seemed very solid and strong and enduring. In the kitchen Clarissa hummed a song.

Mary Alice Cross shut the door to the Campus Corner behind her and made a face at the sound of the tinkling bell. She had had to come in early every day for two weeks for end-of-January inventory and stay late every night. She was sleepy, irritable, and tired. The student help she'd gotten this semester wasn't worth a damn and her daughter, Shari, was still at home with the baby. She and Sue Winston were holding it up alone and they just weren't enough.

It was a neat well-run dress shop. Only last year she'd been able to do a minimum of remodeling and she still enjoyed the softer lights, thicker carpet, and the cozy space behind the cash register where they kept the coffeepot. She hurried back and put it on.

The Campus Corner had been a ploy. Once, so long ago now it didn't seem real, she'd told Lew Cross if he couldn't make any more money she would. Well, she had. She put her purse under the counter and sat down. She'd started out with a loan from B. J. Finch, a year's lease on the store from Old Scrooge, Oscar Ridley, and a good mad on. She had, ten years later, one of the best businesses in Druid City.

She looked at her racks of dresses, her neat shelves of lingerie, the costume jewelry in a glass case, the sweaters and purses and umbrellas and leather belts, depleted now from the January sales, and at the stack of boxes containing the first part of the spring line. They had to be unpacked today. She switched on the lights, watching fluorescence bathe the baubles. She poured her cup of coffee. The phone rang.

"Mother!" Shari said.

Mary Alice glanced at her watch. "What are you doing up at this hour?" she said.

"Well, what do you *think?* This baby got me up. It's the hungriest baby in the whole wide world, and I just couldn't ask Bill to get up and do it today. He had a lab practical till all *hours* last night."

"So what is it, baby?" Mary Alice said.

"I need ten dollars."

Mary Alice sighed. "Shari, I just gave you twenty dollars."

"I know it, but I had to pay the TV man."

Mary Alice looked at her purse. She knew what was in it: one lipstick, keys, Kleenex, three notes to herself on scratch paper, her glasses, and ten dollars. She'd been trying not to mess up the bank account by writing a check before she finished inventory. "Come get it," she said.

"Well, I haven't got the car. Bill . . ."

Mary Alice permitted herself just a little irritation. "I haven't had my coffee yet," she said. "I'll call you back when Sue gets here."

"All right, Mother," Shari said meekly. She hung up.

Mary Alice tasted her coffee, made a face, said, "Oh shit," and took it and poured it down the sink and poured a hot cup. She looked down at her neat Italian shoes and felt better. She'd always loved shoes and only lately had she been able to afford the kind she liked. Her feet, well shod, elegant, detached, reassured her. She was able to enjoy her coffee.

She saw Edyth Innes drive up in her beat-up old Dodge. Edyth looked tired too. January was hard on everybody.

23

Usually she was at work by this time, but Shari had upset her concentration. Back when they were all having their first babies Sandy Mackintosh had said, "Children interrupt your continuity of thought." She smiled. How right Sandy had been. They interrupted it as soon as you missed your first period and as near as she could figure that was the end of concentrated thought for the female of the species. For everybody, that is, except B. J. Finch whose five didn't faze her. But then maybe B.J. had never had any continuity of thought. Though she'd been smart enough to invest in the Campus Corner, and smart enough so that Mary Alice had had to move heaven and earth to buy her out.

The bell tinkled and Sue came in. Mary Alice set another cup out and poured coffee.

"God," Sue said.

"Yeah," Mary Alice said. "Shari's already called this morning, and two more boxes came in after you left last night."

"Do you think anybody would believe running a nice high-toned dress shop is a job for a wrestler?" Sue said.

"Nope. Drink your coffee."

Sue Winston was Mary Alice's age, forty-two, but she hadn't held up like Mary Alice. Few women did. Mary Alice was tall, slender, her hair still black, her eyes still a large surprised blue. People always found it difficult to believe Shari was her daughter. The year Shari had been a Year Book Beauty, Mary Alice had gotten enough compliments on her own looks to last a lifetime. Shari looked like her, but there was a certain softness in her face that had never been in Mary Alice's. Artists and people who knew bone structure had no problem choosing between the two faces. Sue Winston had been a pretty girl too, but she'd put on weight and her blond hair had faded. This morning her eyes were puffy. She took the coffee gratefully.

Mary Alice stood up. "I'm going to open the first damned box and start," she said. "There's nobody to make me do it but me."

B. J. Finch was up early too. She was always up early. She always had been. In college she used to play a set of

24

tennis before breakfast. Nowadays there was always a project afoot with the children. Today they were going to climb Gunter's Hill over behind the campus and go to the drugstore for lunch. The kids always loved to eat at the drugstore. They thought cheeseburgers, and milkshakes were better than anything in the world, except possibly pizza. She helped the maid get them into hiking clothes and settled down at oatmeal before waking J.D. He grumbled a little, like he always did, but he woke up. He'd never had the get up and go his father did, but B.J. figured just having her around had kept him from getting fat and lazy. Just because the Finch Paper Mill kept them all in money was no reason to relax. Life had to be gone at. B.J. had always gone at it. She put on slacks and sneakers and a sweater. J.D. watched her from the bed.

"What is it today?" he said. "Mount Everest? The Channel? Disneyland?"

"Grouch," she said affectionately.

"You're putting on weight again," J.D. said, pushing himself up against the headboard of the bed. "You aren't pregnant, are you?"

"Why, no," B.J. said. A look of doubt crossed her face. "I don't think so."

"Jesus," J.D. said. "I like big families, but this is ridiculous."

"I'll remind you of that at the strategic moment sometime," B.J. said. "Get up and have your breakfast." She tied a kerchief around her hair.

"You aren't going already, are you?" J.D. said.

"Well, we'll have to hike all the way back past the river . . ."

"Goodbye," J.D. said. "Don't lose any of them."

Sandy Mackintosh was up early because a ballet student's mother who had to be at work early had gotten her up. The phone had rung and she'd grabbed it still half-asleep to keep it from waking Kurt. She knew what it would be. She had assigned the recital parts last week. The phone had been ringing ever since.

"But Marcia was doing so well," the voice rattled in her

25

ear. "I just knew she'd have a bigger solo part this year. After all, the little Green girl—"

"All the children have very nice solos, Mrs. Hayes. I'm sure if you come for parents' day next week and see the whole thing run through you'll be much happier."

"But the little Green girl . . ."

Sandy gritted her teeth. "Candace Green has had ballet since she was four, Mrs. Hayes," she said sweetly. "She is much more advanced than any other child in the class. There is only one lead in a ballet. It is only fair she have it." She held the receiver away from her ear and wished she hadn't given up smoking.

"Hi, Mama," Kim said from the bedroom door.

She grimaced and mouthed, "Go back to bed," at him.

"Mark's already up and got the cereal," he said.

"Well, my money's as good as the *Greens'*," the voice said in her ear.

She had a vision of the kitchen counter full of cereal, sugar, and milk.

"I understood Marcia was very good," the voice said.

Kurt turned over. "Good God, already?" he said.

Sandy made a face at him and rolled over on her back and stuck both feet up in the air. The voice on the telephone went on.

"You have very good legs, Madam," Kurt whispered in her ear. She poked him with her elbow.

"I may consider taking her out of the class," Mrs. Hayes said.

"If that's the way you feel," Sandy said.

"Mama," Kim said.

"Eat it," she mouthed.

There was a click and Mrs. Hayes's voice was mercifully cut off.

Kurt was smoking a cigarette. She hated him for a moment.

"Why do you put up with them?" he said.

"Why do you put up with the idiots that come into your office?" she said.

"O.K., lady, you win. Going to try to go back to sleep or give in and get up?"

"It's too late, but I better go check the kitchen. Eggs?"

"Eggs."

"Oh, Lord, I've got to go to the beauty parlor this morning," Sandy said, swinging her legs off the edge of the bed and picking her slippers up with her toes.

"Don't let them put anything on your hair," Kurt said.

"Why do I have to be the only woman in town who's beginning to get gray in her hair?" she said.

"It's because you're so old, baby. You're ancient. Don't you notice how you creak when you do those damned exercises?"

She planted one foot on his stomach and pushed lightly until he rolled out of bed on the other side. "I'm glad our kids are boys," she said. "Just think, I don't have to worry about their blond curls or what part they get in the recital."

Kurt got up off the floor. "They'll have to marry girls," he said ominously.

"Oh, good God," Sandy said.

Meredith and Syd Green were up early too. They owned a shoe store on Main Street and they were completing their year-end inventory. They drove into town together. Syd had a headache. He'd been up too late and had too much to drink and he wished to hell they'd never said yes to Frank Plowden when he asked them to dinner. But Meredith had been pleased and Meredith wasn't always pleased these days about their social life. Of course, he knew why they were asked to Dr. Frank Plowden's. Frank was scraping the bottom of the barrel to get people to be nice to Layne. Not that there was anything wrong with Layne. On the contrary. Still, she was the usurper, the second wife who had taken over from Martha—sainted Martha whom everyone in Druid City thought of as the most injured of injured parties. Not that Syd didn't like Martha too. But great God, when a marriage fails, anybody with any perception knows there are many reasons. Layne Christian wasn't the only one. Women were all crazy anyway. When it was them it was

27

always L-O-V-E. When it was another woman it was nasty ole sex.

"What's the matter with you?" Meredith said.

"I'm hung over," he said. "That answer your question?"

"I didn't notice you complaining about having another one when Layne Plowden kept asking you last night," Meredith said.

"We went because you wanted to go. Don't start."

"Yeah. Reluctant Syd, the life of the party."

"Aw, come on, Meredith. You know damned well I hate that sort of conspicuous consumption we get at places like the Plowdens."

Without looking around he knew she was glaring at him. He waited.

"Well, it's a hell of a lot better than drinking Manische-witz with your parents," she said.

"Oy vey, Miss WASP of 1966," Syd said.

Layne Plowden didn't get up early. She seldom did. At ten o'clock she remembered she had a beauty parlor appointment and came up out of a half-doze to light a cigarette and listen to her head to see if she'd outslept the hangover. She'd waked up at four in the morning with a pounding head and a mouth like the trenches and swallowed two glasses of water and three aspirin and watched the sky seem to lighten and then give up and remain dark before she went back to bed.

She looked at the pillow beside her, wondering when Frank had gone to the office. She pushed the buzzer and hoped Madge had the coffee hot. She pushed her hands through her short blond curls. The headache was gone. Thank God for small favors. She couldn't figure out why she'd drunk so much last night anyway. Especially with that ass, Syd Green. Maybe because she was grateful to him for not mentioning Martha once all night. It was quite an accomplishment. Why did every woman in town have to be a dear old sorority sister of Martha's? Jesus.

She remembered that she was supposed to call Joan Friday about the charter membership to the new country club this morning and for a moment she thought the headache had come back. She didn't want to talk to Joan Friday anytime and especially not this morning.

Madge came with the coffee. She drank a cup and watched while Madge laid out her new white suit. Then she shrugged and picked up the phone.

Dylan answered it. She'd heard he'd flunked out of Princeton and was at home, but she hadn't been sure it was true. He sounded polite and sleepy. Then Joan came on, sounding polite and wide awake.

"Good morning, dear," Joan said, with only a small edge on the dear. "Did you talk to Frank about the club thing?"

"I'm sorry, Joan," Layne said. "We had the Greens over last night and I simply didn't want to bring up anything about the new club while they were here."

"Oh, my," Joan said. "That little problem."

"Mmmp," Layne said.

"I mean, really, I don't know just what the membership committee *is* going to do," Joan said. "After all, Meredith is Meredith and a sorority sister and all that, but one of the main reasons for the new club is to . . . well . . . have people who are a little more *simpático*. And Syd *is* . . . Syd." She sighed. "It's awfully hard sometimes to understand why your friends marry the people they do," she said.

"Yes, isn't it?" Layne said.

The University Beauty Shoppe was warm and steamy. It smelled of shampoo and wave lotion and coffee. Edyth Innes had just finished perking a new pot for the late-morning customers. There were three girls working the booths now, so that often, this year, she had time to have a cup of coffee herself, though not as often as an owner should have, because so many of the customers insisted she do them personally. She really wasn't that good a beautician, but the fact of ownership seemed to make them think so. That and the other reason she didn't let herself think about except on days like this one when she was sick of winter and the long haul toward spring. A large percentage of the women whose hair she rolled regularly at set weekly appointments had gone to college with her and been in a sorority with her back in the days when everybody was

29

going to marry a doctor-lawyer-Indian chief. And even if she knew she'd gotten something a hell of a lot better than the doctors-lawyers-Indian chiefs the rest of them had snared, they didn't know it. You couldn't expect them to. They were sorry for Edyth Innes because she owned a beauty shop and didn't belong to the country club. She could feel smug all she wanted about Miley and the comfortable house outside town. They patronized her. They sat there at her table in the steamed booth and enjoyed having her dress their hair. And that was the way the world was made.

She had Sandy this morning, which wasn't bad. Sandy was the pick of the bunch. And the only one who had a Monday appointment. Most women wanted to finish the week with a fresh hairdo, not start it. Friday was always the really busy day. She poured herself a cup of coffee and leafed through the appointment book. She had Mrs. Frank Plowden down just after Sandy. It had been the best she could do. She tried to avoid getting people in at the same time who would hate being in the same room together all dressed up, much less with their hair soaking wet or half-dyed. That made Friday impossible for the second Mrs. Plowden. The first Mrs. Plowden came in then. Edyth had nightmares sometimes about getting her appointment book mixed up and finding Martha and Layne Plowden sitting together waiting for a booth. Once she'd gotten Oscar Ridley's wife in at the front while his girl friend was in the back having a facial. Her nerves still hadn't recovered from that. Because, Lord, why couldn't women keep their mouths shut in a beauty parlor? It was worse than a psychiatrist's office. What was it about having your hair washed or dyed that made women talk about anything on earth to a girl they didn't even know who was fixing their hair, or to whoever else happened to be around? They'd even say things to their friends in here they wouldn't dare say at a party or in the privacy of their own kitchens. It was a good thing she didn't want to write a book.

She lit a cigarette and put it out abruptly in the ashtray when she heard Sandy Mackintosh's voice up front. Sandy came on back to the little room where the coffeepot was. She looked bright and alert and excited.

"Edyth," she said, "what on earth is going on over at the Delta House job?"

"Edyth felt a small clutching fear. Miley wasn't as young as springtime anymore and he worked like a damned slave. But Sandy didn't look alarmed, just interested.

"What do you mean?" Edyth said.

Sandy shrugged. "I walked over from the studio," she said, "and just as I passed there Miley came scaling down the scaffold like a flyer hitting the net. Then he ran down the street to the drugstore. All the work crew had quit and were just standing around gossiping like a bunch of women. I walked on up this way and saw Miley in the phone booth by the drugstore, talking like crazy. I thought maybe he'd phoned you."

Edyth shook her head. "It didn't look like anybody was hurt?"

"No. I got the impression some of them were laughing and some of them were scared. But it sure didn't look like an accident."

Edyth shrugged. "They probably found out it's going to cost Oscar sixty-seven cents more than they thought it was to tear that damned house down," she said. "Come on and let's get you started."

They went into her front booth and Sandy took her ponytail down and fluffed at her hair with her hands. It was nice hair, still thick and shiny and just beginning to go gray in front.

"No rinse?" Edyth said automatically.

"No rinse."

"He'd never know the difference."

Sandy was contemplating her red hair, her green eyes, and her pointed face in the mirror. "Oh, yes he would," she said. "He counts every one of them." She leaned over and peered into the glass. "Maybe I'll get a streak. It'd be sort of nice."

Edyth had Sandy shampooed and set and ready to go under the dryer when Layne Plowden came in smelling of

31

something expensive and looking expensive. Edyth stared at the plain little white suit, wondering just exactly what it was about it that made it look the way it looked.

"Morning, Edyth," Layne said. "Hello Sandy." She took a silver cigarette case from her pocket and lit a cigarette with a silver lighter. She sat down on the pouf in front of the window and crossed her legs. "What's going on down the street?" she said.

"What does it look like?" Edyth said.

"Well, there are a bunch of cars down at the Delta House, including the university cops and Mr. Ridley himself. Miley's all right though," she added quickly. "I saw him standing there talking to Oscar a mile a minute. I've got the curiosity of a cat, but I couldn't just stay parked at the traffic light all morning. People were blowing horns behind me like crazy after the light changed."

"I hate to get under the dryer," Sandy said. "I'm afraid I might miss something."

"You're not going to miss anything," Edyth said. "Here comes B.J., and whatever's happening she'll know."

B.J. was coming up the street from the drugstore at the corner at a fast trot. Two of the children trailed behind her and she kept stopping to say over her shoulder, "Go on back and eat your cheeseburgers. I'll be back in a minute." They continued behind her.

She came through the door like a tank, turned and gave both kids a swat on the rump, dug in her pocket and produced a handful of pennies. "Go play the bubble-gum machine," she said. "I'll be back in a minute." They turned and ran back toward the drugstore. B.J. watched them for a moment, then came on in the beauty shop and closed the door.

"Hello, Edyth," she said. "Have you heard yet? Sandy, my God, why do you fix your hair on a Monday? Hello, Layne, you look a little hung."

One of the operators, who was putting a college girl under a dryer, giggled. Edyth frowned at her.

"Don't mind me, honey," B.J. said. "I've been tramping all over hell's half with those kids and I know I look hideous." She laughed. "Oh, girls, if you could see the look on all their faces. I haven't had so much fun in years. Oscar Ridley looks like he swallowed poison. But the prize is our dear and beloved college president, E. K. Edwards. Oh, if you could see his face. The last time he was at our house he was giving the business to everybody in sight about New Trends in College Thinking. You should see what he's thinking now."

"B.J.," Sandy said, "if you don't tell us what the hell you're talking about I am going to personally stick your head under a faucet."

B.J. grinned. "You haven't heard," she said smugly. "Get me a cup of coffee, Edyth."

"The hell I will," Edyth said.

"I'll get it then," B.J. said. She went away toward the back of the shop.

"B.J., come back here," Sandy said.

Mary Alice stuck her head in the door. "Is it true?" she said.

B.J. exploded out of the back room, cup sloshing coffee as she came. "Don't you dare tell it," she said. "I got here first."

Mary Alice laughed. "I wouldn't deprive you for the world, B.J.," she said.

"O.K.," B.J. said. "I'm mean, but not cruel. They just found a baby in the walls of the Delta House."

There was a shocked silence and the humming of the dryers seemed very loud. The college girl stuck her head out. "What did you say?" she said.

"But that's impossible," Sandy said. "A baby? What on earth are you talking about, B.J.? You've got it mixed up."

Layne Plowden smiled a slow little cornered smile. She lit another cigarette. "She doesn't mean a real live baby. Do you, B.J.?"

"Well, no," B.J. said. "I didn't say that, did I? It's a skeleton. Bones, you know."

"Bones?" the college girl said.

"It was in the airshaft," Mary Alice said. "The one in that back bathroom over the kitchen."

33

Layne Plowden stood up. She smiled again. "That's right, isn't it?" she said sweetly. "All you girls were Deltas. Gee, how dull things were in my day around the Kappa House."

They all turned and stared at her.

"Well, of course, it must have been the help," B.J. said finally.

"Maybe so," Layne said. "Back whenever it must have been there wasn't much welfare."

"Oh hell, Layne," Sandy said.

Edyth sat down in the chair in front of the appointment desk. "Do they have any way of knowing how long it's been there?" she said.

They all looked at each other.

"I don't think there's any way they could tell . . . is there?" Mary Alice said.

Edyth looked thoughtful. "Where did you say it was?" she said.

"In the airshaft in the bathroom over the kitchen . . ." Mary Alice said. She stopped, a blank look on her face.

"That airshaft was closed, wasn't it?" B.J. said.

Sandy sighed. "Um-hmm," she said. "They had it open when they put in that bathroom. Then they closed it up again." She smiled grimly. "They closed it after they finished that bathroom . . . that summer," she said.

"What summer?" Mary Alice said. "Oh!"

"Yeah," Sandy said. "That summer. Nineteen forty-four, wasn't it?"

The college girl was listening avidly, as were the operators. Edyth motioned them to get back to work.

"Well, what the hell," B.J. said. She looked around at all of them and shrugged.

The phone rang and Edyth reached out automatically.

"I think I'll just put myself under the dryer," Sandy said.

"I better go check on the house-apes," B.J. said.

"I may have a customer," Mary Alice said.

"Beauty shop," Edyth said into the phone. "No, Joan, I haven't seen Miley yet. Yes, I'm afraid so. Um-hmm. I guess I could work you in for an extra appointment this afternoon. Yes, facials are relaxing."

34

"I'll be back in the booth when you're ready for me, Edyth," Layne said. For the first time all day she felt really good.

They called Dr. Frank Plowden because his office was closest and because he could keep his mouth shut. At least that was the idea that crossed E. K. Edwards' mind when they got him over to the work site and dumped it in his lap. "We'd better get Frank Plowden," he said. "Good man." Actually, he thought this because he had had a wonderful time at Frank Plowden's house last New Year's Eve where nobody, not even Mrs. Plowden, had acted as though a college president shouldn't be imbibing champagne and dancing with a most attractive assortment of local ladies. Besides E.K. admired Frank's establishment considerably. If he ever got a new position at a more progressive institution and could quit living in an antebellum mansion with doubtful plumbing he was going to have one just like it. "Yes," he told Oscar Ridley and the campus police, "let's get a good man here." They called Frank.

Frank had just finished telling an OB patient that he didn't think she was a candidate for natural childbirth, and he felt disgruntled. Frank hated women's magazines. They had caused him more trouble during his years of practice than any other factor. This silly bitch, for instance, could no more go through natural childbirth than he could. But she'd read an article in a magazine that told her she simply had to have a wonderful experience like that. He could imagine her husband in the delivery room, too. Some people yes, these people no. But tell that to the magazine editors. Then there were diseases, rare and obscure ones, or small variations in human structure. He always knew when an article on some such damfool thing had come out in a magazine. His office would be flooded with people with all the right symptoms. And new miracle diets. God save him from another one of those.

He picked up a medical journal, thankful the public didn't have easy access to them. There was a new article on DNA that he'd been trying to read all week. He folded the

35

magazine and started trying again. As always, when he started to read, he remembered that Martha used to read out loud to him while he was shaving or having supper or drinking a sundowner. It didn't make him miss Martha. It irritated him. Layne was exactly what he wanted. A wife, not a mother. You did not miss Mother after you finally cut the cord. The phone rang. He heard Miss Collins answer it and then his phone buzzed. He sighed and picked it up.

He listened in silence for a moment, said, "Well, good Lord," and stood up and went out to his car. He didn't bring the SL to work. He felt it wouldn't inspire confidence. He drove a neat black Pontiac to the office and left the sports car for Layne. She had a little Kharmann Ghia, but she didn't drive it much anymore. He wondered if he ought to trade it in on something a little more sporty, maybe a Sunbeam, a white one. He drove the few blocks to the campus thinking about how she'd look in it.

E.K. met him at the curb. He looked excited. His usually neat hair was rumpled and you could see the sag under his jawline. Usually you couldn't—he held his chin at the right angle.

"Well, I don't reckon you'd want to trade jobs with me this morning, Frank," he said, putting out his hand automatically.

"No," Frank said, shaking the hand automatically. "I don't guess I would."

"I don't really know what you can do about this," E.K. said, gesturing toward a small piece of canvas lying on the ground. "But I do think the law calls this a body. Don't they?"

"That's right," Frank said. He walked past E.K. and turned back the ground sheet and looked at the collection of minute bones. If it hadn't been for the skull you could have thought it was a dog or cat and he wished that whoever had found the damned thing had assumed it was a dog or cat and tossed it onto a pile of rubble and forgotten about it.

He looked up at the remains of the Delta House, remembering the nights he'd picked Martha up here, seeing viv-

36

idly for no reason he knew a huge silly sign they used to put on the door during finals: CLOSED HOUSE, with cartoons, a boy tearing his hair, a girl hitting the book. "There'll be trouble about the time," he said.

"Naw there won't," Oscar Ridley said behind him. Oscar was a wiry compact man. He had sandy hair and keen blue eyes behind round glasses. He radiated a kinetic energy that made people uneasy in his presence. He seemed to bounce on the balls of his feet. Frank thought that he looked as though he were getting ready to serve a tennis ball across the net. He served it. "The only time the damn thing could have gone in there was while we were completing that bathroom back there," he said. "It's pinpointed right well, Doctor. I got it all written down somewhere."

Dr. Edwards looked around distractedly. There were a lot of cars parked along the curbs and a lot of students around, some walking by slowly, some just standing and staring. The work crew were sitting around on planks smoking cigarettes. The campus cops had gone to put in a call to the sheriff's office. "I don't guess there's going to be any hushing it up," he said.

Frank laughed. "Not a chance, E.K.," he said.

"Well," E.K. said. "Things *have* been. Worse things than this, believe me."

"I bet they didn't happen in broad open daylight at eleven o'clock in the morning," Frank said.

"Not usually."

Miley Innes came across the lot toward them. He looked dusty and dirty and tired. He took a cigarette from behind his ear and lit it, dirty hands with clipped nails showing a dirtier line beneath them, cupping the flame. "Some days it don't pay . . ." he said.

"You're the man who found it?" Dr. Edwards said.

Miley nodded. "It's a pity we didn't take the crane to that airshaft," he said.

"You said you needed it on another job," Oscar said. "You told me that Friday when we laid off. Said you could handle that one little corner all right."

37

"I handled it all right," Miley said. He shook his head at E.K. "Sorry, Doctor, I'd just as soon have let this one lay."

E. K. Edwards was devoutly wishing he'd taken a chance on that new college in Florida. He summoned up his best smile, but it felt sticky, even to him. "Well," he said. "Hmmm."

"Hmmm, indeed," Frank said.

"The whole thing seems unlikely as hell to me anyway," Miley said. "How come anybody could have a baby to hide? Wouldn't everybody notice a thing like that?"

"Ah," Oscar said portentously.

"Oh, hell, I reckon you got an answer to that too, Oscar," Miley said. "You say you can give us the date and now you're going to give us the reasons. You got the name maybe so we can save a lot of folks in a lot of places a lot of trouble?"

"No, Miley," Oscar said, "but I got the reason. That remodeling job was done during a summer term. There wasn't any regular quota of girls living in the house at the time. They had it all shut up except one wing. There was just a few of them doing summer school work and staying on through the long vacation before the fall semester. I figure a lot could be worked out and covered up during a time like that."

"Remind me to hire you, Oscar, if I ever need a detective," Miley said.

Frank looked at E.K. "You're probably going to need one, E.K.," he said. "And a lawyer and a few fast talkers. Why don't you hire Oscar?"

E.K.'s smile came back. "Very amusing, Frank," he said.

"I've had a great morning," Frank said.

E.K. smiled impartially at everyone with well-concealed distaste and dismay. His well-trained PR mind had assessed the situation as soon as the phone call came in. He'd hope, beyond that assessment, that it wouldn't be as bad as it was, but hope was a silly snare and he knew it. The cold hard facts were that the Delta Sorority had always been the local one. That was the reason the damned house was getting rebuilt—local alumni money. And Druid City was not a big town. It was getting smaller every minute.

He saw the sheriff's car drive up and park. The sheriff and his deputies came across the rubble, almost daintily, he thought, like cats. He showed them the bones. Mercifully, they wanted to take them away. He was beginning to wonder if there was any way at all to keep the students off the sidewalks, knowing there wasn't, but getting and discarding ideas about it anyway. He'd come to Druid City because it was a step up, a bigger school and more money. He had been making a good record here. He wished he could curse. The sheriff talked politely to him, to Miley, to Oscar. Then they said they'd be in touch, told Frank Plowden to come with them, and left.

"Might as well knock off for lunch, Miley," Oscar said. "We've wasted the last hour and I reckon that damned union'll want you people paid right on. When do you think you can finish her up?"

"Thursday, maybe," Miley said.

Oscar shook his head. "I reckon there isn't anything that can't happen to slow down a job," he said. He turned and started toward his car, stopped, looked back over his shoulder at Miley. "It was the summer of 1944," he said blandly.

"Was it?" Miley said.

"Does that mean anything significant, Mr. . . . er . . . Innes?" E.K. said.

"Means my wife was here then," Miley said. "Nothing really significant."

E.K. blanched. It had started. "I guess I'd better get back home and start some checking into records," he said.

"Where are you from, Mr. Edwards?" Miley said.

"The Midwest," E.K. said.

"Small town or city?" Miley said.

"Small town," E.K. said shortly. "Small town, Mr. Innes."

"I don't envy you, Dr. Edwards," Miley said.

E.K. wondered if Miley was offering to shoot him maybe, like a horse with a broken leg. He said, "Glad to have made your acquaintance," shook hands briskly, and began to walk back to the president's mansion.

39

He cut through an alley that led between the first and second circles of sorority row and ran into Dylan Friday coming down the alley. Dylan was wearing sneakers and a white raincoat hanging open over tight black slacks and a pale blue shirt. "Good morning, Dylan," E.K. said. "Get signed in?"

"Yessir. Looks as though I'll be all set for next semester," Dylan said.

"Good, good," Edwards said. He walked on through the alley, thinking of Dylan Friday and his problems with nostalgia. Only this morning he had thought of him as a problem of his own.

He entered his house through the kitchen, much to the surprise of the cook, and walked through into the cool spaciousness of the front hall. He looked at the curve of the staircase with dislike and went to the phone on a small gilt table. He called the housemother of the Delta Sorority at her office in the temporary house the sorority was using.

"Yes, Dr. Edwards," she told him. "We keep the records. They're on file both here and in the district and national offices. It's no trouble to get them. But Mrs. Friday might know offhand. She's head of the local alumni chapter."

"I want the records," Dr. Edwards said blandly.

"They'll be in your office within the hour," she said. The tone of her voice did not change.

He hung up and went in to lunch.

E. K. Edwards was forty-nine years old. He didn't believe it yet, but his birth certificate said so. He didn't look it either, he told the man in the looking glass every morning. His hair was still black, his eyes bright, his stance erect, and his jaw firm—almost. His wife was forty-nine too, but unfortunately, he thought, she looked it. He looked at her now across the table. She was impeccably coiffed and made up, but she looked forty-nine all the same. It annoyed him for the simple reason that if she was, he was. Time was passing. And there wasn't a damned thing you could do about it. On days like this one he felt that he hadn't done a damned thing *with* it either. He had been a college student, a graduate student, a high school principal, an assistant dean, the president of a small college, and now a southern university. After today he'd probably never make it any further.

"Troubles?" his wife said.

"My God," he said. "Haven't you heard?"

"No. I went downtown this morning. Something on the campus? Nothing like at Southeastern, surely?"

"Worse," he said bitterly.

"You're kidding."

"I wish I were." He stared belligerently at his shrimp salad. "Homosexuality ain't in it with this one, baby."

"Oh, dear," she said. "And we just got asked to become charter members of the new country club."

"What in hell has that got to do with it?"

"Well, you sound as though we might be leaving."

He laughed shortly. "What I'm afraid of, my dear, is that we won't be. Ever."

"Oh," she said.

"Aren't you curious about it?"

"Of course, Ed," she said, continuing to eat. "But just telling me probably isn't going to help much."

He reminded himself that she was a very good hostess. "They just found a baby's skeleton in the old Delta House," he said.

That changed her expression. He watched her look surprised, shocked, then sly. "Well," she said finally. She actually put her fork down. "That might involve a lot of people in Druid City, mightn't it?"

He folded his napkin neatly and put it beside his untouched plate. "When they give the prize for understatement be sure to wear something black," he said. "It becomes you."

"Don't be sarcastic," she said.

The doorbell rang before he had time to think of a good enough reply.

A blond girl in a white skirt and blue sweater handed him a manila envelope. "Mrs. Wills at the Delta House sent this over," she said.

41

She was a pretty girl. He smiled at her. "Thank you," he said.

"She said to ask for a receipt," she said.

"Fine," he said. "Come in and wait here."

She stood in the hallway, a little hipshot. He thought he detected a certain insolence in the stance. He ignored it, but it spoiled some of his pleasure in looking at her, and he hurriedly went into his office and made out the receipt. He gave it to her and let her let herself out the door.

Back in his office he opened the envelope and looked at the papers. The one on top was a roster of names and pledges for Delta Sorority for the years 1941–45 inclusive, the second was a complete list of sorority residents enrolled in college for the year 1944, the third was a list of the girls who had lived in it for the summer session and long vacation. It was considerably shorter than the others. He read it through in complete bewilderment. There was not a familiar name on it. Then he realized that of course these were maiden names.

Edyth Perkins	Druid City, Alabama
Joan Holmes	Newcastle, Alabama
Mary Alice Burns	Druid City, Alabama
B.J. (Barbara Jean) Lowe	Mobile, Alabama
Sandra MacPherson	Druid City, Alabama
Martha Lovett	Druid City, Alabama
Meredith Smith	Druid City, Alabama

Under the names there was a note in Mrs. Wills' neat script: *These girls all now reside in Druid City.* He could have choked her. There were only two other names on the list:

Kathryn Hodges	Newcastle	Now resides there
Dolores Powell	Memphis	Now resides in Sarasota, Fla.

Well, thank God for you, Kat and Dolores, E.K. thought. I hope one of you is guilty as sin. He went to the door and called his wife. "Who are they?" he said, handing her the list.

She read it through carefully. "Oh dear," she kept muttering at strategic intervals. "Oh, dear."

"Who?" he said. "I haven't got time to figure them all out."

She looked at him and sighed. "Well, dear, there's Joan Friday. You know her, of course. And there's Martha Plowden, Frank's first wife. And there's that girl that runs the dress shop, and that nice little ballet teacher, and the Smith girl that married a Jew. They own the shoe store. And, I'm not sure, but I think Edyth Perkins is the Innes woman who runs the beauty parlor."

"Yes, indeed," E.K. said. "I've already heard about her. God almighty. It's the damnedest cross section I ever heard of."

"I've saved the best for last, dear," Jean Edwards said. She put a look of sympathy on her face, but he could hear the malice. "B.J. Finch," she said. "She's on here. Isn't that lovely?"

"I wonder if those damned tranquilizers really work," E.K. said.

Dylan Friday watched Dr. Edwards walk away from him down the alley. Well, he looks fit to be tied, he thought happily. He was not fond of E. K. Edwards. He had had a thoroughly unpleasant session with him earlier this morning. Edwards had informed him he could enroll at the university, but he knew damned well Edwards wished he hadn't had to. Dylan silently toasted the ghost of his father who had been a department head at dear old Druid City U. That might not have gotten him in, but his father had also been a very nice guy loved by one and all, and that had. He was now a new student in Humanities and he didn't have to start to class for two more weeks, and Miranda was waiting. Princeton, like Camelot, existed somewhere, but Dylan was here, and this was now, and Miranda was waiting.

He walked through the first circle and past the demolished Delta House. The sun was warm now and he considered taking off his trench coat, but it would spoil the effect he had carefully created when he dressed this morning. He left it on, preferring discomfort to disenchantment. He had to be enchanted with Dylan Friday. Nobody else was. Miranda might be, someday soon, but she wasn't yet. By maintaining his own sense of returned Ivy League man he kept it from mattering too much. She was going to cut lab this afternoon and go down to Chuck's Place and drink beer with him. It was a good way to spend a spring afternoon.

She was waiting in the back booth at the drugstore, reading a book. He walked quietly up behind her and looked over her shoulder. Camus. He smiled. He'd talked about Camus most of last night. Boy, that had been a weird scene—a psych student, a creative writing major, and some idiot with a guitar, and him and Miranda. They'd all been drinking California port and had somehow ended up at the house of a psych prof. He remembered swaggering in with the bottle in one pocket and a glass in the other and sitting on a bar stool talking Camus with this character and his wife, a nice gal with good legs who kept drinking beer out of the bottle and looking amused. She and Miranda had gotten on like a house afire though. But then, Miranda got on with everybody . . . except his mother, and that didn't really have anything to do with Miranda. It had to do with the fact that Miranda's father never got beyond the sixth grade even though he was the best farmer in the county, and with the fact that Dylan's mother was a Southern Belle who had been married to a department head.

"What is a southern belle?" Dylan said.

Miranda didn't even look up. "Something that rings in the welkin," she said.

I love you, Miranda, Dylan thought, but he didn't say it. He was afraid she might say, *I know, Dylan.*

He sat down and said, "How is *The Fall?*"

Miranda's brown eyes looked up at him. "As good as it was the first time," she said. "You peddling apples?"

"Oh, you are sharp, today, my love," he said. He permitted himself that. You could say "my love" to almost anybody.

44

His father had said "my love" to Joan Holmes a long time ago, but what Bill Friday meant by it was something not understood by a generation who thought it could be said casually. He had meant like Romeo, "beauty too rich for use, for earth too dear," or that like Abelard he could die of and for it, or that like Robert Browning he could cure her of all the world's ills and take her somewhere where the sun would always shine. He never knew she didn't know what he was talking about. And, actually, it didn't matter. Bill Friday had his love, in the fastnesses of his heart and by and with the aid of English poetry. He could look at her pretty face and put behind it all the dreams he had.

But Dylan was made of this and this. He had tried the romantic route once and found out there wasn't anything behind the pretty face. She had been a Vassar girl whom he never really knew except as a face across a dance floor. He had written poetry for her and letters to her and it hadn't been easy for him to find out she didn't know what he was talking about.

Miranda he had grown up with because her father's farm bordered on the lakefront where Bill Friday had built the house for his dream girl. Miranda wasn't beautiful, not as Dylan had grown up thinking about beauty, not with regular pink and white features, not like that, so he had never believed you could project the dreamstuff onto her. He hadn't ever tried. She would have known what he was talking about—Miranda was a smart gal—but he hadn't thought intelligence and emotion went together. Not until Princeton and Dylan failed each other and he came home and really saw his mother for the first time in his life. And there was Miranda, Miranda still. And what if she said, "I know what you mean when you say 'my love'?"

But she didn't. She said, "I have a message for you from your psych major friend. He'll be at Chuck's and he says for you to bring the skittles. I think he means that life *is* all that if you want to play."

"I lost my skittle box," he said.

45

"It doesn't matter," Miranda said. "We can settle for cakes and ale."

By one o'clock Joan Friday had had three telephone calls about the scandal at the Delta House. The first one was from the housemother of the ADPi House next door to the Delta House. From the speed of the phone call Joan figured she must have been looking out the window when it happened. The second was from B.J. Finch who called from the drugstore, the third was from the Delta housemother after she'd talked to E. K. Edwards.

It *had* been a very good day, Joan thought. The sun was shining on the wide polished floorboards of her house, the cook was making curry, a February rose was blooming outside the front door. Dylan was home and had gotten registered in school. An unladylike word came into her mind, but she didn't use it, even to herself. Instead she went into the bedroom and slowly and carefully and with concentration made up her face. In a soft light she could still look like Bill Friday's beauty, but she didn't allow herself soft light to make up in. She had a glaring fluorescent fixture over the dressing table and a makeup mirror that magnified. There wasn't any point in kidding yourself. Besides, she was through with all that. She only wanted to be gracious, charming, Dylan's pretty mother. She could carry that off without too much effort. It was the trying for what Bill would have called "the first fine careless" that made the strain lines. It was trying for *men*, an unessential and silly pastime that most women never seemed to grow up enough to stop. Men were so unimportant, really. It was a pity society had set things up so that it was impossible to get along without them.

She finished the job on her face and methodically rubbed cream into her hands for ten minutes. Luckily she had dressed for the day in a good dress. It was probably a premonition. She turned out the dressing table light and went across the room to her French provincial desk. She took out a white fountain pen and sat looking at the blank paper in front of her. She had to start organizing her thoughts, because she was going to have to do something

46

about this thing. Every girl in town who had belonged to that sorority was going to start calling her any minute now. She had to have some attitude to take, some damned thing to say.

She wrote: *Clarissa was cooking for us that summer. Where is she working now?* Then she stared at the blank paper. She wished suddenly that Bill were here. Not because he could do anything about it, but because she knew he would think it was funny.

She wrote: *B.J. was dating that tennis player.* And stared at that. She wondered why that had come to mind so quickly. Probably because they had all been so hung up on him. What was his name? One of those clever things, like a TV hero. No. Clark That's what it was, Clark Davidson. She wrote that down and looked at it and laughed. Not a TV hero name at all. Superman. Clark Kent. And Bill never thought I had any sense of humor, she thought. She drew a line uner that name and thought, Miley was overseas and Edyth was being awfully faithful-faithful. Except for the 4F from Eutaw that she had some sort of mother complex about. She wrote down *Edyth, 4F from Eutaw. Meredith, several boy friends, Mary Alice, Trueblue Lew, Sandy?, Martha, dear doctor.* She looked at the list, added *Kat Hodges, Homer; Dolores Powell, homely, Me, Bill already.*

It was a silly sort of list, but it had settled her mind. She looked at it carefully, then tore it up and threw it in the wastebasket. She went into the kitchen and asked Cora if Dylan had said whether he'd be home to lunch.

"Yessum," Cora said. "Said he wouldn't."

"I'll just have a salad then," she said. "Save the curry for supper. I've got to go in to the beauty parlor and if Dylan gets in before I get back tell him he's to dress decently for dinner. We may be having guests."

"Yessum."

"Cora?"

"Yessum?"

"Where's Clarissa working now?"

Cora sighed. She put down the spoon she was stirring

curry with and folded her hands. "Ummm," she said portentously.

"Cora, don't start that," Joan said. "Tell it, please."

"Well, Clarissa's had troubles, Miss Joan. Her boy done got in with a knife-toting crowd and her daughter ain't much. She ain't working steady. She does day work here and there."

"Here and where, Cora?"

"Mrs. Edwards, when she need an extra hand. Miss Sandy some."

"Stir the curry," Joan said. "I'll eat in the breakfast room."

She had lunch on a blue place mat with the good silver. She needed that. Then she put on her black hat and got her white gloves and went out and drove to the beauty parlor.

Under the relaxing pressure of Edyth's hands she felt the tension go out of her. She shut her eyes and let Edyth talk. As long as she kept talking she didn't have to think at all.

"Remember that summer, Joan!" Edyth said. "It was a crazy kind of summer. Those times just happen seems like, or at least they used to then. Maybe that's some special thing about being young, those crazy times. You look back on them and you remember all kinds of silly little details because there were so many things that happened out of the ordinary. It's like science fiction. Something somewhere was out of kilter and all the coincidences had a chance to work. That summer was like that."

"There was a war on," Joan said.

"That isn't what I mean," Edyth said.

"I know it but the clichés are comforting sometimes," Joan said.

"Bill used to come and see you for just one minute, right at check-in time," Edyth said. "We all thought that was so romantic."

"It was because he wasn't supposed to be dating a student," Joan said.

"No. It was because he was Bill."

Joan didn't answer her and she worked in silence for a

minute. Then she went on. "Remember B.J.'s tennis player?" she said.

Joan laughed. "Clark Kent."

"What?"

"Nothing," Joan said.

"Jesus, he was good-looking," Edyth said. "Even *I* thought so, and I plain never did go for good-looking men. But every once in a while I guess one is so spectacular everybody has to notice. Some women are beautiful that way too. It's enough all by itself. Those people serve their function by just standing around letting everybody else gape."

"I don't remember that he was that good-looking," Joan said. She sat up. "That's enough massaging." She peered at her face in the mirror. "It feels better anyway . . . No, I think he was sexy. We just didn't know that was what we meant about him."

"Maybe," Edyth said. "But he looked a lot like that actor Paul Newman."

Joan laughed again. "You see," she said. "*I* remembered him as looking like Robert Mitchum. I don't believe he was really good-looking at all."

"This thing seems to have given you a sense of humor," Edyth said.

Well, Joan thought. She didn't think I had one either. "There really isn't anything funny about it," she said. "Laughing is just a way of whistling in the dark."

"That one comfort you too?" Edyth said.

"Edyth, what was that 4F's name?" Joan said.

"I'd better use a little extra cream around the eyes," Edyth said.

"Go home with me for supper, Miranda," Dylan said.

She tilted her beer glass and looked at him over the rim. "Unh-unh, dear."

"Why not? You used to come to supper with us."

"I am now old enough to have to be asked formally," Miranda said. "Haven't you noticed?"

"Shut up and drink your beer."

"All right." Miranda drained the glass and smiled.

"We could go out in the country," Dylan said, "and look at the trees."

"Should I leave?" Wes Melton said. He took a beer can and folded it neatly and pushed it to one side.

"Probably not," Dylan said.

"One more beer," Miranda said. "Then I've got to go home and study Philosophy."

"That's a useless endeavor," Wes said. "Come on over to the Psych department. We explain the same things much more scientifically."

"And not half so pretty," Miranda said.

"Well, if it's pretty you want you're in the wrong universe anyhow, baby."

"Ha," Miranda said. "Let's do go out in the country and watch the trees budding. I believe in it."

"We all believe in it," Wes said. "We have to, being hung up on it. We merely differ as to what it means."

"It means what it means to me, it means what it means to you," Miranda said. "That's simple enough."

Wes laughed. "What about Dylan here?" he said. "He hasn't made up his mind what it means to him. Where do we work him into our varying universes?"

"Oh, Dylan's purpose is to let us argue," Miranda said. "I'm convinced, you're convinced. We are really talking to Dylan."

"I'm not even listening," Dylan said. "I'm trying to catch somebody's eye and order us another beer."

He wasn't listening. He was watching Miranda's face while she talked.

"I don't really want any more beer," Miranda said. "Let's go look at trees." She gathered up her books and stood up.

"Bless you, my children," Wes said. "I'll stay and get drunk enough for everybody."

They went out into the brightness of the street, blinking at the sunlight.

"Do you really want to drive out in the country?" Dylan said.

"Yes. Why not? Probably the trees *are* budding."

"All right."

They got into Dylan's Ford and drove out the highway past the school. Miranda sat silently, watching the sunlight.

"A penny?" Dylan said.

"Not worth it."

Halfway to the lake Dylan turned off onto a side road and stopped the car. Miranda smiled and came into his arms. He hadn't really had time to think about it, but he held her very tightly as though she might suddenly go away some place. After a long moment he kissed her. Her mouth was very soft and she tasted faintly of beer. Her eyes were open, watching him. Her lips parted.

He drew away from her. "Miranda?" he said quietly. "Why?"

"Oh, Dylan," Miranda said. "Try Religion 101."

When Joan got home from the beauty parlor she went to the phone and called all of them. Martha she asked to supper because she was the only one she could get without her bringing a husband along. The others she asked to lunch the next day. It's all I can do now, she thought. She went into her white bedroom and took her nap.

Martha Plowden put down the telephone and looked around the newspaper office. It was sunny, cluttered, and dusty. Her desk was neat and clean. She was through for the day. She had interviewed a new poverty program official, a kindergarten expert, and a boy who had killed two girls in an automobile accident. Her columns were typed, headed, filed. She couldn't find another thing to do. It was five o'clock. She had to go home. But at least she was going out tonight, even if it was somewhere she didn't want to go for reasons she didn't want to think about. At least she could shower and dress and drive out to Joan Friday's. Reluctantly she got up and put on her coat and gloves and went out into the hall. It was empty. She waited for the elevator and put herself in it and took herself downstairs. She walked out of the building, hearing the silence. Lately she had begun to notice the presses again. It was odd. When she'd first come to work here they had almost driven her crazy, then she never heard them at all, now she was

51

hearing them again. She didn't wonder what it meant, she didn't like to wonder about things like that. That was the sort of thing Frank used to do—wonder, discuss, analyze. The answer never amounted to anything anyway. If it was important you'd just know one day. If it wasn't it didn't matter. She went to the parking lot and got her car and drove to the apartment house on the edge of the campus. The stairs almost defeated her. They always did. She simply didn't want to climb them. But she did, and took out her key and opened the door, and went into the neat empty living room and turned up the thermostat.

In the kitchen she made herself a very light drink. She set it on the drainboard and carefully put away the bottle and mixer and shot glass. Then she took the drink into the living room and sat down and drank it. She couldn't tell that it improved her spirits any. It occurred to her that she hadn't taken off her coat, so she stood up and removed it and hung it neatly in the closet. "Maybe I should get a cat," she said aloud, then shut her mouth firmly because she was not going to start talking to herself. She went into the bedroom and took off her clothes.

There was a full-length mirror on the bathroom door and she stood and looked honestly into it for a moment. It is not a really young body, she thought. It was never spectacular. But it is good enough. It is still reasonably firm and reasonably slim, and she is not really young either. She went into the bathroom and turned on the water and got in the shower. After a few moments she could feel herself start to relax and she waited for the question. She got it at this time every day, as though it were hidden away somewhere and needed solitude and hot water to bring it out. *What did I do wrong?* was the question. She didn't have any answer for it.

This wasn't a thing like the sound of the presses either. No answer for this was going to pop up. If it had been it would have by now. The unconscious places didn't know the answer to it either.

She got out of the shower. In the bedroom again she kept her eyes away from the mirror, dressing carefully in clean

52

underwear and a new dress. She made up her face and combed her hair and put two neat dabs of perfume behind her ears. A nasty little thought crossed her mind. It was very graphic. She wondered about the places Layne put perfume. It made her a little sick with herself. She didn't have that kind of thoughts often, but when they came they clawed at her. Her mind skittered away and came to rest against Joan Friday's phone call. She didn't want to think about that either, but it was better than this sort of thing.

Joan could make anything sound like afternoon tea party conversation. "Have you heard about what happened at the University today?" she'd said.

"Yes," Martha said. "Grotesque isn't it? But kids nowadays . . ."

Joan's voice had gone on sweetly. "Of course, that sort of thing shouldn't concern any of us, but the really ridiculous thing is it was in the airshaft. You know the one they closed up when they put that extra bathroom in?"

That is supposed to tell me something, Martha had thought. But she didn't know what. Joan told her.

"Dear," she said. "Don't you remember when they put that bath in? It was that summer we all decided to stay in the house even though it was supposed to be closed."

Oh, yes, Martha remembered that summer all right. She wasn't likely to have lost that summer. That summer had been all Frank. And damn it, damn it, damn it. What had she done wrong?

She had met him the fall term before in the silliest way. He'd lost his anatomy notes somewhere on the quadrangle and he was quartering the grounds with a flashlight when she came out of the library after her two hours' work on a Monday night. He'd shined the light right in her face.

"I'm sorry," he'd said. "I didn't know there was anybody around."

"What are you doing?" she asked him, not really caring because she could see he was one of those charming boys who didn't interest her.

"I seem to have lost something," he said. And smiled.

I don't want to believe that, Martha told herself, remem-

53

bering that smile with a physical stab. I do not want to believe I fell in love with a smile.

Maybe she had and maybe she hadn't. At any rate she'd found the notes for him. They were lying in plain sight beside the monument to the Confederate dead. So they had gone to the College Inn. And by the next summer . . .

She stood up from the dressing table and went and turned the bed down so it would be ready when she came home. She always turned the bed down. She wondered if Layne—no, she did not. She fixed her water carafe and put it on her bedside table, and turned out the bedroom lights. She went into the living room and got her coat out of the closet and put it on. She turned out the lights in the living room and carefully locked her door before she went down the stairs.

The Friday house showed through the trees above the lake, lights in every window and on the patio. Martha slowed her car and looked at the view. Pines, thick and tall, led toward the house and behind the house darkness hid, she knew, a slope toward the water. It was quiet here, and private, and beautiful. It was also sad. She parked the car and rang the back doorbell. Everybody always went in through the Friday kitchen, which was half sitting room.

Joan answered the door. She was wearing a pink dress and she looked very fresh and pretty. Involuntarily Martha smiled at her. Beauty affected her that way. At least, this kind of beauty. "Hi," she said.

"Hi." Joan grimaced. "Let's wait till after supper to talk," she said. "Dylan's brought somebody home."

Dylan and Miranda were seated in front of the kitchen fire. He got up and spoke to Martha, introducing Miranda. Martha looked at the girl. There was something about her that reminded her of Layne. She couldn't imagine what it was. This girl had long straight hair and her face was all angles. Layne was a curly-haired blonde and seemed soft. But maybe she wasn't really; maybe the angles were there. Martha breathed deeply and said something polite.

Dylan was standing at the bar. "What's your poison, Martha?" he said. "Still martinis?"

"Heavens, no, Dylan," Martha said. "You remember nicely, but I long ago went to vodka and juice."

"Orange?"

"Grapefruit, if you've got it."

"Coming up, lady," Dylan said. "Mother?"

"A little bourbon, dear, with a lot of ice."

Dylan made the drinks and brought them over.

"When are you going back to school?" Martha said politely.

"I'm not," Dylan said. "I'm going here next semester."

"Oh, that's nice," Martha said. "Aren't you glad, Joan?"

"Yes." The word was short and Martha didn't pursue the subject. She sat down on a hassock and sipped at her drink. Behind them Cora was humming as she steamed the rice.

Dylan grinned at his mother. "A lot of excitement today, huh?" he said.

Joan shook her head at him. He laughed. "Hell, Mother, it's going to be all over town by tomorrow," he said. "The funny thing is I was downtown and didn't even hear it till I got home tonight."

"Oh, Dylan," Joan said. "You're impossible."

"That's what all you people keep telling us, the younger generation," he said. "And just look at this."

"Oh, come on, Dylan," Miranda said. "You're just trying to tease your mother."

"That's right," Dylan said. "It's an old habit I picked up from Dad."

Joan smiled in spite of her annoyance. "I know it," she said. "Sometimes you're just like him. Neither of you ever thought I had a sense of humor."

Martha stiffened. "That's one of those silly things people say that always gripes me," she said. "Everybody has a sense of humor. People just say that when they're trying to get your goat."

"There are degrees though, aren't there?" Miranda said.

"I really don't know," Martha said. "But everybody has one."

"Well, I don't know," Joan said. "Dylan and Bill could

55

always sit around saying perfectly asinine things that I never thought were funny at all and going into stitches about them."

"Maybe they *were* asinine," Martha said.

"Martha," Joan said, "I believe you *need* a martini."

Martha laughed. "I'm sorry," she said. "Maybe I do."

"You folks had better hurry then," Cora said. "Dinner's about ready."

"Oh, Cora," Joan said. "Don't be a tyrant. We'll all have another drink. Dylan."

Dylan collected the glasses. "Anybody for amontillado?" he said, and he and Miranda both burst out laughing.

"You see," Joan said.

"Mother," Dylan said, "you follow that. You just don't want to admit it for some deep and devious female reason."

"Amontillado is a wine," Joan said.

"It comes in casks," Miranda said.

"Who casked you?" Dylan said.

"Nobody," Miranda said. "I'm not even ripe yet, much less withered on the vine."

"That little ole winemaker, me," Dylan said.

"Will you stop it?" Joan said. "Honestly."

Martha finished her drink in one gulp and set the glass down. "They meant Poe," she said. "And it really isn't very funny."

"Martha," Dylan said, "we left that way back yonder."

"Don't be disrespectful, Dylan," Joan said. "I don't care if you have known Martha all your life."

"He isn't," Martha said. "I'm just in a foul mood. It was hectic around the office today. And now this thing . . ."

"Let's go to the table," Joan said.

Oh, God, Martha thought. What an idiot I am. How could they possibly know about Frank throwing that at me that last terrible time, banging the door and then sticking his head back around it and saying, "You don't have any sense of humor." How could they possibly understand that.

Joan thought, That girl is as bad as Dylan and Bill. How strange for a girl, and a pretty one too. At least I *think* she's pretty. Not in the usual way, but pretty. I hope that's all it is, that Dylan thinks she's pretty. I wouldn't mind *that* sort of thing. But good heavens! Lee Benson's daughter!

Miranda thought, My God, how I love him.

And Dylan thought, My love, my love.

After dinner Dylan and Miranda went to the basement to play records. Cora cleaned up and poked up the fire and went home.

"Let's do have a martini, Martha," Joan said. "You look tired."

"No, thanks," Martha said. "A little brandy maybe."

Joan got the snifters and poured from one of the last of Bill's bottles of Courvoisier. She felt Martha needed it. She sat down in a chair and curled her legs under her. "I'm sorry Dylan was so sarcastic tonight," she said. "It isn't like him."

"Dylan's a delightful boy and you know it, Joan," Martha said. "I didn't mind anything he said. I just feel lousy."

"I'm sorry, dear. Maybe we'd better wait till tomorrow to talk."

"No," Martha said. "If you're determined to talk about this thing let's get it over with."

Joan looked into her brandy glass. "Well, it isn't just going to go away if we don't talk about it," she said.

"No."

"Well, then . . ." Joan shrugged.

"What are we going to say about it?" Martha said.

"Well . . . do you have any idea?"

"Who it might have been, you mean? No."

"To tell you the truth," Joan said, "I'm not sure I want to know. Maybe it was the help. Only I don't believe that and neither do you and neither will anybody else." She sighed. "It's like *Beau Geste*, you know. Somebody did it, and somebody nice at that. And everybody is going to think it was one of us and they'll take their choice. and no matter who it was we'll all come in for the blame. It isn't pretty."

"It *would* have to be that summer," Martha said.

"Edyth said today that that summer the whole world was out of kilter," Joan said.

57

"Maybe it was," Martha said. "Maybe that was what was wrong."

"Wrong with what?" Joan said.

"Everything," Martha said.

Joan giggled. "The awful thing," she said, "is we all put on weight that summer. Do you remember that? Clarissa was so damned tickled at having so few of us to cook for that she stuffed us. She used to take all the ration books and go out and do unbelievable things with them. Probably black market. But we all ate like pigs. I do believe anybody could have covered it up with little jackets and things."

"Not B.J.," Martha said. "She was always running around in a tennis dress."

"But she's so big she never shows. Heavens, you know that. You've seen her that way enough. Nobody is ever sure until J.D. drags her to the hospital."

"That's right," Martha said. "What was that tennis player's name?"

"Clark Davidson. Who did he look like?"

"Tony Perkins."

"Oh, my God," Joan said.

Layne and Frank Plowden were eating chocolate cake in their kitchen. Layne had on a shorty nightgown and Frank had on a T shirt and khaki pants. He liked to wear T shirts and sit in the kitchen with Layne. It made him feel slightly disreputable, and terribly young. The chocolate cake had the same effect. He hadn't allowed himself any chocolate cake in fifteen years.

Layne had scrubbed her face and sat looking at him with pale lips in a half smile. "So, what do you think the law is going to do about it?" she said. She licked icing off her fingers.

"My God, you're sexy," Frank said.

"Not really, I'm not. But you think so, so I am."

"Let's make some coffee," he said.

"Not Sanka?"

"Not Sanka."

"All right." She got up and went to the cabinets. He

watched her, wondering how anybody as old as he knew she was could have legs like that.

"Well, come on," she said. "What do you think?"

"About what?"

"Oh, Frank."

"I don't know," he said. "It's a touchy situation. Dem bones is dem bones. It *could* have been infanticide, you know."

"Frank! You don't think they really want to go around arresting somebody for something like that, that happened all that long ago, do you?"

"No. What they want to do is forget it ever happened. But as you and I well know, my dear, that ain't always exactly possible."

"Are you glad it ain't?"

"Yes."

"All right." She kissed him. "I'm a bitch," she said.

"No, you're not."

"Yes, I am. I think it's funny. And that really is a bitchy thing. I know better. I know it's going to maybe ruin somebody's life. But there's this awful little corner of my mind that wants to laugh."

"Well, it doesn't really concern us."

"Doesn't it?"

"No. I assure you it does not."

"That's sweet, dear, but don't you think everybody involved is sitting around reassuring each other about that same little point right now?"

"Maybe. But I do not lie to you. I never have. I don't now. It doesn't concern us."

"You lied to Martha," she said. "For a hell of a long time you were lying every minute of every day."

"Don't."

"I'm sorry."

For a long moment they didn't say anything to each other. Then Layne got up and poured the coffee. "Come on, Doctor," she said softly. "Drink up. I promise you. It won't keep you awake."

"I love you," Dr. Frank Plowden told his second wife.

"Yes," she said, "I know that."

The baby was crying again. Shari Cross Adams went across the small bedroom and looked at him. He lay on his back, both hands held over his head in the position he always put them in when he was sleepy. The small fists were clenched tightly, the face was creased and screwed into a mass of rage. She smiled at him, she felt his bottom. He was dry. She turned him over on his stomach and patted his back. Gradually the howls ceased and were replaced by small whimpers. Then he was quiet.

"Well, thank God for small favors," Bill Adams said from his desk across the room.

"Shh," Shari said. "Why don't you study in the living room?"

"You can hear him just as well in there," he said.

"You want anything?" Shari whispered.

He shook his head. "Might as well wait till your mother gets here," he said.

"She may not come tonight," Shari said. "She sounded awful bushed when I talked to her awhile ago."

"You get the money?"

"Yes."

"Good. I got five out of the old man today. Put together that ought to just about bail us out."

"I just can't understand how so little can come to so much every month when the payments are due."

"That last department store bill didn't help matters," Bill said.

"The baby had to have things."

"We could try Penney's."

"Oh, Bill. You know you want us to have *nice* things."

"Did you ask the Dows to supper Saturday?"

"Yes. Didn't you want to?"

"Yes, but what are we going to feed them?"

"We'll get pizza. They like it."

"Yeah. I guess they get enough steak at home anyway."

"You wouldn't want us to live with your parents or mine, would you?" Shari said.

"No. I damned well wouldn't. Even if your mother cooked us steak every night and twice on Sundays. She's a nice gal and so is mine. But I don't see that living-in bit."

"But the Dows never have to spend any money," Shari said.

"They pay for it," Bill said.

Shari tucked a blue blanket around her blue-clad baby and tiptoed away from him toward Bill. She kissed him on the cheek and went into her living room. It still looked bare to her, but it looked nice. There was the sofa, a really good one, and the TV set, the very best one made the salesman had assured her, and one very nice chair. It ought to be nice anyway. It had cost one hundred and fifty dollars and it wasn't a very big chair. There was a coffee table with wedding ashtrays and a stack of colored cushions. That was it. She still hadn't gotten a rug. But maybe Christmas. She got a piece of Kleenex and dusted all the furniture for the third time that day. Then she sat down on her couch and looked at her living room and at her diamond ring and at the neat tweed of her blue skirt. She was completely and sensuously happy.

Mary Alice and Lew came at eight o'clock. She let them in and kissed them each on the cheek.

"Is he asleep?" Mary Alice said.

Shari nodded. "Bill's studying, but he wants to have coffee with us. How was your day, Mother?"

"Hell," Mary Alice said shortly. She sat down and took her shoes off.

"I'll go make the coffee," Shari said. She went into the kitchen. Mary Alice sighed, got up and followed her. She took the ten dollars out of her purse and stuck it under the sugar canister. "Here, baby," she said. "I could not get over here sooner. The shop's been a madhouse. Sue and I just got the first part of the new line unpacked."

"You work too hard," Shari said. "Why don't you make the girl you hired do the scut work?"

"Because then I'd never find anything," Mary Alice said.

"Did Daddy take you out to eat?"

"Yes. We went to Morrison's. It was nourishing, but not

exciting. One good thing though. We think we may be able to start the house next spring. If things keep going like they are."

"Oh, Mother, that's really great. You deserve it."

"Tonight I'm not even sure I want it."

Shari turned around and looked at her. "What's the matter?" she said.

"Nothing. Just tired. I've been remembering when your father and I first got married. I have those days. They don't mean anything."

"What's that got to do with not wanting your house? You know you've wanted it for years."

"Oh, I don't know. In those days I wouldn't have cared if I'd lived in the Black Hole of Calcutta as long as Lew was with me."

Shari frowned. "Wanting things doesn't mean you don't love somebody, for heaven's sake," she said worriedly. "That's part of it, getting married and living together in your own place with your own things and all that . . ."

"I told you," Mary Alice said. "I'm just tired."

She watched the coffee breaking against the glass top of the percolator. She remembered the way she had watched it with Lew that first year. She remembered coffee in the College Inn for breakfast dates before they were married. It was this damned thing happening today. It had made her remember all sorts of things she'd forgotten completely.

That summer they used to sit around the kitchen table and kid Clarissa about the black market. There was always coffee and she never told how she managed to get it. They would come down late on weekends and eat in their house-coats, all except B.J. who would come in about the time they all got up, looking flushed and energetic after two sets of tennis. "My Lord," she'd say, "that man is better than I am. He's all over the court. He's unbelievable."

"Hummph," Clarissa would say. Clarissa believed all men were put on earth purely to devil women. She used to give them all lectures about it along with breakfast.

"They ain't one of 'em worth the powder to blow 'em to hell," she'd say. "If you want some advice, and naturally you don't, forget 'em. They will sweet talk and sweetheart you and then either leave you or make you take care of them forever and one is as bad as the other and there's no choosing between, so what you think you're getting? It's God's mercy most of them are off fighting the war. It keeps them out of trouble."

It was hot that summer—unbelievably hot. And that was before air conditioning. You didn't sit around nowadays blessing air conditioning, but you ought to. You had only to remember the sweat trickling down inside your bra, the feel of all that long hair on the back of your neck. It had been murderous. They all took so many showers she and Meredith had gotten little warts all over their legs. They'd thought they had cancer or leprosy, but the doctor at the infirmary had told them it was purely too many showers. He'd limited them to one a day and sure enough the warts or whatever had gone away.

She realized she was trying to remember whom she'd seen in the shower that summer and that she couldn't. They hadn't gone around clothed, but they put a towel around themselves when they went down the hall. She felt sick.

"Isn't that coffee ready yet?" she said.

"Nigh 'bout," Shari said. "You want an aspirin? Or a drink? There's sherry and some vodka."

"No, thanks."

"I know I ought to keep some scotch for you, but we don't drink it and—"

"Don't be silly," Mary Alice said. "I don't need a drink. If I did I could go home and get one."

Lew had brought her the first scotch she'd ever tasted. There wasn't a lot of it around during the war. She wondered where he'd gotten it. It's funny I've never asked him, she thought.

It had been a Saturday night and Lew had driven a hundred miles from camp. She could see him now standing at the door, his overseas cap on the side of his head, the scotch, in a brown paper sack, in one hand. She'd brought what they hadn't drunk back into the house in a cracker box. Sandy had made a drink out of it with tap water and a lemon she'd talked Clarissa out of. Sandy said the first scotch she'd ever had was in Newcastle. A railroad man had bought it for her.

"What were you doing with a railroad man?" Mary Alice had said.

Sandy had said, "I loved him, but I didn't have the nerve."

"What nerve?" she'd said.

"You know," Sandy said. "The nerve to really love him. I wanted him and I wouldn't do it because he *was* a railroad man. And yet that was the reason I loved him."

Martha had said, "What *are* you talking about, Sandy?"

And Joan had said, "She means he was common and she liked that, but she had better sense than to do anything about it."

And Sandy had said, "Oh, God, I'm a fool. I always will be."

"Mother?" Shari said. "The coffee's ready."

"Oh. Thanks." Mary Alice took the cup and went back into the living room. Lew was reading a copy of *Reader's Digest.*

"Where did you get that bottle of scotch?" she said.

"I won it in a crap game," Lewis said. He didn't even look up.

"How did you know what bottle of scotch I was talking about?"

"Oh, come on, baby," Lew said. "What other bottle of scotch has there ever been?"

"Do you want an after-dinner drink?" Syd Green said.

Meredith put down her knitting. "Like what?"

"Like a beer."

"No."

"I could fix something a little more elegant," Syd said. "I could make you a grasshopper."

"No, thanks."

"All right." He got up and went into the kitchen and opened a bottle of beer and brought it back to the living room. Meredith looked up at him.

"No," he said. "I don't want a glass."

She shrugged. "What time are they coming over?" she said.

"Eightish."

"I was hoping to have the kids in bed."

"You know they'll bring them something."

"Yes. Of course."

"Isn't there anything on TV?"

"Not fit to watch."

He went over and picked up the *TV Guide* anyway. There wasn't anything fit to watch, but he turned it on. He sat down and drank his beer and enjoyed the sound it made.

Meredith knitted until the back doorbell rang. Then she got up and went to let Mr. and Mrs. Green in. The children exploded out of their rooms as soon as the buzzer sounded. Candace was wearing the blue jeans that she had purposefully dipped in salt water and that Meredith had told her she simply couldn't wear. Syd Jr. was already in his pajamas and robe. The presents appeared and Meredith went back to her knitting.

Mrs. Green was a short dumpy woman with a warm friendly face. Her husband was thin, short and wiry. He was, Meredith always thought angrily, the happiest man she had ever known. He dressed very well in perfect taste, his white hair was so expertly cut he made everybody want to get white-headed overnight, his shoes were something he would never sell in his store—Italian and handmade. He was the only man Meredith had ever known who looked perfectly at home in either bermuda shorts or a dinner jacket. Just this year he had bought himself an Aston Martin—an honest-to-God Aston Martin. What really griped Meredith was that it was the most beautiful thing she had ever seen.

The presents were distributed—a new record for Candace, a book for Syd. Meredith went over and turned off the TV, not that you could hear it over the other noise. "You can stay up thirty minutes," she said. "Then back to your rooms. The grown folks like to talk too sometimes."

"You always say that," Syd Jr. said.

"I always have to," Meredith said.

"They're nice kids," Mrs. Green said.

"They're spoiled rotten," Mr. Green said. "But what can you do? We do it." He winked at Meredith.

"Why don't you fix everybody a drink, Syd?" she said.

"What would everybody like?"

"Nothing for me, thanks," Mrs. Green said.

"What are you drinking?" Mr. Green said.

"He's drinking beer," Meredith said. "I'm going to have some scotch."

"I'll have some with you, dear."

Syd Jr. had sat down by Mrs. Green. He watched her with solemn brown eyes. Candace was banging around the living room.

"You're going to turn something over," Meredith said.

"Leave her alone, Meredith," Mrs. Green said. "She's fine."

Meredith shrugged. She got up and went to the kitchen door. "A lot of scotch," she mouthed at Syd.

His father was leaning over the sink looking at her potted zinnias. "You need some of that new fertilizer," he said. "I'll have them send some out. How were things at the store today? I just couldn't get in. Mother had a thousand things lined up for me to do. But tomorrow I'll work till midnight and we'll finish the inventory."

The hell of it was, Meredith thought, he would. There simply wasn't anything in the whole wide world wrong with Irving P. Green. Why then did he irritate her so much? She got along a lot better with Mother, who was hardly her type.

"It was a fiendish day," she said. "Inventory means nothing to customers. They come right on."

"To you, dear," Irving said. He lifted his glass and Meredith lifted hers back and drank gratefully.

They finally got the children to bed at nine. Meredith shut the doors and came back to the living room. They were already talking about it.

"What do you think?" Mrs. Green said. "Was it really something that happened a long time ago? It's not something this new generation did?"

"It happened a long time ago," Meredith said firmly. "They know."

"How's that, dear?" Mrs. Green said.

Meredith looked at Syd. He didn't look at her. They'd discussed it briefly and unhappily in the car on the way home tonight. "It was that summer," she had said. And Syd had said, "Oh, shit."

"They know because that airshaft was where you could get to it for one brief time, Mother," Meredith said. "It was the summer Syd and I got engaged." She got up and went in and poured herself another scotch.

Mr. Green came into the kitchen. "Don't I get another one?"

Meredith jumped. "Of course," she said, wiping scotch up off the counter. She took his glass and fixed him a drink, not looking at him.

"What's the matter, Meredith?" he said.

"Nothing."

"Oh, come on. I'm an old man, but my eyesight's good."

"Nothing. I'm tired, that's all."

"Why don't you go out, and drive the Aston Martin now, dear?" Irving said. "It'll make you feel better."

There was nothing else in the world Meredith wanted as much as to drive that damned car, and she wouldn't have done it for all the tea in China.

"No, thanks, Dad," she said. "Some other time."

"You have any idea who could have done that thing?" he said.

"Not the foggiest."

"Such a pity they found it," he said. He sipped his drink. "It doesn't seem quite fair. Good God, twenty years."

"Kismet," Meredith said.

"Whose?"

"Everybody's." She went back into the living room.

"Meredith," Mrs. Green said, "weren't there a lot of girls in the house?"

"No, ma'm," Meredith said. She made a face. "Unfortunately, no, ma'm. There were precious few of us. In fact, most of us are right here in Druid City now. We're all going out to Joan Friday's to lunch tomorrow. I'm not sure what for. To look at each other in a wild surmise, I guess."

Mrs. Green clicked her tongue. "It's sad," she said.

"It was once, I guess," Syd said. "Now it's grotesque."

"That's an unfortunate choice of words, son," Irving said.

"That's what it is," Syd said.

"Hell, so is a rose if you look at it that way," Irving said.

"You stole that," Syd said.

"I steal all my good lines," Irving said. "I'm not witty, but I've read a lot."

Meredith couldn't help it, she laughed. Not at Irving, at the look on Syd's face. "Let's talk about something else," she said.

"The children," Mrs. Green said.

"Of course."

"What is this round black oilcloth patch doing on the lavatory?" Kurt Macintosh said.

"Sorry. It's part of something I was trying out for a costume." Sandy stuck her head in the door, grabbed the oilcloth dot, and went away. Kurt could hear her throwing her mat on the floor for her exercises.

"How'd it go today?" he said over the sound of running water.

"All right." Sandy banged onto the floor.

"You're shaking the furniture," Kurt said.

"I'm shaping the body," Sandy said.

"You really going out to that dame's tomorrow?"

"I can't hear you."

He turned off the water. "Are you going to that luncheon?"

"Baby, I wouldn't miss it for the world."

"Well just what is it you're all going to do? Play truth? Draw straws? Count potatoes?"

"I don't know. That's why I wouldn't miss it. I want to hear what everybody's going to say."

"You should blame it all on the war," Kurt said. "That always works. You can all say, 'It was wartime,' and smile and nod at one another and forget it."

"Oh, sure."

He came into the bedroom. "Sandy, I don't think any of you realize what this damned thing is," he said. He sat down on the edge of the bed.

Sandy gazed up at him from the floor, then stood up and wrestled the mat back into the closet. "Yes we do," she said. "That's the reason we have to keep kidding about it." She sat down by him on the bed. "Could I have one of your cigarettes?"

He grinned and handed her the pack. She took one lovingly and rolled it between her fingers for a long moment. "I haven't smoked one in almost two years," she said. She stuck the cigarette in her mouth and lit it. Kurt watched her face, the dilation of her nostrils, the greedy mouth she made. She sighed and exhaled.

"How's it taste?" he said.

She stared at him. "Good," she said shortly.

"O.K."

"Don't start."

"I didn't say a word. You quit on your own. It's your business. I didn't quit. What right have I to say anything?"

"You're *looking*."

"I'm not."

"You're thinking I don't have any will power." She drew on the cigarette again.

"You're talking. I haven't said anything."

"O.K. *I* think I haven't got any will power. But I just wanted a taste. Just to see."

"And?"

She sighed. "I told you. It tastes good!"

Kurt laughed.

"Oh, shut up," she said. "I need to think. I've been trying all evening to remember things about that summer. It's funny but the only things that I can remember are that it was hot as hell and some silly tennis player B. J. Finch was dating."

"Tennis player?"

"Uh-huh. He looked like Lee Marvin."

"Been around the block a few times, huh?"

"No. That's not what I meant. A young Lee Marvin."

69

"Ah."

"Now you're saying Ah like that."

"Like what? All I said was ah. You are always trying to give me ulterior motives."

"Ha." She finished the cigarette down to the last quarter inch and put it out reluctantly. "Oh, there was Lawson," she said.

"Lawson?"

"The gay one. I used to date him. After all you said it. It was wartime."

"The one who painted those pictures you have?"

"Well, naturally. How many do you think I had on the string?"

"I don't know. You might have been running a harem."

"Very funny," Sandy said.

"B.J.," J.D. said, "quit stomping around the room and talk to me."

"All right." B.J. sat down on the chaise longue and looked at J.D. "Let's see," she said. "Guess what E.K. Edwards is doing right now." She laughed.

"B.J., it isn't funny."

"Oh, sure it is, honey. And you know it. He tries so hard. He has such a public image—such a private image of a public image I mean. It kills me. Are you hungry?"

"No. Good Lord, we had a huge supper."

"I'm hungry. Come on. Let's go down to the kitchen and have a snack."

"All right." He followed her out of the room and down the stairs. She took cold chicken and milk out of the refrigerator and set it on the kitchen table. "Great," she said.

"B.J.," J.D. said, "tell me about this thing. What was going on in that house that summer anyhow?"

"My God, everything was going on that summer. Isn't it always? Those workmen were all over the place banging and hammering and everything smelled of paint. It was hot as the hinges of hell and everybody was sweating gallons and gaining weight anyway because we ate all the time. Yes, everybody, not just me. The housemother was a stupid old doll who didn't know the time of day. She couldn't even play bridge. Just a wing?" She thrust it at him and he took it and nibbled obligingly. "That was during my tennis phase," she said. "I played every day."

"Do you realize what everybody in town is saying by now?" J.D. said.

"Well of course I do. I'm not a complete idiot. They haven't had so much fun since Ingrid Bergman fell off the volcano. This is a lot better. It's people they know and a whole slate to choose from."

"B.J., you're on the slate."

"I know. But there really isn't much I can do about it, is there? I was there that summer just like everybody else." She finished her milk and took the remains of the chicken back to the refrigerator. "I guess I'll live now," she said.

"This really doesn't bother you, does it?"

She sighed and sat back down. She reached across the table and took his hand. "Of course it bothers me," she said in a surprisingly low voice. "But it doesn't help to go around wringing your hands. I found that out a long time ago. I'm just not the type. Can you imagine what people would think if B.J. ever acted coy or neurotic, or even upset? I can't get away with it, honey. I realized that when I was fourteen and had to start wearing half-size dresses."

"The whole thing should have been handled better," J.D. said. "The idiots shouldn't have blabbed it all over."

"Well, they didn't. Not really. It was just unfortunate that people were standing around. I bet ole E.K. is running around like a cat trying to throw dirt."

J.D. laughed. "You're right," he said. "It's better to laugh."

"It always is," B.J. said. "I look hideous when I cry."

"Miley," Edyth Innes said, "what am I going to wear out to Joan Friday's to lunch?"

"What difference does it make?"

"Well, now that you mention it, probably none. But I want to look nice anyway."

"All of you are going to be too busy wondering about each other twenty years ago to care how you look," Miley

71

said. "My God, I wish we'd taken the crane to that bathroom."

"Yes. What good can it do anybody? And Lord the harm. You'd like to think a thing like this would make people choose up sides and love each other harder, but it never does, Miley. It never does. Right now you're wondering what I was doing while you were dodging Japs."

"Ah, hell, Edyth."

"Yes, you are. And I could talk all night and you'd still wonder. We've had one of the best marriages I know of, we've been closer than most people ever are, and you still wonder. Because that's the way things are. I could bawl."

"I haven't accused you of anything."

"No, not yet. But that doesn't change anything. You wonder."

"Let's go to bed," Miley said. "I'll lock up."

"All right." Edyth picked up the coffee cups and took them to the sink. She stood for a moment looking at her kitchen. Miley had done all the cabinet work himself. It would have cost a fortune hired. It looked beautiful. There was a small nagging pain in the small of her back. She always had it when she'd had to give a lot of shampoos. She shook two aspirin out of a bottle, ran water from the tap into a glass, and took them. Then she stood there, staring down into the sink. After a while she dumped the rest of the water, turned off the light, and went upstairs to bed.

Sandy woke up at three o'clock in the morning. She lay there, half awake, half still dreaming, and she couldn't remember either the dream or why she was awake. She could smell gardenias. The scent was very strong and she put her hand out to touch . . . something. Then she knew that it wasn't gardenias at all and was fully awake. It was the furniture polish she used. It was so ridiculous. She used it because it did smell that way, like gardenias and that summer. She'd told Kurt about it once and he'd said it was a new subliminal the manufacturers had discovered. That particular furniture polish probably made every middle-aged housewife in the country remember her own particular summer. It was a menacing thought.

She wished that it were raining. Then she could close her eyes and listen and feel and go to sleep again very quickly. But it wasn't. It was still and the room felt cold and she was wide awake. She listened to Kurt's even breathing beside her but it didn't tempt her back to sleep. I won't start tossing and turning and doing things to the pillow, she told herself sternly. I'll be very still and recite poems. That almost always works. She shut her eyes, then opened them again. What do I mean that works? she thought. I never have any trouble sleeping. I never have. Except once.

Oh, that's why I'm awake, she thought. I might as well get up. She got out of bed quietly and put on her robe and slippers and felt her way to the kitchen. The refrigerator was cycling and the sound was loud in the stillness. The windows were black. She peered out, but there wasn't even a false dawn to look at. The moon was down and there didn't seem to be any stars.

Eighteen-year-old Sandy MacPherson had had the world all figured out. She wasn't terribly pleased with it, not in all its manifestations, but she understood it. It had terrible beauty and terrible ugliness, but if you just hung on and believed in some indescribable and waiting future you would make it. So said Sandy when she went off to class in the mornings, her books under her arm, her ballet shoes in a black bag over her wrist, smelling of Straw Hat and morning, waiting for a train—any train, but probably the one that went a long, long way. It was a random universe, but you could structure it. She structured it daily with ballet exercises and books.

College was the best part of the world that had happened to her yet. There were people to talk to and places to go. There were things to look at and taste and touch. She joined the Players. At that time she thought she might be an actress. She painted a lot of scenery and moved a lot of flats, and had a walk-on in one production. Joan Holmes, her sorority sister, had a bigger role. That was because Joan was a beauty. She couldn't act, but she looked marvelous and the people in the back who couldn't hear what she was saying leaned closer trying and saw more of her.

She met Lawson at the Players. He came to tryouts on a rainy Wednesday when she was wearing a red velvet dress.

"That dress is really and truly ruby," he said.

She looked up from her notes she was studying for tomorrow's exam. Well, Jesus, she thought. Nobody is that beautiful.

He looked like Michelangelo's David, and she knew he was gay. You couldn't be male and have a face like that and not be gay. Somebody, somewhere would have seen to it.

"Redheads really shouldn't wear red," she said.

"That's a stupid statement. Are you being stupid or funny?"

"Defensive."

"All right."

He walked her back to the College Inn and at the foot of the steps going down to the arcade she slipped and fell down in a puddle of water. So much for red velvet. They went on in anyway because it was too close to check-in time to go home and change. She kept dripping little puddles of water all over the floor. It was very funny. The next night he took her to an art movie. I'm going to have to go through the whole thing, Sandy thought. Because if I don't I won't get back to sleep and I've got a class to teach at eight in the morning.

It had been like all the poems in all the books because they loved each other because each one thought the other one was beautiful. It was completely and grotesquely impossible, and that made it all the more beautiful. They spent hours in the College Inn making puns, and more hours walking along streets under trees, and still more hours in his apartment where they read poetry and he sketched her in a hundred poses. They held hands and listened to Ravel on a portable phonograph. They got hand holding down to a fine art. Thinking about it now, she knew that nothing since had ever been quite that sensuous to her and it made her, after twenty years, want to cry.

Eventually she got to know all his friends and learned to be very campy and very funny. She met his family, who too anxiously wanted her to marry him. And finally he took her to a real drag party, where everybody got stinking on martinis, and let her watch the whole thing deteriorate until she had to leave.

"So, that's the way it is," he told her the next night.

She was sitting in a wicker chair, smoking a cigarette in a long gold holder, wearing the jade earrings he'd brought her from New Orleans, trying to feel very sophisticated, and wanting to bawl her head off. "It's a dirty mean way of life and there's nothing gay about it at all, and that's why calling it that is such a camp."

"Get you, dahling," she'd said. Because there wasn't anything else to say.

"I want to want you, don't you understand that?" he said. "You don't know it now, but someday after you've been wanted and wanted by people with nothing else for you you'll know how much that means. I *want* to want you. I don't think you have any conception of what a compliment that is."

It took it a long time to fall apart because they were both sentimental and romantic people. There were a couple of ridiculous fights and some agonizing smooching that did at least one thing for her. It made her more tolerant of people with problems for the rest of her life.

And he made the statue—a beautiful statue of a naked Sandy he had never seen, but that nevertheless looked exactly like naked Sandy really looked. So much for the power of the mind. And probably somewhere in some attic a beautiful naked Sandy MacPherson at eighteen was getting layered over by dust, and right now, remembering all those nights when she couldn't sleep, she thought he should have made it thumbing its nose.

The gardenias were an afterthought. They came during the summer, after it was all over, and Sandy had decided life was not beautiful. It was hot as hell and the house smelled of turpentine just the way Lawson's studio used to smell when she went with him to paint at night. He sent them over every once in a while, just like they still had coffee together every once in a while, and laughed a lot while they were having it. After all they were both very funny people.

Sandy Mackintosh, mother of two, teacher of ballet, wife of Kurt, and beginning to have a lot of gray in her hair, suddenly laughed. Because she hadn't really thought about it in a long time, and because she knew suddenly, feeling sleepy, she probably never would have to think about it again.

She taught a class in beginning ballet at eight o'clock. There were ten little girls in it, ranging in age from four to eight. They all adored her. This morning she adored them. They were blond, down to the last one, a thing she'd marveled at for years. Why did mothers think only cute little blondes need ballet lessons? They really didn't need them at all.

She lined them up at the bar and watched the feet make awkward first positions, all except the Wilfred child. There was at least one in every class, a child who danced as she smiled and walked and ran. That one—sometimes it was even two—made it all worth it.

She could see the sun shining outside the window, turning the brown grass to gold. Two college boys lay on it, heads pillowed on their arms, shirts off, getting the illusion of a suntan from the still thin late-winter light. There was a red rose blooming in front of the garage apartment next door. There were six buttercups beside the drive. Here in the big room with the polished floor the sun struck into the mirrors and turned dust motes into something tangible. The little girls lifted thin legs and arms and squinted at the sun.

The world is very beautiful, Sandy thought. Even today. It never goes back on you. I guess that's what last night was all about. I needed to remember that. The world is not like people. It can stab you with all that beauty, but it will not take it away, or turn small or mean, or cease to mean what it means. It cannot betray you by being less than you think it is. It is every bit as immense and wonderful and strange as you thought when you were five years old, pirouetting in

76

sunlight on too-thin legs. I need to tell myself that, to say it very loud, because if you don't do that on the good days how are you going to get through the bad ones?

"Mrs. Mackintosh, Mrs. Mackintosh."

"What, baby?"

"Is this right?"

Trudy Helms, two arms lifted like a bird trying to learn to fly, smiled at her.

She went to her and lifted the arms higher, strightened the leg. Trudy looked lovely. Trudy's mother was a mean bitch, and maybe someday Trudy, who looked just like her, was going to be a mean bitch too, but right now she was sincere, pathetic and lovely. And that, Sandy thought, is important too. Take people as they are and when they are and if it goes bad don't let that ruin the days when the sun shone on them. It does not take it away. It was. It is. Beauty is not skin deep.

"I love you, Mrs. Mackintosh," Trudy said.

"I love you too, Trudy. Now hold your arm just like that."

"I don't do it very well. I never look as pretty as Wilfred."

"Do the best you can, Trudy," Sandy said. "That's good enough for anybody. It's all there is."

When she got to Joan's at twelve forty-five there was only one car in the drive, B.J.'s beat-up station wagon, looking strangely empty without its normal cargo of children. B.J. was in the kitchen, sitting on a counter and eating a stalk of celery.

"Hello, Sandy," she said. "Joan's still dressing. I didn't know whether this was formal or what so I wore a sweater dress. I wonder what in God's name I'd do without the sweater dress."

"Invent it," Sandy said.

"You ladies want one of them tomato things while you're waiting?" Cora said.

"You're damned right we do," B.J. said. "I'll mix 'em. This is a formal-type luncheon after all, drinks and everything. It feels like when they were trying to ram old Tricky

Dick down our throats. Everybody in town had luncheons and coffees and teas and bridge parties. It was even fun."

"B.J.," Sandy said. "I'd be willing to bet a nickel you and J.D. voted for Nixon."

"He did. I didn't. I voted for ole Barry though."

"Why?"

"Well, it wasn't why you think, I assure you. No. It was because his pore ole wife was such a dud."

"B.J., honestly. Your politics floor me."

B.J. got down off the counter and mixed them both a bloody mary. "You remember the time J.D.'s father had me out to look me over?" she said. "Poor ole J.D. was about ready to have a conniption. He just knew I wasn't going to make it. Well, Papa—you knew Papa, grand old man of the paper mill and all that crap—he had us all sitting around the living room sipping lapsang souchong, or whatever it was, out of the thin cups, and he'd hidden all the ashtrays, not knowing I didn't smoke. And he says in this portentous voice, 'Well, my dear, what do you think of this terrible Pumpkin Papers affair?' And I said, 'I think anybody that would hide anything in a pumpkin is some kind of nut.' Well, he laughed so hard he spilled his tea and I was in, and J.D. doesn't understand it to this day. What are you looking so funny about, Sandy? You're making one of those awful connections of yours."

"Yes, I was thinking he hid the papers in the bathroom first."

"You've made my day," B.J. said. "Drink your drink."

Joan came into the room. "Hello, girls," she said. "Guess who was just on the phone?"

"The White House," B.J. said. "We've been declared a disaster area."

Joan smiled. "Well, nearly as bad," she said. "It was our esteemed president, E.K. Edwards."

"I'll mix you a drink," B.J. said.

"I don't know exactly what he wanted to convey," Joan said. "Let's go into the living room."

"Hmmph," Cora said.

They trailed behind Joan into the front room where there

was a magnificent view of the lake, but less atmosphere. "Dr. Edwards said he thought the police were going to be cooperative," Joan said. "Doesn't that sound ominous?"

"Oh, hell," B.J. said. "He watches too much TV. Do you know they've got it hid in a dry sink?"

"What?" Joan said.

"The TV, of course."

"Oh."

Sandy giggled. "The Plowdens have theirs behind an abstract painting."

"Why don't they just leave it out and call it pop art?" B.J. said.

"Somebody's at the door," Joan said. "I think it's Martha. So . . ."

B.J. shrugged. She leaned over and whispered to Sandy. "Layne Plowden's got a bidet in the bathroom, too. Did you know that?"

"I never got past the wallpaper," Sandy said. "It's got all these NEKKID WOMEN holding up pears and pomegranates in strategic spots."

"Hello, everybody," Martha said from the door.

"Hello, Martha," B.J. said. "You here officially or unofficially?"

Martha grimaced. "Don't mention that damned paper to me," she said. "I've never been so glad to get out and look at the trees."

"You're looking good," Sandy said. "It must agree with you."

"I look like a witch and you know it," Martha said. "I've been trying to get to Edyth's all week, but with no success. I missed my last Friday's appointment due to a masquerade deal at the country club."

"Carrie Evans' little do," B.J. said. "My God. Old women in cute little costumes. I can't bear it . . . either way." She slapped herself on the hip. "Still, it's better than scrawny. Somebody told me Carrie actually took a bikini to Nassau last year. I'd give a year's desserts to have seen her trotting around the beach in that."

"Give a year's desserts and maybe you can trot around the beach in a bikini," Joan said.

B.J. laughed. "Stupid I may be, insane I ain't."

"Somebody just drove up," Sandy said.

"It's Edyth. And there's Meredith too. She looks absolutely lethal."

"She's probably thinking about Papa's automobile," B.J. said. "She always was a nut about cars. She went with the worst creep for a whole year once just because he had the most beautiful restored A model you ever saw."

"Then why do they drive a Chevrolet?" Martha said. "You know damned well they can afford something else."

"I think she's doing penance," Joan said. "It's a form of sackcloth and ashes."

"Do I get a drink?" Martha said.

"Tell Cora while I let them in," Joan said.

Martha got up and wandered off to the kitchen. Sandy and B.J. looked at each other. "How do you think she's doing?" B.J. said.

Sandy shook her head. "How can you tell? She was always a little put upon."

"God. Remember the time Frank had the thing with that girl who flew the airplane?"

"I heard that," Martha said. She was standing in the doorway, balancing her bloody mary.

"Well, we all do remember it, honey," B.J. said. "It was quite a thing."

"As I remember he got air sick," Martha said shortly. "Hello, Edyth, Meredith. Join the wake."

"Is everybody here?" Joan said. "No, not Mary Alice. I'll have Cora bring the mixings in here."

They all sat down and crossed their legs and sipped their drinks, and looked at each other.

"Why don't we all get some paper and pencils and write down what we're thinking and then read it out loud?" B.J. said.

"I've never known you to have to resort to anything like that, B.J.," Meredith said.

80

"No. I'm uninhibited. And hungry. I wish Mary Alice would get here."

"She's probably baby-sitting," Martha said. "Shari puts everything off on her."

"I think that's her now," Joan said. "We're having a salad, by the way. I don't know how hungry everybody is. I'm not." She went to the door and let Mary Alice in.

"Sorry," Mary Alice said. "Customers at the last minute. Why didn't you go on and eat?"

"We're not exactly hungry," Joan said.

"Chirk up, dear," Mary Alice said. "It can't be as bad as we all think."

They went into Joan's sunny breakfast room and sat around a glass-topped table. "I thought I'd call Kat and Dolores tonight," Joan said.

"That sounds mighty like whistling in the dark to me," Mary Alice said.

Joan shrugged. A smile appeared at the corner of her mouth. "Remember how Clarissa used to lecture us about men?" she said. "I reckon she might have been right."

"Oh God," B.J. said. "I'd forgotten that. She thought my Clark was a pretty boy."

"He was," Sandy said.

"What do you mean by that?" B.J. said.

"Just what Clarissa did. That he was a guy who got through life on looks and charm and little else."

"I'll buy that," Martha said.

"Why do we all keep thinking about him?" Edyth said.

There was a small silence.

"I know," Sandy said.

"Why?" Mary Alice said.

"I'm not sure I want to say it," Sandy said.

They all looked at her.

"I'll say it," Martha said. "It's because we've all sat around wondering about which one of us it might be and pretending we're not wondering which one of us it might be, but none of us has admitted she's wondering just as much who the other party might be. And that damned tennis player has crossed everybody's mind for the simple

81

reason we all thought he was the bee's knees, cat's pajamas, la-di-da boy. That's it, isn't it?"

"Well I'll be damned," B.J. said. "I never even knew that."

"Oh, B.J.," Edyth said.

"But I didn't. All of you had the mad hots for somebody or other. It never occurred to me you even saw ole Clark. Heck. I'd have been so set up if I'd known it." A wistful look appeared briefly on her face, was replaced quickly by a smile. "It's a real pity."

"B.J.," Sandy said, "he was like somebody you meet on a train. You know what I mean?"

"Vaguely."

"Really. There are people you love and people you like and people you hate and people you can leave alone, but all of them fit into your life somewhere. People like Clark don't. So you can afford to think whatever you want about them in odd moments. They're not real. They're like a movie star or—well—somebody you meet on a train. It don't count. You know?"

"He sure improved my tennis game," B.J. said.

"Then he did count for you," Sandy said. "I meant for the rest of us."

"I think life is a bitch," Meredith said suddenly.

"Oh, my dear. Don't get on that track," Joan said.

"O.K., Joan, this is your little party," Meredith said. "What is it you suggest we do about this mess?"

"I don't know, dear," Joan said. "I just don't want any of us to push the panic button, as Dylan says."

Six people inquired about Dylan.

"Dylan's fine," Joan said. "But every time we start to talk about this somebody changes the subject."

"Well, there really isn't a whole lot to say," Mary Alice said. "Not, that is, unless somebody is feeling in a very confessional mood, which somehow I doubt. We're the wrong generation for it. This bunch of kids that come into my shop nowadays to get their cute little clothes to take to the Florida beaches for spring vacation would probably be falling all over each other to confess. But we just aren't put together that way and we all know it. Do you know I actually heard one of them telling another in the fitting room the other day that she'd been trying for three months to lose her cherry? We're the generation that tried to preserve ours and there just isn't any getting around it. Just because we're getting older doesn't change our attitudes. We might as well face it."

Sandy laughed. "Who, sir? Me, sir? Not I, sir," she said.

Edyth folded her napkin and put it beside her plate. "You know, Joan," she said, "you and Martha are the lucky ones in this mess."

"How do you figure that?" Joan said.

"No men," Edyth said crisply.

"Oh," Joan said. "Yes. I see your point."

"I don't know," Martha said.

"Oh, yes, you do," Meredith said.

"I am a grandmother," Mary Alice said.

They all looked at her. "Well, I am. It's ridiculous, but there it is. I am too old to go through this mess."

"Aren't we all?" Joan said. "But here it is."

"Well, damn it," Sandy said, "we all know what she means. You live through all the things you're sure are going to kill you at sixteen and twenty and thirty, and you think, Boy, at least I've made it through *that*. I may be getting old and I may look like hell, and a lot of the excitement may be gone, but so is all that dratted pain. I've made it. I'm mature. And then some son-of-a-bitch opens you all up again."

"Miley didn't mean to," Edyth said.

They all laughed. "Oh, Edyth," Sandy said. "Don't you know we all know that? Nobody ever means to do anything anyway. That's what Meredith means about life being a bitch."

"It makes me wish I were a Hindu," Meredith said. "Then you could say, Well, it's karma and therefore only partly my fault, and if I do the best I can with it it'll be better the next time around."

"It is a comforting religion at that," Sandy said.

"You sound like Bill used to," Joan said.

"You see, you're thinking about Bill. We've all gotten opened up again," Sandy said. "B.J., you're not talking. What's the matter?"

"I don't know," B.J. said. "I feel a little sick."

"Maybe you're pregnant again," Martha said.

"Thanks a lot," B.J. said.

"I've got to get back to the paper," Martha said.

"Yes, we've all got to get back somewhere," Mary Alice said, "and we haven't said anything, have we?"

"Maybe it was Dolores Powell after all," Joan said. "She was so homely she might have been a pushover."

"She might have been homely," Mary Alice said, "but she married a cool million bucks. Did you all know that?"

"Hell, I didn't know what ever happened to her," Meredith said.

"Well, I saw her last year when we went to Florida," Mary Alice said. "They've got a forty-foot boat and a house that knocks your eye out, and she wears designer dresses. You'd hardly notice how homely she is at all."

"He's real old," Joan said.

"Who isn't?" Meredith said.

Meredith started back to the store, but halfway there she changed her mind. She just kept driving, through town and out of town on the other side. There wasn't much to look at on this side of Druid City, some pretty terrible developments, courtesy of Oscar Ridley, a rubber plant, and a hell of a lot of gas stations. She drove through it all and came out into country finally, trees and a curving road that led to the county line where they used to have to come to buy beer because Druid City hadn't gone wet until they got big enough to hold a town referendum without the county. She slowed down for the curves and said, "Where the hell am I going?"

Nowhere, she guessed, so she kept driving, remembering all the times of coming over this road, all the hours of driving just to get a couple of beers, all the talk and all the wrestling in back seats, and all the love, and the clear lucid moments of sheer identification with the universe. *Bill Fri-*

day, reading out of a thick green book in Lit. 3 . . . AND MALT DOES MORE THAN MILTON CAN, TO JUSTIFY GOD'S WAYS TO MAN.

So what's wrong? she thought. I loved Syd, and I got him against all the odds in the universe. We have each other and the kids and the house and the money and the work. So what was this discontent that gnawed at her and made her snappish and impossible, that hurt Syd and then hurt her because it had hurt him? What was this ridiculous game she played of not taking advantage of Irving's love, generosity, openness? They hadn't wanted Syd to marry a shikse, but when they gave in they gave in all the way, and she knew it. She belonged—particularly after she produced the son.

She realized she was driving too fast and slowed down. I will think the unthinkable, she thought. Is it that? Is it that I have a prejudice I will not face? Am I the kind of no-good bitch who says, 'Some of my best friends are . . .' No. It was not that and she knew it. It simply was not that. Which meant it was probably some stupid everyday sort of silliness like on a soap opera. Middle-aged housewife bored with life. Where did it go? Whatever happened to me? And what, she thought, *did* ever happen to me—to Meredith Smith who had beautiful hair and bit her fingernails, who fought the good fight against prejudice and injustice and beat the bastards? Whatever happened to her?

Al Weisberg had introduced her to Syd. Al was in her psych class and he was dating a shikse too. That made him amenable to shikses. Al was always psychoanalyzing her. She fascinated him, he said, because she had so many dates and she didn't have a love. He didn't think it was normal. But then he didn't think anything was normal. And wasn't he right? Even now she wouldn't be able to muster much of an argument against him. So she'd found a love, a sort of love, a nice boy who almost wanted to marry her, but didn't quite, so she'd quit dating him. God, and thrown away that perfume he liked so much. She hadn't loved him, not really. She'd wanted to love him, but that was different. Just the same she still couldn't bear the smell of that perfume. Which went to show that Al was probably exactly right. There is no normal in this world.

It had been raining for two weeks. It rained a lot in Druid City. There was an old story about a former student getting on a radio program and being told he'd win a hundred bucks if he named a town in the United States where it was raining. They'd call the station there and verify. He didn't even hesitate. He said, Druid City, Alabama. They made the call and came back and gave him his hundred bucks. "They say it's raining like you know what," they said. So it was raining, a slow, steady, gray rain, turning the world to sog. She was sitting in the College Inn, so dispirited she hadn't even taken off her raincoat and she felt damp and sniffly and down. Oh, way down. And here came Al, moving purposefully, as he moved through all of life, books in a neat oilskin parcel under his arm, looking like the only dry human left in the universe. He bought her a cup of coffee and plunked it down in front of her. "What's wrong with Meredith?" he said.

"I threw away my ten-dollar bottle of Song of India perfume," she said.

"That was probably very good for the soul," he said.

"No."

"Yes."

She shrugged and sipped the coffee and burned her tongue. "Oh, damn, damn, damn," she said.

Al watched her. "Meredith," he said finally, "I have just discovered the secret of life. I know exactly what it is."

"Oh, Jesus," she said. "Couldn't you spare me that today?"

"No. It is you who have given it to me. Here you sit in your damp raincoat on a rainy day with a burned mouth, having thrown away your feminine embellishments, and I know what you want, and from this I know what everyone wants, and from that I have discovered what the world is all about."

"Write it down in your next bluebook," Meredith said.

"Don't you want to be the first person to hear the Theory of Weisberg?"

"I don't want to be singled out," Meredith said. "Not even for a signal honor. I want to disappear."

"Ah," Al said. "You are bearing out my theory with every breath. Are you ready?"

"I gather it's inevitable."

"It is Escape from Reality," Al said. "That is all anything is. Now, think carefully, and if you can think of a single act of your own or anyone else's which will not fit this theory I'll buy you a drink."

"Buy me one anyway. I'm cold."

"You just have goose bumps because of my great insight. But think about it. It is true."

He waited. "Have you thought of anything to refute me?"

"No."

"You won't."

She gave up and took off her raincoat because he always managed to get her to talking. "Love?" she said.

"Escape from the reality of not being in love."

She stared at him. "It's awful," she said. "Everything does fit."

"I told you."

"Money—escape from poverty," she said. "Sex—escape from discomfort. Books—oh, that is a really good one. Food, drink, noise, conversation. Hell, Al."

"I told you. Now you can cease to worry about why you do anything. You know. So enjoy. You threw away your nice perfume because you wanted to escape the reality of smelling thataway. So, sweet, now Dr. Weisberg is going to mess around with fate and give you a real good escape."

"Please don't."

"His name is Syd and he is my esteemed roommate and fraternity brother, and you will like him very much and buy a new bottle of some other kind of perfume."

So Syd was therapy; and it turned out just the way Al said it would. He was therapy she liked.

Al and Syd lived in a fantastic old house on the edge of the campus. The house was falling apart and a completely demented old lady owned it and rented it all out except for one room. She never used the door, but went in and out by her window, and she would forget to pay the electric bill and suddenly all the lights in the house would go off. But it was a cheap place to live and it had big rooms and nobody gave a damn who came in or out or how long they stayed. During her college days Meredith was in that house often because somebody she knew was always living there. It was at a party there that she'd seen a divorce happen right before her eyes.

Evelyn and Burke. What ever happened to them? Evelyn had looked like a girl in a teenage novel, with long wispy blond hair, a pensive face, and a thin little body that managed to look sexy just the same. Burke was a brunet, short and stocky and terribly masculine. They had been sitting on the floor in front of the fireplace, looking into it, and Meredith had thought she'd never seen two people look as happy and as right together. Then that wonderful-looking girl, Irene Somebody, had walked out of the kitchen with a mint julep she'd spent an hour concocting and said, "Who wants a taste?"

Burke had looked up at her and said, "I do."

The moment hung like a crystal in Meredith's mind. Irene had held out the glass. It was silver and there was frost on it, and the mint smelled like summer in the chilly room. Burke took a sip of it and looked at Irene and said, Thanks. And she said, Yes. Then Evelyn had exploded off the floor like somebody crazy. Irene had already turned away to offer the glass somewhere else and Burke was looking back into the fire again, but there was Evelyn, looking like a Fury, tears running down her face and screaming at him.

"I told you," she said. "I told you. It is not the way you said it would be. You wanted her. I saw you. Damn you forever, I saw you."

And Burke saying, "No, baby. What the hell, baby?"

All the rest of them, pretty well stoned by this time, quit talking and stared at them. Because they all knew that was the end of the fairy tale. They weren't married more than a month after that. Not that anything ever happened between Burke and Irene either. Nothing that neat. Evelyn just quit believing in something. Meredith wondered if she'd ever learned to believe in anything again.

Meredith, slowing the car, saw that she was already across the county line. She drove on to the next side road and turned the car and started back. Sandy was right. Somehow this damned thing had opened up all the closed chests and boxes and bales in the attic and under the bed. She hadn't thought of that Burke-Evelyn thing in years.

So why am I thinking about it now? she wondered. Because I started out to think about Syd and me and maybe that's all there is to that? Magic dying . . . Tristram and the cup. But that should be magic starting. Or maybe when any magic starts some other magic somewhere was to die. Clap your hands, everybody, and save Tinker Bell. Dear Lord, I'm crying.

The countryside whipped past the window, all the rows of trees and fields of dried and dead cotton and corn, that had been here then and now and probably tomorrow. But she slowed down for the curve anyway. They hadn't even finished inventory at the store.

Miranda and Dylan were making magic on the river bank. It was chilly so they had the car heater on and their breath and cigarette smoke had fogged the inside of the panes so that they were in a world away from the world, and because they were modern children they didn't mind that the world was made of chrome and steel and leather, and that it had cost more money than they either had, or that it could kill them both in some quick moment on the roadway, or that it took a certain amount of gasoline to make it go. *The barge she sat in like a burnished throne . . .*

"Miranda," Dylan said, "do you really have a two o'clock class?"

"I have one and I can't cut it—not again."

"I would have to have a conscientious girl."

"Am I your girl, Dylan?"

"Yes."

"What does that mean?"

"I don't know."

Don't push him, Miranda thought. Don't push him, and get that tight-lipped look and that blank stare and that What have I to do with you? bit. Don't do that, Miranda. Make him smile.

She kissed him just beneath the jawbone. "That is a sweet place," she said. "An absolutely delicious place. Now I will comb my hair and go to Philosophy and tell them there is a teleological universe. It means, sweet places are for kissing. That is its meaning." She pushed him away and combed her hair and straightened her clothes and lit a cigarette. "Onward and upward, darling. Excelsior."

Dylan looked at her. He smiled. He turned the key in the ignition and took her back to school.

E. K. Edwards was practicing all the magic at his command. He had practiced it with the board of trustees and with the deans and with the alumni president and with the police and with the reporters and with the housemothers and with the department heads. He had no need to practice with his wife. She sat across the table from him.

"So?" she said.

"I still don't know," he said. "Everybody would like to hush it up. Everybody would like to forget it happened. Nobody quite sees how we can."

"I've seen worse," she said. "That hazing thing. God."

"Yes. But the boy's family cooperated very well."

"That's because his father had belonged to that frat. I hate to think if he'd been another type."

"It was an accident. I truly believe myself it was an accident," E.K. said. "This wasn't."

"Oh, yes, it was, dear," she said.

"Don't be crude," he said.

"Crude? Good Lord. When I think of the things I've heard and seen while being a gracious college president's wife, this seems almost disgustingly normal. But I'll tell you one thing. This time I'm all for hushing it up. What good is it going to do to bring hell back into somebody's life who has lived through it and past it and maybe even forgotten

90

it? Yes. Don't raise your eyebrows at me, Ed. I said maybe even forgotten it. People do. There are places where the blocks go up. It's known as survival. It happens."

"Do you have any suggestions?"

"Yes. For one thing there's election coming up for our esteemed sheriff within the next year. For another there's a lot of alumni money in that sorority. For another there's Oscar Ridley. But I'm sure you've thought of all this."

"What about Oscar?"

"Ed, Oscar is the only person who pinpointed the thing. Why he found it necessary to do it only he knows, but if it weren't for that no policeman would be interested in screening every girl who ever lived in that house."

"And what do you think Oscar's lever is, love?"

"Oh, Ed, for God sakes."

"I can't resort to bribery."

"I was thinking about that land over by the river."

"Oh. That," E.K. said.

Martha entered the newspaper office by the side door and there was the sound of the presses, waiting for her. She went on upstairs. There was a memo sheet on her desk and she was glad of it. There were two calls to make during the afternoon. She left her coat on and took the addresses and went back down and got in the car.

The sun shone and she drove along Main Street watching people—old people, young people, children. They all seemed to have somewhere to go. So did she. She was going to interview Walden P. Kranmer, new resident of Druid City. He lived on Clover Lane and to get there she had to pass the new house Frank had built for Layne. She'd never seen it. She didn't want to see it. Of course she wanted to see it. She turned into Warrior Shores. She knew which house it was. She'd heard about every board and brick that went into it. It was at the end of the street. It looked just the way she had thought it would, all planes and angles and straight blank walls, everything hidden away somewhere inside. I shouldn't have stayed here, she thought, but where was I going to go? They offered me the job. There were two cars parked in the drive, Frank's SL and a Kharmann

Ghia. There were azalea bushes in the yard. There was a neat bronze sign, Frank Plowden, M.D. She drove on by.

They had met Layne at one of those enormous parties Joan Friday gave every year during the Christmas season. The country club had been decorated with poinsettias, hundreds of bright red stars. They were late because Frank had had a last-minute patient, and they didn't expect to be able to stay because there was a full moon and Frank said everybody in their ninth month would come to term tonight. The room was crowded and noisy and full of smoke. Everybody had already had at least two drinks. She'd said, "Hurry and get us one, I feel positively frighteningly sober."

Frank had wandered off toward the bar and Joan came up and said, "Merry Christmas, darling, you know everybody—oh, well, not Layne. She's a house guest of the Bernhams." She brought her over, a blond girl with a spectacular body, but very nicely dressed in something black. She was holding a glass in one hand and a cigarette in the other. She smiled at Martha and Martha liked the smile. Then Frank came with her drink and she said, "Frank, this is Layne Christian. She's visiting the Bernhams." Frank said, "Hello," and right there, right then, in the middle of all that damnable smoke and noise and drunken palaver she had one of those awful insights that came to her sometimes. It said, quite clearly, *Frank is going to fall in love with that girl.* It was so ridiculous she almost said out loud, Nonsense. She looked at Frank. He was applying himself to his martini. She looked at the girl. She was quite obviously looking around the room and fidgeting to get away. She thought, I'm a complete idiot. I must be fixing to have the change early. She always told herself that when she got silly thoughts and Frank always made fun of her. The girl went away and they didn't see her again for the rest of the party.

On the way home she said, "Wasn't that a pretty girl?"

"What girl?" Frank said. "Oh, the new one."

"Yes."

"Her nerves are too close to the surface," he said.

And she said, "She didn't look that way to me. She seemed very poised."

And he said, "That wasn't exactly what I meant."

It took him three years to know exactly what he did mean.

"What did I do wrong?" Martha said aloud. It was the first time the question had ever come to her like this in the sun of daytime going about the work of the world.

She'd gotten through other things. There was that damned girl with the airplane B.J. and Sandy had been talking about today. She'd nearly lost that time. And there had been that nurse while he was interning. Once she'd even wondered about Sandy. That was after they were married and everybody was having so many drunken brawls and he and Sandy were always dancing together, only that was probably simply Sandy's dancing. Still, whatever it was, she'd handled that all right too. But Layne. Maybe it was because Layne was a quintessence of all those other girls, the airplane one, and the nurse, and Sandy, and even of her too. Not that any of them looked alike or were alike. It was just that Layne had all the things a part of which had been in all those others, and something in her had known that. So maybe she hadn't done anything wrong after all. Maybe there simply wasn't anything she could have done.

Only there should have been. Other women's husbands had affairs, but they didn't go away. She might not have been able to stop the falling in love, but she should have been able to stop chaos. Anybody with twenty years on their side ought to be able to stop that.

The girl with the airplane had been named Dixie. My God, she'd forgotten that. She was a thin little girl, with mousy hair and huge gray eyes. She wasn't sorority. She lived over in one of the old dorms and she was, of all unbelievable things, in engineering school. She used to wear tweed skirts and a leather jacket with patches on the elbows. She and a bunch of independents had gone in together and bought this airplane to take people up for money. Dixie flew the damned thing. Her crop-dusting father had taught her when she was eight years old.

Everything was understood between her and Frank by that time. He would finish med school and then intern in Newcastle, and then they would get married. She wasn't going to burden him with a wife before that. He had an apartment over behind the stadium and she used to go over in the afternoon and type up his notes for him. At night she helped him study. They went out on Saturdays.

It was a Tuesday afternoon. She never forgot that because of what B.J. said that night when everybody came in. She'd walked over after class like she always did, enjoying the walk by the stadium, the feel of late afternoon, the smell of grass. She'd gone around the old brick house where the landlord lived and through the alley and toward the second-floor garage apartment. It was always very quiet in the afternoons because Frank would just have finished lab and would be resting until she got there. But today she could hear the noise before she put her foot on the steps. It sounded mightily as though they were having a party. She went on up and peeped through the glass in the door. The room was full of people and cigarette smoke and talk. She let herself in.

"Hi, honey," Frank said. "We've got company." He was wearing khaki pants and a white T shirt and he had a glass of wine in his hand. He took her around the room. She knew most of them by sight. They hung around the College Inn. But they weren't anybody she and Frank ever had anything to do with. There was a Jewish boy she recognized as having seen with Meredith—Al something. There was an Australian boy who was supposed to be a genius, but who looked like Mortimer Snerd. There were two med students who were working their way through school. She supposed they had prompted this gathering. One of them was a girl, Jo Griffith, who wanted to become a doctor and go back to her home town somewhere in Mississippi and treat Negroes. There was a girl from Sandy's ballet class. And there was Dixie Smith. They all nodded at her and went back to talking.

"Have a drink, honey," Frank said.

"I've got to type up your notes," she said.

"Oh, hell. Let it go for once."

"You'll be sorry tomorrow. I'd better go on and do it."

"They're not in very good shape today."

"How long's the party been going on?" She said.

"Well, not *that* long," he said, looking sullen. "I went to class."

She shrugged and went on into the bedroom where the typewriter was and typed up the notes. He came in once and set a glass of wine at her elbow. She drank it, but she finished the notes. Then she went back to the living room. They'd all reached the argumentative stage by that time and were standing around shouting at each other. Martha had felt very sober and very out of it and very mad at Frank. But she didn't let him know any of that. She smiled and shouted back at everybody and helped them drink up the rest of the wine. Then that Dixie had gotten up and cooked scrambled eggs and everybody had eaten them and left the dishes. By that time Martha was tight and so mad she almost left them, but she didn't. She washed every blasted one of them and cleaned up the living room and drank what was left in a bottle of bourbon Frank had. He was sound asleep on the couch and she had to walk home by herself, cussing all the way.

She'd gone into the house and up the steps and B.J. had been standing by the phone in the hall. She'd said, "My God, Martha, you're drunk."

"Yes," she said. "I am."

B.J. had said, "What next? What next? What a night! And it's Tuesday. Nothing is supposed to happen on Tuesday."

"What did happen?" she said.

"What hasn't?" B.J. said. "Edyth is down the hall bawling her head off because Miley's going overseas. Mary Alice is screaming about all of us being old maids. Sandy is drunk as a coot because she went to Newcastle to the movies with that damned queer and he left her and went off to some wild party somewhere and she had to come home on the bus. And now you. Dammit, it's Tuesday. I just don't understand it."

And that, Martha thought, was entrance stage right for Dixie. She never knew how long it went on before she found out about it, but there finally came the weekend when he flew off to Memphis with her and just flat out told her he was going to. "We're going to fly up to Memphis for the weekend," he said, just like that, standing in the middle of the apartment, looking at her with a mixture of bravado and guilt and just plain silliness.

"O.K.," she'd said. "Fly to Memphis, but I won't be here when you get back."

"Where *will* you be?" he'd said.

"Who knows. I'll think of something."

"One of these days," he'd said, "this med school exemption is going to play out on me and I'm going to have to go to the war."

"Don't be an idiot," she'd said, and walked out.

Well, he'd gone to Memphis, but he was back by Saturday night. Dixie brought him back and called her up to come do something about him. He'd been sick all the way up there and all over a hotel room and all the way back. He was still sick when she got to the apartment; he'd been green. But Martha hadn't laughed. She hadn't even said, I told you so. She'd held his head and held his hand and fixed him milk and crackers.

"You'd better join the infantry before you get drafted into the air corps or the navy," was all she'd permitted herself to say.

Mr. Walden P. Kranmer lived in a new house on a new street. He was short and fat and cheerful and he had come to Druid City to supervise the rubber plant. He said he liked it. Martha went back to the newspaper office and typed up the story.

Joan Friday still had all of Bill's papers. They had been crammed into boxes and bookcases, they had dripped off his desk and the tables in his office. They were that way when he died. She hadn't left them like that, but she hadn't thrown them away either. She'd just had Cora bring in some strong boxes from the attic and put it all in indiscriminately—old bluebooks, old exams, bits and pieces of paper with cryptic notes on them, poems he had written, poems Dylan had written, bills, receipts, and names of friends. She hadn't gone through any of it. The books she'd put back on the shelves. The boxes were stored neatly away in the built-in cabinets in what had been Bill's office. At least once a year she told herself, I have to do something about those papers of Bill's. But she never did.

Today she thought it again. Standing in the breakfast room, looking at the table still full of half-eaten food, she thought, I have to do something about those papers of Bill's. I can do it now because Dylan is here to help me.

"You want the table cleared, Miss Joan?" Cora said.

"All right, Cora." She moved to the window and stood looking out at the lake and the trees. When they had first gotten married they had had a little sailboat. There really wasn't enough wind on the lake for it, so that any expedition in it had been full of frustration and hard work and a good deal of cussing from Bill's corner, but they always came in feeling brown and lean and healthy, and the first drink had tasted like nectar. The boat was still in the boathouse, but the canvas was gone and the dry rot had set in.

Bill had lived in one of the few antebellum houses in Druid City. It was on the far end of what was now Main Street, a towering white ghost with filling stations encroaching on it. But it had a veranda all the way around and the trees shaded it and cooled it and there were rocking chairs on the porch. It belonged to the Carltons and they had made apartments out of the back wing. Bill lived in one of them. They all knew where he lived because they used to discuss it after his Lit Class. He would walk around the room, and their heads turned to watch him. He talked in a wry monotone, and they knew he wrote poetry because a good bit of it had been published in quarterlies and they used to go to the library and look it up. He wore atrocious old brown suits and a watch chain and fob across his stomach, and he would suddenly turn away from the window and say, "What the hell do you think Elaine wanted with this guy's shield anyway, Miss Holmes?" or, "Do you know
97

that when Swinburne proposed to the reason for all this poetry, she laughed, Miss MacPherson? She had red hair, too, and I guess you'd call her a show girl nowadays. She nearly killed herself laughing. You see, he didn't look like much. But look what we have here, just because he didn't. What if he'd been her prince charming? No poetry for me to quiz you on tomorrow morning. Class dismissed."

One Friday they went over there—she and Sandy and Mary Alice and B.J. B.J. was kin to the Carltons. Mrs. Carlton and her mother had one of those awful second-cousin-twice-removed relationships. Philip Carlton was in the army then. "We'll just go over and see ole Philip tonight," B.J. had said. "He's on furlough." They had taken the bus downtown and walked up Main Street. It was eight o'clock and the air had smelled sweet. She remembered that but not what it had smelled of. They had had on skirts and blouses and loafers, she remembered that, and Sandy had danced ahead of them, laughing.

There had been lights in the house, but the porch was dark. They'd walked up the cracked sidewalk, beginning to feel a little silly now they were actually doing it. From the porch there was the sound of rockers creaking across floorboards and male conversation and the smell of tobacco, mixing with that other smell she still couldn't name.

"My God, it's a committee," somebody said, and Philip Carlton came down off the porch and hugged B.J. and winked at the rest of them and said, "What have I done to deserve it?"

The voice from the porch said, "We don't dare offer them any refreshment. It's against the rules."

Philip said, "What about elderberry wine?"

And Bill said, "O.K. Call it elderberry wine. I'll pour it out of an old bottle."

They went up on the porch and sat around on the banisters and on the edge of rockers and Philip went into the house and brought out glasses and a pitcher of water and Bill poured out of a bottle that was sitting on the floor between his and Philip's rockers.

They didn't have anything to talk about, so they all sipped tentatively at blended whiskey and did a lot of unnecessary smiling in the darkness. Philip kidded them and Bill talked about southern belles.

"Why do you reckon the good Lord saw fit to make me a college professor, Philip?" he'd said. "Sometimes I think he made a terrible mistake. But then maybe he didn't know there would be a war and I would be teaching so many beautiful girls. I should have had a post in a boy's school somewhere in the frozen north. It's really sheer sybaritism for me to be teaching southern belles literature in a land that smells of flowers in the night."

Philip had walked them home, all the way back to the University, which was two miles away. They had walked through a lot of moonlight, and laughed a lot, and Bill had stayed behind on the porch in his rocker, drinking up the rest of the blended whiskey, no doubt, and thinking antebellum thoughts.

Joan turned away from the window and went into the den that used to be Bill's office. It seemed, as it had ever since he died, terribly neat. It smelled of polish and leather and roses because she had put the first ones on the desk in a silver bud vase. The smell that night had been wisteria. She knew it suddenly in her nasal passages, not really a thought, but a nostalgia, strong enough to overcome roses, strong enough to make her feel eighteen.

She went to the closed cupboards and dragged out the box in front. It was heavy, but she heaved it onto the floor and sat down in a chair and looked at it. Then she opened the top and took out the first paper. It was a bluebook marked Joan Holmes and it said, among other things, "Lancelot was really the innocent party." Beside this in Bill's red-penciled scrawl was, "Are you really sure of your facts, Miss Holmes?"

She put the bluebook back in the box and stood up. "I'll go find Clarissa and talk to her," she said out loud. "That's something to do anyway."

B.J. stopped at the store outside town and bought all the kids a Hershey Bar. She bought herself one too. Then she drove home slowly, still bemused by the fact that had come out at lunch. They had all had a thing about her Clark. It made her feel good, and strange too, as though she had been missing something all the time, and maybe was as dumb as she pretended. After all, any woman should be able to tell when other women wanted their man. It was supposed to be instinct. You shouldn't have to think about it. But she'd always thought of Clark as an athlete, and all that bunch of girls had considered themselves above athletes. Hell, Sandy had run around with that bunch of queers and Joan had married a college professor, and even Miley and Lew weren't athletic types.

Not that Clark was a real college-type athlete like the coal-mining football players or the gangling basketball players, or those track boys. But Jesus he had a backhand! B.J. had never been visually orientated, neither did she hang on to things that were over and gone and had no use in her life. But suddenly, driving along the road, she had a vivid picture of Clark Davidson, white shorts and shirt, brown legs, arm upraised in a serve. She supposed he had been good-looking, though she'd never thought much about it one way or the other. Looks didn't have much to do with anything as far as she could see.

They used to go out at sunrise, when there were just the two of them on the courts. The whole world would smell fresh and the court would feel springy under your feet. They'd play two sets, and both be tired and sweaty and yet toned up. Then they'd go out in Grant's Woods over behind the old quadrangle and make love. It seemed like part of the same thing somehow, using all of you the best you could for a good purpose—tennis or love—both of them something they were both pretty good at. She'd loved him, but she'd known, even then, that it wasn't anything that was going to last or that had anything to do with marriage and children and the rest of her life. It was funny how when you were that age there were so many choices, and you knew it, so you could do a lot of things and feel a lot of ways and it was all good. Then somewhere someday that wasn't true anymore. You'd made this choice here and that

100

one there and there kept being fewer of them as you went along, and one day you realized there really weren't any left at all. Not unless you wanted to tear up the pea patch which people, being conservative at heart, really didn't want to do. She thought about Frank Plowden. He'd done it. But hell, that was because he hadn't had all the choices along the way. He'd made a big irrevocable one too quick. "Gee, B.J.," she told herself, "you're thinking like a heavyweight. It's got something to do with them finding that damned baby in the wall."

She turned into her driveway and slowed down as she saw Jim and Timmy coming to meet her. Timmy was ten and serious. Sometimes she was afraid he was her favorite, and she didn't believe in having favorites. Children were all too unique, too wonderful as what they were, and so incredibly different. It always seemed strange to her that the same two genetic sources could get together over and over again and keep turning out something completely unique. Timmy came toward the car, Jim tagging behind him. Jim was her youngest, and irresistible. Not just to her, but to everybody. He charmed utter strangers and children haters. Now he was dragging a packing box with the bottom out. His face was smeared with jam and he was smiling. Timmy was carrying a plastic model of a guillotine, balancing it carefully in both hands. She stopped the car.

"Say, Mother," Timmy said, "isn't this keen?" He cocked his head and grinned at her, waiting to see if she would get the pun. If she didn't he'd say, "Get it?"

She cocked her head back at him. "It's hard to say," she said. "When was it sharpened last?"

He laughed. Jim tugged at the car door. "Let me in, Mama," he said. "I want you to carry this."

"Carry it where?" she said, looking at the box.

"Garage," he said grandly. "I'm tired of carrying it."

"Hop in," she said. She reached around and opened the back door. "Help him get it in, Timmy," she said. "I'll hold the guillotine."

"Don't drop it, please."

101

"I'll try."

She drove around to the garage and deposited Jim and the box. Timmy stood in the doorway waiting for her.

"You bring a surprise?" Jim said.

"Don't I always?"

They trailed her to the back door. The girls were in the kitchen pasting something together on the kitchen table. "God, what's all that?" she asked the maid.

"Some one of them damfool school projects Liza got to do. They all been helping her and messing up my kitchen."

"So I see. Candy, everybody."

She distributed the Hersheys. "Where's Bill?" she said, holding the last one in her hand.

"Oh, he's reading," Liza said.

"Somebody take him the Hershey. Not you, Liza, you always nibble. Timmy." She handed it over and looked at the conglomeration of paper, paste, paint, and magazines on the table. "What is it?"

"Products of the Midwestern states," Liza said. "Pictures and text."

"That's my new *Journal*," B.J. said.

"Oh Mother . . ."

"Nope." She swooped it up and leafed through it. "You only got one story and an article," she said. "I guess that isn't too bad."

She went into the den and turned off the television that nobody was watching, picked up two shoes and three odd socks, and went upstairs. Her bedroom seemed unnaturally clean and still, though her dressing table drawer was open where they'd gotten her nail scissors out and she knew the sewing kit would be a mess. She shut her door and went over to the window and looked out. The lawn was still brown, but buttercups were blooming down the drive and around the playhouse. When she'd been a little girl there had been a sweet-bubby bush by her playhouse. She could still smell the sweet, peppery, overpowering odor, and see the tiny curled dark purple buds. When you chewed the twigs they tasted of . . . what? Peppermint? Something tangy and good and satisfying. "There are so many things," she said. "Just so many. All kinds. I want the kids to all grow up seeing that."

The door opened. She assessed the sound of steps on the rug without turning around. "Please knock, Mary," she said.

"Sorry, Mama. There's somebody downstairs to see you."

"Who, love?"

"It's Aunt Sandy," Mary said. Mary had J.D.'s hair and eyes and B.J.'s movements and body. Her quiet determined voice was all her own.

"Tell her I'll be right down," B.J. said. She glanced in the mirror, tugged at her blouse, shrugged and went downstairs.

Sandy was in Timmy's room, admiring his models. B.J. put her head around the door. "Could I have my company, please sir?" she said.

"She just wanted to see the new ones," Timmy said.

"I bet. Come on, Sandy. I have a feeling it's warm enough to sit out back on the terrace if we move the chairs into the sun. You want some coffee?"

"Yes."

They went out through the kitchen, B.J. grabbing the pot as they went.

"One of these days you going to pull the plug right out the wall, doing that," Sue said.

"Nonsense," B.J. said. "I just want to plug it in outside. Would you bring the cups, please?"

They pulled chairs into the patch of sunlight on the terrace and sat down.

"Well, aren't you going to ask me why I came out?" Sandy said.

"Hell, no, I'd rather think you wanted to see me," B.J. said.

"Well, I did. I started back to that damned studio and I thought, I just do not want to do that this afternoon. So I called Kurt's sister and had her take over for me. Then I thought, I want to talk to B.J. some more. She cheers me up."

"You need cheering?"

"Oh, not really. But it's a pretty day. Why spoil it by having to go back and change and teach?"

103

"This thing worry you?" B.J. said.

"Some."

"It does all of us. We'd be real nuts if it didn't. But, hell, you aren't going to change it by worrying about it."

"I don't know," Sandy said. She stopped and waited while Sue moved a table over and set cups out. "It isn't the thing itself so much, it's an awful feeling I have that it's going to do all sorts of things to all of us."

"Maybe that's good," B.J. said. "We're all pretty much in a rut. I was thinking driving home about the choices being all gone, that sort of thing. Maybe this will shake everybody up and . . . oh, I don't know."

"That doesn't sound like you, B.J." Sandy said. "If I ever knew anybody that got up in the morning full of choices it's you."

"You know what I mean," B.J. said.

"Yeah." Sandy sipped her coffee. "I guess I do. Say, B.J., were you in love with that tennis bum?"

"Oh . . . yeah. Like you are at that age. In love with love and with the whole idea of a sort of person, sort of time. Yeah."

"Like my railroad man," Sandy said.

"Maybe. You never talked about that."

"There wasn't anything to talk about. He used to take me out and buy me wonderful meals at wonderful restaurants in Newcastle when the checks came in. Blow it all, that's the way those railroad boys used to think. Drink and eat and live it up, dance till three o'clock in the morning, smooch the rest of the night, stagger in half-killed, and sleep like the dead till the middle of the morning, then get up and start in all over again. He'd come to my cousin's house and get me and we'd go on a picnic out in the country somewhere and smooch some more. Real torture stuff. Good Lord."

"No," B.J. said. "Mine wasn't like that. Was that what you wanted to know?"

"Oh, B.J.," Sandy said, "I wasn't fishing. Honestly. We can't all start in trying to make each other feel that way."

"Joan wants to," B.J. said. "She'd love to dig up all sorts

of dirt and feel justified in putting the knife to whoever she can."

"I don't think so," Sandy said. "She just doesn't really think. Not about how things may have been for other people. Everything was always so easy for her. She was so pretty. Pronounced pritty."

"Ho, ho," B.J. said. "You've cheered *me* up. Have you ever gotten a look at her face when anybody mentions Dylan's girl?"

"What's wrong with her? The girl?" Sandy said.

"She is, I believe," B.J. said, "what my Liza would term a swinger."

Sandy smiled. "Is she pritty?" she said.

"No," B.J. said. "But she's going to be beautiful, give her a few years."

"Ah," Sandy said.

"Besides, her father's a farmer or something equally distasteful to poor Joan. Remember the time she tried to talk Edyth out of marrying Miley?"

"I'd forgotten that. Ole Edyth really came through that time, didn't she? She used to let Joan put it on her about Bob Allen. But, boy, she let Joan have it about Miley. I think that's the first time in my life I really believed in the solid kind of thing. You know, the love that's supposed to light your old age bit. As I remember, she said, 'A man is a rarity on this earth only equaled in rarity by a woman. There aren't many of either. I've got a man.' Oh, my. At the time my sentiments weren't exactly with her, but she got through to me. She got through to all of us. I remember nobody said a damned word for five minutes."

"Not even Martha," B.J. said.

Sandy looked at her. "No, not even Martha," she said. "How do you think she is?"

"Lonely. Wouldn't you be?"

"But why the hell doesn't she get out of Druid City? That's some sort of insanity."

"Well, all her friends are here," B.J. said. "I think she feels like *they* should have gotten out."

"He had his practice," Sandy said. "I don't give Frank a whole lot of house room, but he did have his practice."

"I thought you always liked him," B.J. said.

"Yes . . . and no. I guess I always liked both of them more than I would have normally because I saw something there that was . . . I don't know how to put it . . . saying doomed sounds pretentious. Saying anything after the fact does."

"But everybody thought they had a perfect marriage," B.J. said.

"That was just it."

"Evidently," B.J. said. "What do you think of *her*?"

"I don't know her. Not really. None of us do. But I have to say—and you can call me unfair or anything else—I have to say he isn't looking for anything anymore."

"I didn't know he ever was."

"He was."

"Hey, we're gossiping," B.J. said. "What fun."

"Uh-huh," Sandy said. "You have any more unkind cuts?"

"Not right offhand. Maybe I could think up a few."

"You should know some of my ballet students' mothers. You wouldn't have any trouble."

"Hey, I'm one."

"Yes, and so is Meredith, and thank God that's two that leave me alone."

"What's the matter with *Meredith*, anyway?"

"I don't know. Creeping middle-age, maybe."

"Oh, everybody's got that. It's something else."

"Hell, B.J.," Sandy said, "it's always something else. That's the deal. Life is one damn thing after another, and you know it."

"Well, this thing is a good one, I'll say that."

"Yeah," Sandy said. "It's a pretty good one. But it could have been worse."

"How?"

"Well, they could have discovered it twenty years ago."

Mary Alice took the house plans out from under the counter and spread them out beside the cash register and stood looking at them. She had an appointment to talk to

106

Oscar Ridley at three o'clock. She'd considered breaking it, but she couldn't help feeling it would look worse to break it than to go through with it. Lew was going to leave the office and come in, that was something. She didn't relish the idea of Oscar without Lew.

"It's a beautiful plan," Sue said.

Mary Alice looked up at her. "I've wanted this house for fifteen years," she said. "And now it's all spoiled."

"Why?"

"I don't know. I just don't want it anymore. When we first got the final plans I could sit and look at them and think about sitting on my terrace in the sunshine. I could look at this little square right here and say, There is my beautiful bedroom with all the space in the world and everything built-in. Now it's just a bunch of lines on paper."

"Is it because of this baby thing?"

"I don't know. I think it was that way all the time and I was kidding myself. Then this thing happened and I could admit it."

Sue shrugged. "Don't build it," she said. "Save your money and go to Europe."

"Why?"

"Because it's there."

"Yes. So it is. But Lew saw it and I don't really want to. I wouldn't mind going somewhere else, though. The Caribbean, maybe. I was only there once for a weekend when Lew won that sales trip, but I liked it. We had a room that opened on a little balcony with a courtyard underneath. It smelled of bananas—or maybe I only thought it did. But the sun was always shining, except for an hour in the afternoon when it rained very hard and very quickly and then it was all over and the sun would come out and dry up all the drops of water hanging on everything."

"Where was it? Jamaica?"

"Yes. We stayed a day in Port Antonio and one in Montego Bay. That was before Ocho Rios got started. At Port Antonio there was never anybody in the bar because it was the off-season and we sat there with this English manager and drank all sorts of rum things, and there was a calypso band. Errol Flynn used to own it."

"The calypso band?"

"The hotel. We had tea in the afternoon."

"Build your house around a courtyard," Sue said.

Mary Alice laughed. "Can't you see Oscar's face if I suggested that?"

"Whose house is it?" Sue said.

"That's what I don't know," Mary Alice said.

Oscar Ridley leaned back in his chair and looked at his office. He liked what he saw. The building was new; it had been put up only last year on the corner of Main and Elberta. There had once been an old house on the lot, but he had waited out the old woman who lived there and gotten it at his price from the absentee landlord son after her death. The office was bare and functional. There was a pale gray carpet and pale gray furniture and on the walls were the abstracts he'd commissioned Ken Brinkley in the Art Department to do for him. They were all very bright and very cheerful with a lot of red and yellows. They looked damned good. They were good for business, too. People looked at them and knew Oscar Ridley was not just a hack builder. He'd worked long and hard to create his image and the pictures were the final symbol of it. Sometimes he sat and looked at them for five whole minutes. Like his very good small cigars, they told him that all was right with Oscar Ridley's world.

Miss Benson came to the door of the office. He had two secretaries, one for show and one who did the work. Miss Benson did the work. She was sixty years old and the best shorthand-typist in the county. She had once worked as a court reporter. She was worth every cent of the hundred and fifty dollars a week he paid her. His other secretary was Miss Wilson. She had been an airline hostess until she got too old. She was thirty-two. She couldn't do anything, but she had very wide-open blue eyes which she focused on whoever walked into the office, and she sounded so completely stupid it convinced anybody with an IQ over 100 that Oscar must be pretty stupid too. She still had a good figure, though Oscar suspected her of falsies. But her looks weren't her real worth. Oscar had seen a lot of otherwise shrewd men get the idea they could take him just because Miss Wilson had convinced them he couldn't even hire a secretary. He paid her seventy-five dollars a week. She was worth it too. Miss Wilson had the front office. Miss Benson was in the back. It was from the back office door that she grimaced at him.

"E. K. Edwards is on the phone," she said.

"Put him through," Oscar said. He picked up the phone, laid it down on the blotter and carefully cut and lit a cigar He leaned back and picked up the phone again. "What can I do for you, Doctor?" he said.

"Oscar," E. K. said, "Mrs. Edwards and I have been thinking that you and your lady should have dinner with us some night soon. I know we're all busy people, but we're not that busy. We've had a good many business contacts during the past year or so, but we never seem to give the ladies a chance to dress up and get to know one another. Don't you think it might be a good idea if we did?"

"Um-hmm," Oscar said.

"Well, now, then I'll just have Mrs. Edwards call Mrs. Ridley and see if we can't arrange something . . . soon."

"Sounds fine to me, Doc," Oscar said. "Why don't we take them out somewhere, save wear and tear on them?"

"Fine, fine," E.K. said. "We could go to the club."

"The faculty club?" Oscar said.

"Well . . . we can't get a drink there, you know. The food's good, but maybe the country club would be better."

"All right," Oscar said. "Let's tell the ladies to set it up."

"Fine," E.K. said. "I know it's short notice, but I wonder if you're busy tonight."

"Well, you'll have to ask Mrs. Ridley. There's nothing I know of, but sometimes these things slip up on me. You just have your wife call."

"Fine, Oscar," E.K. said. "We'll be seeing you."

Oscar, with the phone still in one hand was dialing out on the other one. He got Betty on the second ring.

"Mrs. E. K. Edwards is about to call you about going out tonight," he said. "We're going."

"Oh? Where?"

"The country club, I reckon, to dinner anyway. We don't have anything else, do we? If we do, drop it."

"There isn't anything."

"Fine, baby," Oscar said. "Lay it on, be gracious, be surprised."

"Has this got anything to do with that mess out there at the university?"

"We'll talk about it when I get home." He looked at his watch. "Which will be early. I've got to talk to Lew Cross about his house and I'll just come on home from there."

"Wasn't Mary Alice involved in this?"

"As far as I know *nobody* was involved in it. Remember that."

"Yes, dear. I'll wear the black."

"Fine," Oscar said. "I better get off and let the president's lady talk to you. Bye."

He hung up, butted his cigar, and looked at the painting across from his desk for sixty seconds. There was a kidney-shaped thing in the corner of it that gave him the fantods, but he guessed everybody had some crazy thing that bothered them. That's what all these psychiatrists said anyway.

He stood up and went to Miss Benson's door and told her where he could be reached for the rest of the afternoon. Then he went out through the front office. Miss Wilson was staring into customary space. He told her goodbye. Sometimes she gave him the fantods too.

He got into his new Imperial and drove out toward the campus, assessing the lots he drove past. Druid City still had a long way to go. There were too many old houses standing on what could be valuable commercial lots, too many residential sections that had never made up their minds just what they wanted to be, too many run-down neighborhoods that were hanging on by the expedient of renting rooms to indigent students. The outskirts were a different matter. Things were going well there. Most of the land between town and the rubber plant was coming along nicely with middle-priced developments, and on the other side of the university the higher-priced developments were replacing the scattered private homes that had been built back before World War II. That damned lake out there was still a sore spot in his mind. Bill Friday had tied that land up in such a way it was going to remain useless to any builder for just about forever. He forgot it, as he always had to, and concentrated instead on the land between the university and the river. At least four high-rise apartments. And that land, which he'd thought tied up too, looked more possible every minute. Oscar thought of E.K. Edwards and smiled.

He parked in front of Mary Alice's shop and went in. As always when he entered a place of business, he checked it mentally. He liked this one; it was a neat well-run operation. Mary Alice was not only a good-looking woman but a shrewd one. She had taken a shoestring and some of B.J. Finch's money and made a going concern out of this place. She reminded him of his wife, Betty. Fine women, both of them. But he bet Mary Alice wasn't going to be easy to do business with. He preferred Lew, but Mary Alice was building as much house as Lew was and he might as well face it.

"Hello," he said. "I see you've got the plans out looking at them. It's going to be a beautiful job if I do say so myself. Every bit as good as if you'd sent to Newcastle for an architect. Between us, my dear, we've worked it out right well."

"Hello, Oscar," Mary Alice said. "Lew's on his way out from the office. You want a cup of coffee while we're waiting?"

"Fine, fine. How are you, Sue?"

"Tired, Oscar. How're you?"

"Fit." He sat down on the chair Sue pushed out from behind the counter for him. "How's the dress business?" he said.

"It must be pretty good, Oscar, if I'm even considering letting you put me up a house," Mary Alice said.

He laughed. "Oh, come on, Mary Alice. You know I give fair deals."

"Oscar," Mary Alice said, "you stole the Plowdens blind. I thought I'd mention that."

Oscar was beginning to enjoy himself. "Not at all," he said. "The little lady wanted a lot of things. We provided them for her. Second wives, you know."

"Well, I'm not one, "Mary Alice said.

"No. No. Good heavens, I remember when you and Lew got married. Doesn't seem possible that Shari is grown up and with a family of her own."

Is he going to start something? Mary Alice thought. Where in hell is Lew?

But Oscar went quickly away from families and the old days. He knew how to be discreet with a client. "They say we might be going to get an architect of our own right here in town," he said. "A young fellow from the coast, new ideas, new blood. May be good for all of us."

"Is he going to work with you, Oscar?" Mary Alice said.

"How else, dear?"

"I meant out in the open is he going to work with you?"

Oscar laughed. "Mary Alice," he said, "you're probably going to skin me on this house."

"I'll do my damnedest," Mary Alice said.

Edyth stood at the front window of the beauty shop watching Oscar get out of his car and go into Mary Alice's. "I guess they're finally going to start that house this spring," she said aloud to whoever might be listening. "They've rumbled long enough in the prologue."

"Who?" one of the girls said behind her.

"Lew and Mary Alice. I see Oscar going in over there. He doesn't go anywhere unless it's business."

"Why they want to build a big house now with Shari gone?" Glennis said.

"Why does everybody?" Edyth said. "But they always do. I don't know. People live for years with a house full of kids and not enough bedrooms or closets and trying to entertain in the kitchen. Then all the kids are gone and they build a huge house and sit and look at it, I guess."

"Well, kids *are* messy," Glennis said.

"Yes," Edyth said, "I guess they are." I don't want to

sound like that, she thought. I sound sorry for myself. Poor little Glennis probably thinks, Well, the old girl is thinking about kids again. And Glennis comes from a family of ten and never once had a room of her own or enough clothes or nickels. She probably thinks I'm some kind of nut. Maybe I am. I've been lucky enough to have Miley all these years and that's about as much luck as one woman can ask for in this world. Mooning about babies is silly. It's because of this thing that's happened. I've been resigned to it for a long time now. God knows I only have to look around at some of the kids my friends have to feel blessed not benighted. That Janice of Martha's. What good was she to her when the chips were down? She sucked up to Layne as soon as she found out which way the wind was blowing. Before most people knew which way it was blowing. An instinct for the money. Jesus!

"Mrs. Innes," Glennis said.

She turned from the window. "What, Glennis?"

"Who's our next appointment?"

"Miranda Benson."

"Has she ever been in before?"

"No. Not that I remember. But you know who she is, don't you? Mr. Lee Benson's daughter out on the highway."

"Oh yeah. She's going to school over at the university."

"Um-hmm," Edyth said. "She's dating Dylan Friday."

"Oh, he's something," Glennis said.

"Dylan? I'd have thought he was a little anemic for your taste, my girl."

"He looks like a poet," Glennis said.

Edyth laughed. "He is, I understand," she said. "At any rate he was begot by one."

"Ma'm?"

"Just a figure of speech," Edyth said.

Miranda came along a sunlit street. She had sat through class without knowing what had been said or what she had done. It bothered her because more and more she was that way lately. She just sat there, abandoned to Dylan, Dylan alive in her mind and senses, banishing words and worlds and work.

113

"The world well lost," Miranda told herself. But she knew it wasn't true. The world was right there going on and if she flunked a subject it was flunked, no matter about love or being lost in it.

She had never gone to the beauty parlor before except on special occasions, like a dance. Today she was going just because she wanted Miranda to be beautiful. She'd never thought much about being beautiful before either, but now she wanted to be. Beauty for Dylan, because he believed in it. She felt herself smiling. That was something else. Just walking along the street there she'd be smiling, for no reason. Just smiling. She cried sometimes like that too. There the tears would be. For no reason. Hey, Miranda, she told herself. You're cracking up.

Tonight she was going to make herself a new dress. She had the material, a soft pink spring wool, the color of ice cream and parties and certain roses. She'd make the bodice with darts so she'd look more . . . more like a girl. Then she'd have to figure how to get a new pair of shoes. She really didn't have the money for them, but the dress would have to have the shoes. Her feet were really the very best feature that she had.

She passed a stranger and smiled at him, she saw a poodle in the street and smiled at him. I'm becoming like the duke's last duchess, she told herself. My God, the whole thing's true. All the words in all the books. I am in love.

She abandoned the street for the beauty parlor and the warm smells of steam and hair spray. She liked that too.

"Hello, Miranda," Edyth Innes said.

"Hello, Mrs. Innes. It's a lovely day."

Edyth smiled at her and she smiled back. "Do something very special with it," Miranda said.

"A party?"

"No. It's just be-kind-to-me day."

"I think it's perfect," Edyth said. "Just the way it is."

"Is it?" Miranda looked in the mirror. Her hair was long and straight and brushed, but that was all. "Nothing special, Mrs. Innes? You can't think of something to make me utterly devastating?"

114

"You've already thought of it, honey," Edyth said.

Tuesday evening came with a breeze from the southeast, so that instead of getting cooler the town warmed with evening. Along the streets people were going home with coats and sweaters over their arms and rolling down car windows to smell the scents of afternoon. There was another smell in the air too. It was an old one, with a tang of brimstone. They called it scandal. People were looking for people, to talk to, for nothing really exists until we say it, a lesson the human animal either can't or doesn't want to learn. *They say that Miley Innes found it and that Edyth was actually one of the ones that was living there in the house that summer. They say that Martha Plowden was there too then. It makes you wonder if it isn't a judgment on Frank. They say that Sandy MacPherson used to run around with everything on the campus. They say that Joan Holmes was already carrying on with Bill Friday. He was teaching out there way back then. They say that Lew Cross was in the army and didn't know what Mary Alice was up to. B. J. Finch gets p.g. every time J.D. takes off his pants. Once that way always that way.*

"Mother," Shari said into the telephone. "I have been through absolute hell today."

"You have?" Mary Alice said. "Just what now?"

"You, Mother," Shari said. "I've been having to defend you. Isn't that absolutely ridiculous?"

"It's pretty silly," Mary Alice said.

"Honestly, Mother, everybody I know keeps calling or coming by and asking me the most ridiculous questions in the most innocent voices with an absolute smirk on their faces. I have never heard anything get around so fast in my life."

"Shari," Mary Alice said, "they have been walking into this shop all day long today and none of them have bought a damned thing yet. They are smirking at *me*. So you just tend to your husband and your baby and your apartment and leave me alone about it. The smirks are mine, my girl."

"Mother."

"Good night, Shari." She hung up the phone.

"That's the sixth one that's called today," Sandy said, putting down her phone.

"What's their excuse?" Kurt said.

"Oh, recital plans, costumes, when they should put the check in the mail—anything they can think of. But you should hear the cream on the whiskers."

"You *hear* it?"

"You hear it."

"Jesus."

"Yes. Jesus."

"Would you like to go out to dinner?"

"God, no."

"Shall I fix us a drink?"

"God, yes."

When Meredith came out of the store the Aston Martin was sitting by the curb. Irving never brought it to work with him. She turned and looked back through the plate-glass window. He was checking the cash register and didn't look up.

"Syd," she said, "what's the new car doing here?"

"Dad brought it down for you to drive home," he said.

"He's crazy."

"No. He's trying to be nice to you."

"Does he think I need it?" she said as hatefully as she could manage.

"Everybody needs it," Syd said. "Do him a favor for once and drive it home." He put his hand out toward her with the keys dangling from his finger.

She took them and went out to the curb. She stood for a long moment looking at the car. Then she shut her eyes, put her hand on the door handle and pushed.

Martha went straight from the paper to the movie theater. There was no one in line for the early show so she walked up to the glass cubicle and pushed her money through the open space and looked up at the girl in the cage.

The girl looked back at her with what could be a smile. For a moment she thought, Oh, for heaven's sake. She knows. But she had been thinking that for such a long time

116

now about something else entirely that she was almost able to laugh at herself. She took the change and the ticket and went in to sit in the dark and watch the animated faces on a screen.

J.D. got out of his car and went in through the side door. "B.J.," he bellowed, "where the hell are you?"

"Upstairs."

He went up, taking the steps two at a time before he remembered that the doctor had told him at his last checkup that he shouldn't do that. He slowed down and went into the bedroom. B.J. was sitting in front of the dressing table making up her face.

"You better hurry," she said. "They said six-thirty."

"Who said?"

"The Carltons," she said calmly. "We were invited over there a month ago for dinner tonight. You forgot to look at my calendar."

"You don't want to go over there now, do you?" he said. "Hell, B.J., this thing is all over the plant. There was an absolute dead silence when I walked back to the bagging department this afternoon."

"I don't really see how we can get out of it, do you?" she said.

"You could call and beg off."

"Oh, J.D., that *would* look funny."

"What the hell? What's the point of pretending nothing's going on when everybody knows damned well it is?"

"Not with us it isn't. Do you want them thinking you're beating me or something?"

"Frankly I don't give a damn what they think."

"Then go on and get into your suit."

Edyth put the last customer under the dryer. Please do not say anything to me, she thought. Please do not say anything at all to me. With the exception of Miranda everybody who had walked into the place today had had something to say. "I don't want to hear anymore," she said aloud.

The head popped out from under the dryer. "What did you say, Edyth?" her customer said.

117

"I said you don't use that white polish anymore, do you?" Edyth said.

"No, the beige, dear."

She drew up the manicure table and chair and placed the bowl of water by the diamond-clad hand. Miley, she thought silently. I love you. Why is it I'm suddenly not sure you understand that at all?

Joan drove rapidly out of the Negro section. She wanted to be home before dark. There were children ahead of her on the bridge and she slowed down, hoping they would get off before she had to cross. The porches of the houses she passed were full of people enjoying the first really pleasant twilight of the year. There were old men in rockers, grizzled heads looking noble in the going light; there were tired women sitting on the edge of the steps and porches, hands folded, shoulders slumped for the first time that day; there were young girls like all young girls, skirts tight, eyes bright, wonder, challenge, hope; there were children, playing or crying. There weren't any young men and boys. Already they had gone to the barbershop or the poolhall or the cafe on Eighth Street. The children stood back on the side of the bridge and let her pass.

What she had just passed through was the only part of Druid City that could legitimately be called a Negro section. Unlike most Southern towns Druid City did not strictly segregate its Negroes to one area of ground. Long ago the people who had built the big houses on the shady streets had allowed the house Negroes to live in the alleys behind them, convenient to the house, and these alleys still belonged to them, although long ago the big houses had ceased to house either slave or servant owners. But seventy yards behind one of the better streets in Druid City there would be a street of ramshackle, decaying shacks, housing Negroes. Oddly enough, the section she had just come from was the best Negro section in town. Its houses were painted, its yards planted to grass, its people proud. It was near the school and a good store and a cafe. There were even flowers in the yards.

Clarissa had hollyhocks, and her house was painted a

118

cheerful green. Joan had asked directions of the school principal, whom she knew from having met him on one of the biracial committee things the sorority had been involved in last year in Newcastle.

"Leave the car here if you want, Mrs. Friday," he said. "It's just two houses down. I don't know if Clarissa is there or not. Sometimes she works late, sometimes not."

She'd thanked him and walked the few yards down the block, trailed by two small girls in pink dresses with pigtailed hair and the cleanest faces she'd ever seen on a mortal under twelve. There was a swing on Clarissa's porch and a potted mother-in-law's tongue. The two little girls paused behind her at the walk.

"She's home," one of them said. Then both turned and ran away down the street, giggling. Joan knocked on the screen door.

For a moment there was no sound from inside, then she heard a faint creaking, as though someone had gotten up from a chair, and then footsteps. There was a long moment of silence during which she felt herself observed from somewhere inside the house. Then the footsteps again, quickened now and coming straight to the doorway, and there was Clarissa, opening the screen and hugging her.

"Lord, Miss Joan," she said, "what on earth?"

"Hello, Clarissa," Joan said. "It's been a long time since I've seen you."

"You haven't changed a bit," Clarissa said. "Still the prettiest thing I've ever seen. You needing some help? Ain't you still got Cora?"

"I've got Cora," Joan said. "I wanted to talk to you. About . . . something."

Clarissa stood aside. "Come on in, honey," she said. "It ain't much, but it's clean."

Joan went through the door. The living room was small, but it was clean, the cleanest room Joan had ever seen. There were white curtains at the windows, looking as though they'd just that moment been starched and put up, there was a sofa she recognized as one from Sandy's old house, and an old upright piano from the sorority house.

119

There were two wooden chairs, a rickety gate-legged table with a stack of magazines on it, a floor lamp with a crinkled pink shade, and an umbrella stand. She sat down on the couch and Clarissa hovered over her.

"Sit down, Clarissa, and quit standing over me," Joan said.

"All right." Clarissa sat on the edge of one of the straight chairs.

She really did look just the same to Joan, a tall tan-skinned woman with good high cheekbones, full lips, and a thin nose. Her hair had some gray in it now, but she still wore it pulled back tight to her head. She had put on very little weight. "You're looking well, Clarissa," she said.

"I'm making out, I guess," Clarissa said. Her lips tightened, almost imperceptibly, and Joan knew there was no point in pursuing that subject.

"Have you heard the news around town?" she said.

"Yes'm."

Oh, hell, Joan thought. She's going to go sullen on me. "It puts us all in a bind, you know," she said sweetly. She took out a cigarette and lit it.

Clarissa didn't meet her eyes. "No'm," she said. "I don't reckon they'll really do nothing about it."

Joan tapped her cigarette impatiently. "Do you know who it was, Clarissa?" she said firmly.

"No'm."

"And you wouldn't tell me if you did, would you?" Joan said.

Clarissa did look at her then. "None of my business," she said quietly. "I don't remember nothing about it. You was all my babies that summer. Still are."

Joan shrugged. "It was a funny time, wasn't it?" she said in a different tone.

Clarissa smiled at her. "Member what I used to tell you?" she said. "Menfolks. Don't worry, Miss Joan. Nothing's ever as bad as you think it is. Whether that's good or bad though, I don't know. Seems like folks can live through anything." She paused a moment. "Even if it ain't worth it to keep on doing it."

Joan looked at her, but the bland face told her nothing. "Is there anything you need, Clarissa?" she said.

"Need? No, baby. I past that. Want, sometime, wish for, but nothing I need. Need goes begging, and I ain't ever done that."

Joan stared at her, but there was no trace of insolence or arrogance on her face. Nevertheless she felt distinctly put in her place. She stood up. "Well, I'm sorry to have bothered you," she said. "You know you can always call on me if you do need anything."

"Yes'm. I know."

She followed Joan to the door and held it open for her. "How's your boy?" she said as Joan stepped onto the porch.

"Dylan's fine," Joan said. And then for no reason at all that she could think of she added, "He has a girl."

"That's fine," Clarissa said. "I used to talk a lot about things, but it's the way it is right on."

"Yes," Joan said. "I guess it is."

She threw her cigarette into a spirea bush and went down the walk and down the sidewalk and got into her car.

Dylan's car was in the drive when she got home, but she didn't find him in the house. She walked through to the breakfast room and looking out the window saw that the boathouse doors were open. She stood still for a long moment staring out at the gray sides of the building. Then she went out and walked down the steep path to the dock. The boards felt unstable under her feet, full of years and rot. But they were silver and rather beautiful. She could hear Dylan and Miranda's voices now. They sounded very young and very happy. She stopped outside the door and said, "Dylan?"

He stuck his head around the door. "Hi, Mother," he said. "We were taking a look at the old sailboat. I was wondering if we couldn't get some new canvas and re-rig her."

She walked on toward him and looked around the door. Miranda was sitting on the duckboard that ran around the inside of the boathouse. She was wearing blue jeans and a

121

white sweat shirt about three sizes too big for her. Her sneakers, very torn and dirty, dangled just above the water. Her hair shone like silver, too, in the late light.

The boat was down from the wires, but not touching the water. "It's a good thing you didn't put it in the water," Joan said. "It's gone, Dylan. The only thing it might be good for would be a Viking funeral. We could heap it with flowers and aim it toward the middle of the lake. At that, it wouldn't make it very far."

Dylan looked at her in surprise. "Well, well," he said. "A strange thing for you to say, Mother."

"There was nothing strange about it," she said. "I was just pointing out that dry rot's got that boat."

"Hello, Mrs. Friday," Miranda said.

"Hello, Miranda." She hesitated a moment, looking at the lines of the hull. Suddenly she had a terrible impulse to cry. "Well," she said briskly, "when you get through looking her over come on up to the house."

"What was her name, Mrs. Friday?" Miranda said. "You can't read it anymore."

"*The Lady of Shalott*," Joan said. "It was sort of a joke."

She went back up the path and into the house. It was Cora's evening off and she looked into the refrigerator to see what she'd left for supper. There was a casserole and she took it out and stripped the aluminum foil off and put it in the oven. The coffee was measured out and ready to go in the pot. She filled the pot at the sink and plugged it in. Then she stood in the middle of the kitchen and said out loud," I am lonely. I am so lonely I don't know what to do."

For a long time she had thought Bill was making fun of her in class. He would say terribly cute things to her that amused everybody else and made her feel stupid. She had tried very hard in the course, but she could never remember just what he'd said about each poem. She liked some of them, others just bored her, but none of them were to her what they were to Bill, a sort of communion with everything. That was why he had kidded her so much about *The*

122

Lady of Shalott. "You weave your web in a mirror," he'd said, "but I doubt you'll ever be half-sick of shadows."

I'm half-sick of them now, she thought, watching them across her kitchen floor. She felt chilled and went to her room for a sweater. She stood there for a moment, then she put in a call to Dolores Powell Hanson in Sarasota, Florida.

"Dolores," she said when the remembered voice came on the line, "this is Joan Friday. No, I don't want a donation. I want to talk to you about something that's happened up here. I'm fine. Yes. Yes. I know them. I didn't know they were living there. They did what with their boat? *She* did? But where was he? Oh. Oh. Yes, dear, I'm sure it's a lovely community. One of these years . . . Now, listen. It's important. They were tearing down the house, you know. The Delta House. Yes, I know you donated toward the new one. Yes. Well, they found something while they were doing it. No. Certainly not money. Is it ever? It was bones. Yes. Just like in a suspense novel. Yes, dear, only I don't read much. I'm sure they're interesting books. But will you please listen. It was a baby's bones. You what? Yes. That sounds like fun. But listen. They were in the airshaft and so they believe it happened that summer we were there alone. Yes, just the few of us. Who? No, no. You've got it mixed up. *She* never belonged to our sorority. Well, yes, maybe she would have, but she just wasn't there. Yes. Well, you see the possibilities of this. No. It's a little late to hush it up. You bet what? The who? Oh, Dolores, the one who looked like *who*? Humphrey Bogart? Yes, I'm laughing. I know it isn't funny. I'm quite aware it isn't. You're right, Dolores, I'm probably hysterical."

She hung up and sat there still laughing weakly. She simply didn't have the heart to call Kat Hodges, so she went back to the kitchen. She could hear Dylan and Miranda coming up from the boathouse and she went over and stirred the back log on the fire. They came in the door looking flushed and laughing. "You need some more wood?" Dylan said.

"I don't know. It feels chilly in here to me."

"It feels like the fiery furnace," Dylan said. "You must be

123

catching a cold." He took the poker out of her hands and chunked up the fire.

"Did you see what I meant about the boat?" she said.

"Yes," Dylan said. "I'm afraid it's pretty far gone."

"Yes. Well, there never has been enough wind on that lake for it anyway."

"It's a pretty boat," Miranda said.

"Yes," she said. "It was."

The Carlton house looked just the way it always had, B.J. thought, getting out of the car before J.D. had time to come around and open the door. It was almost alone now on Main Street, though there was a church across the way that kept it from being completely surrounded by commercial establishments. Behind it, the old Maynard house had been sold to a beauty school, but they had been smart enough to leave it the way it was, even to the trees in the yard, so it wasn't too bad. But there were filling stations uncomfortably close, and a car agency and a Burger Queen. None of it fazed the Carlton house. There it was, wide, white, with a veranda and oak trees, just the way it had been when B.J. was five years old and used to come here with her mother and grandmother and play with Philip in the back yard. They had squashed china berries and held their noses, and stripped willow switches for fencing swords. She still had a scar from one of those on her middle finger. Once Philip had hit her in the eye with a croquet mallet, too. Jesus, she'd had a shiner. It had been an accident, but it had hurt like blazes all the same.

"You coming in?" J.D. said.

"Um-hmm. I was just thinking about playing here when I was a kid."

"I don't see why Philip and Cassie want to live here," J.D. said.

"Really? I love it."

"So do I, but it's like New York. I wouldn't want to . . ."

"Yes, dear."

The Carltons were waiting for them in the high-ceilinged living room. Cassie had on a pair of black velvet hostess

124

pajamas. "I hate you," B.J. said. "I look like a damned cow in pants and you're every bit as old as I am and you look like Mata Hari."

"No, I don't," Cassie said. "Ask Philip. He complains about my beam proportions at all times."

Philip brought the drinks and swatted Cassie on the behind. "Not so much as you'd notice," he said.

"So who else is coming?" B.J. said. "You don't get yourself up like that just for us."

Cassie shrugged. "The Plowdens. Sorry, this was set up a long time ago."

"I know," B.J. said. "Hell, we can't all hibernate."

"Well, shall we talk about it before they get here?" Cassie said. "They're always late."

"They never used to be," B.J. said. "When one of them was another people, that is."

"Well, damn it," Cassie said, "all of you are always making me feel like Benedict Arnold. Martha was never a close friend of mine. I hardly knew her. Frank has been our doctor for years. I cannot run around changing doctors because doctors change wives. And to be perfectly frank, I'm a horrid old cynic. I just can't get exercised about it. He didn't shoot Martha, and he pays her alimony, and unfortunately I *like* Layne."

"Oh, let's don't talk about it," B.J. said. "It's just one of those things. I'm curious to see what Frank has to say about our scandal anyway."

"He won't say anything," J.D. said. "You know that."

"Wait'll after four martinis," B.J. said.

"Now who's the cynic?" Cassie said.

"I am not a cynic," B.J. said. "I am simply well aware of the weight of your husband's hand on the liquor bottle."

"Well, what do you have to say about it, B.J.?" Cassie said.

"Oh, my, how direct you are," B.J. said. "I don't know. And that's the truth. I wish we could all just forget about it. Life would be so much easier on everybody if there were just ways to turn things off."

"Come on, B.J.," Philip said, "you aren't that way. You'd much rather fight than switch and you know it."

"We all get on," B.J. said.

"Not bloody likely," Philip said. "Remember my esteemed grandfather. He died at ninety-six still laughing and scratching. I intend to emulate him." He stood up. "I'd better fix everybody's drink," he said. "It's too early and too sober to get started on philosophy."

"Well, I'll have another drink," B.J. said. "But I'd just as soon talk, drunk or sober. It's time for it."

"I bet everybody in town is talking right about now," Cassie said.

"You know, that's a real grotesque-type thought," Philip said. "I can just see them, all over town, tongues wagging, mouths gaping, yackety, yackety, yack."

"Yeah," B.J. said. "And about me, among others."

"B.J.," Cassie said, "what do you think will come of it?"

"Hell, I don't know," B.J. said. "One thing that has already, though, is that a lot of us are remembering a lot of things we thought we *had* turned off."

"I hear the Plowdens," Cassie said. She got up and went to the door.

Layne was wearing a plain little yellow dress that made both B.J. and Cassie look and feel five pounds heavier. Frank looked tired. They came in and sat down and everybody looked at each other. Then a small twitch started at the corner of Layne's mouth and B.J. looked at her and they both laughed. Then everybody did.

"It is all rather silly, isn't it?" Cassie said. "Every time anybody gets together now we all sit and feel absolutely miserable until somebody manages to bring it up."

"Well, you and Layne have the advantage tonight," B.J. said. "I'm the only one of the Terrible Seven who's here. Till now I've had a little company."

Philip fixed drinks. "Well, none of us gentlemen are exempt," he said. "We were all around here one way or the other."

"Yeah," B.J. said. "Even World War Two didn't keep

you from getting around to touching home base once in a while."

"Well, meow, or something," J.D. said.

"I'm not quite sure which summer it was," Philip said. "Was it the year old Bill was starting to get ideas about Joan?"

"Yep," B.J. said. "Who did you have ideas about?"

"Anybody that would listen to them," Philip said. "That year there was nothing in the world but girls and whiskey and the day I was gonna get sent overseas."

"The forward area," J.D. said.

"Yes, indeed," Philip said. "Hubba hubba."

"You are all ahead of us," Layne said. "I'm going to have another drink."

"I had one before I left home," Frank said. "I cheat that way."

"And you an upright member of the medical profession," B.J. said. "It pains me."

"Where, dear?"

"Free medical advice," B.J. said. "Goody. There's been this little bitty twinge, Frank."

"Maybe your nose is out of joint," Frank said. "Or is it a pain in the neck or elsewhere? I have a lot of that this season. It's going around, as my patients say."

"My, you're bright these days," B.J. said.

"I had a drink before I left home. I told you."

"Have another. Let's all have another, Philip. I have a feeling this is going to be one of those late supper nights," Cassie said.

"Will it get cold?" B.J. said.

"Nope. Delay as long as you want. It's ready, but not ruining."

B.J. held out her glass. "Hell, let's tie one on," she said. "You got any due mamas tonight, Frank?"

"Nope. Delivered one this afternoon." He stopped. "We're going to get back on the subject in spite of all we can do."

"Well, it's a pretty prevalent-type subject," B.J. said.

"If you can say that, you haven't had enough to drink,"

127

Philip said. He took all the empty glasses over to the bar. "Say," he said, "I just remembered Miss Sandy dancing on that damned writer's grave."

"What *are* you talking about?" Cassie said.

"Oh, it was that summer or the one just before. I was home on furlough and Bill Friday had that apartment out back. All the little gals in his lit classes had the mad hots for him; they used to come over here and see me just to get a chance at him outside the classroom."

"Philip, that's not so," B.J. said.

"Ha, it was so. I never had so much attention in my life. He had the aura of older man and great poet—all that bit. Jesus. It used to get plum sticky around here sometimes."

"We never came over here more than once or twice," B.J. said.

"Well, this time, I'd walked you home and we stopped at that graveyard out by the campus. There was a moon like crazy and Sandy said she had to pay her visit to this Weldon Benson's grave. She did it all the time, she said. She went over there and did a Charleston on the damned slab. I'll never forget it."

"We used to sit over there and drink wine, too," B.J. said. "You and I did once, J.D. Remember?"

"Yes, and it made me uneasy as hell. All of you girls were crazy."

"You're beginning to sound like something out of Tennessee Williams by Scott Fitzgerald," Cassie said.

"Or out of Carson McCullers by Kat Porter," Layne said.

"There you are," Philip said. "I was wondering if you were here."

"I'm here," Layne said.

"But you weren't *there*," B.J. said. "Be thankful."

"I don't think anything is really going to come of all this," Frank said abruptly. "E. K. Edwards is going to pull every string in the state to shut this up and we all know it. Nobody wants this."

"But we got it," B.J. said.

"Yes," Frank said, "I reckon we have."

128

Layne raised her eyebrows. "I don't want to sound cynical," she said, "but is it worth all the turmoil it's causing?"

"Is anything?" B.J. said.

Layne gave her a very straight, very level look. "Yes, dear," she said softly. "You're damned right some things are."

"I think we better eat something," Cassie said.

The Druid City Country Club was just past a Negro section. From the golf course you could lose a ball into one of the yards across the way and have it brought back by a little boy to whom you could give a dime. Then he could go home and sit on his front porch and watch the children swimming in the pool. It was an old building with columns, and not enough parking space in front. There were four tennis courts and the pool had been enlarged only two years before. There was a good pro shop and an excellent dining room and a very nice small bar. There were two good card rooms downstairs and the Nineteenth Hole, another small bar, open in the daytime. The main room was big enough for half the town to dance on orchestra nights. It was old and established and had a beautiful view across the greens toward the river. But already it was fighting for its life. The new country club that was going up out on the interstate was sneaking its members, quietly and one by one, even before the first spade of dirt had been turned by Oscar Ridley's crew.

Years ago Oscar had bought up the tract of land between the state school and the proposed right of way. Bit by bit he had hooked in other investors. Now the lots were going for ten times what they had cost him, and all he was going to be out was the money he'd had to pay the expert to come in and set up the country-club choice-lots deal that had hooked them. Oscar looked at the columns of the old club and sighed. He liked this club. It had beauty and tradition and dignity. The new one wasn't going to have any of that. He wondered if he would be able to swing belonging to both of them without insulting anybody. Decisions, decisions, they made life as difficult as it was interesting. He looked at his wife and smiled at her with approval. She looked every bit as good as Mrs. Edwards, neat, elegant, subdued. He winked at her and the four of them went into the club and sat at the bar.

They talked social niceties through two cocktails and dinner. When the ladies went to the powder room before coffee, E.K. looked across the table at Oscar and said, "Well, Oscar, you still interested in that land between the married students' housing and the river?"

"Who said I ever was interested?" Oscar said.

"Oh, come on, now," E.K. said. He handed a cigar across the table and Oscar took it, sniffed, cut the end off and lit it appreciatively.

"I heard it was pretty well tied up," he said.

"Well, it's one of those weird legal propositions," E.K. said. "If the school has an interest in whatever goes up, it's possible for another party to take a certain option agreement, I believe. I'd have to look into it with the school lawyer and with the board of trustees, but I seem to remember something about an option."

"I don't know," Oscar said. "I'm pretty tied up these days, what with the new country club development. Got approval of final plans today for a house out there for the Crosses. Going to be a beauty, too."

"That's nice," E.K. said. He lit his own cigar. There's still a lot of work to be done on the campus, too."

"Well, we have to bid on those damned houses. You never know."

"You get most of them."

"That's true, but it's because we can afford a low bid. And we don't have to pay an architect. For something the size of what should go on those river lots an architect might be necessary."

E.K. poured more coffee from his silver pot. "Oscar," he said abruptly, "did you say you were absolutely certain about the summer that airshaft was closed up in the Delta House?"

"I ain't never been certain about anything in my life," Oscar Ridley said.

Edyth decided to have swiss steak for supper because it
130

was Miley's favorite. She took the steak out of the refrigerator and put it on the counter and stared at it. Round steak cost as much as sirloin. It never made any sense to her. It didn't used to; it shouldn't now. It wasn't a good cut of meat. Why did you have to pay as much for a tough cut as a good one? Supply and demand? That never made any sense to her either. It was like the stock market—it didn't really exist except in people's minds. If they all stopped believing in it it would go away. When she'd told Miley that he'd laughed and then said, "But of course it's true. That's exactly what did happen in 1929." So how much was real and how much was in people's minds? It was one of those circular thoughts she could play with all day. Like the stars. *Were* they really there? She'd had an idea once that the universe was only different parts of that one huge exploding star that some astronomers believed began it all. It was just that through time warp we saw different parts of it at different times in its history and thought we were seeing a complete set of stars. And the one we were on now, this silly little chunk of burned-out rock, maybe it had ceased to exist for anybody else a long, long time ago.

Cut up the onions, Edyth, and stop the crap, she told herself. We eat, don't we? *Ergo sum.*

Once she and Bob Allen had looked at the stars from a hill on the way to Eutaw and she'd said, "They make me feel so small and insignificant." And he'd said, "That's funny, when I look up at them this way they make me feel like I could take my hand and erase them, every one." The difference in the male and female viewpoint, maybe. A hand to hold and another with which to wipe out all the stars. Or conversely, a hand to hold that makes you part of all the universe and therefore insignificant in your own small self.

Well, Bob Allen hadn't wiped out all the stars. Or maybe he had. The last she'd heard about him he'd been in an asylum in south Alabama. Maybe he had wiped them all out and the rest of us just didn't know it yet. Like the natives who kept the elephants away by snapping their fingers. There sure weren't any elephants around. Maybe if

Bob Allen quit believing in them there wouldn't be any stars.

She cut up the onions and sautéed them in butter. She pounded the steak and put pepper and salt and garlic salt on it. She sliced it and put it in the pan. She cut her finger. She stood still, staring down at the lacerated flesh, watching the blood start to well out before the reaction set in and she grabbed her wrist and moved her hand away from the steak and put a Scott towel over the cut. She'd sliced right through the side of her index finger, just as though it were part of the supper. Now it started to hurt and she moved the pan off the stove and went into the bathroom and put on the antiseptic and the Band-Aid.

Now I'll do it twice more, she thought. I always manage to hurt myself three times before it stops. The good old unconscious protecting me from a big one by giving me three little ones. Accident prone, but not much. Not enough to break a bone or wreck the car or fall down stairs. Just little nicks and cuts and bruises and lacerations, just little tricks to keep the elephants away. Don't think about an elephant. So. There is this baby in the wall. There are all these people you used to know. And today they are all here with you, like they used to be, not customers in your place of business, but the girls you went to school with. So hot that summer, and so many stars.

Of course, she should have known, because she met Bob Allen through Sandy and that damned Lawson. Beautiful Lawson. Oh, shit. She wondered what had ever happened to him. Though she did remember hearing something about him being in New York once . . . naturally. Well, Sandy had always known a lot of odd ones, not necessarily odd in that way, but odd. They had all been mixed up in the Players that year: Sandy and Lawson and Joan and Bob. They used to meet at that all-night cafeteria that was a laundry now. They'd sign out for late rehearsal and then they'd leave early and go to the cafeteria and drink coffee and eat those wonderful doughnuts that nobody seemed to make anymore. Bob was 4F because he had had rheumatic fever when he was a kid and it had done something reason-

ably drastic to his heart. He was tall and thin and had pale
gray eyes and a straight nose and a thin wide mouth and
beautiful hands.

And Miley was in the South Pacific. She wrote letters
and wrote letters, and sometimes she just got lonesome and
needed somebody to talk to. And things happen, dammit.
They happen. You do not go around planning on them and
figuring them out and saying, I will now do so and so and
feel so and so and want so and so. You do not, no matter
what any damned man believes. Things happen, God help
us all. Did Miley plan on finding a set of bones? Did
anybody plan on having to go to World War II? Does the
egg ask for the sperm? Well, maybe it does. But what can
your oh-so-civilized and logical mind *do* about it? What can
you do about fate? Yeah, yeah, her mind laughed. It's
bigger than both of us. But why do we have clichés like
that one? Because they are comforting, as Joan said? No.
Because they are true. Because we do not live in a reasonable, logical world. If we did, we wouldn't go around
cutting our fingers to keep the elephants away.

She went back to the kitchen and put the pan back on
the stove and poured in the tomato sauce and put in the
steak. She looked at her watch and got out the fifth and the
glasses and looked out the window. But she didn't see
Miley's car yet.

She sat down at the kitchen table and stared at the sugar
bowl and wished her finger would quit hurting and then
decided maybe it was a good thing it did. It reminded her
of mortality, and that was a good thing to remember. If we
could all remember it, we'd be nicer to each other and to
ourselves. We'd live a lot more of life. She could smell the
afternoon now, the afternoon of the day Bob Allen had
tried to kill them on the way back from Eutaw. How strong
all her senses had been after that. How alive, alive, alive,
for a whole week, until her nerves forgot and her senses
forgot and the shock of almost ending went away and she
began to live in the world like everybody else again. She'd
heard people say getting real religion did that to you, being
saved, or having a real good psychoanalysis. But she

133

doubted they'd either one be as good as almost buying it and knowing you hadn't. In a way, it had been being saved, at that. Saved for Miley and for postwar and for today. So like it today, Edyth, she told herself. Like the steak on the stove and the house around you and the dark coming down outside. You were saved for it. Enjoy it. Do not let Miley make you defensive and mean and belligerent when he comes home. Count your blessings—another good cliché. And when night comes you can count the stars. They are there. Nobody's managed to wipe them all away.

On the way home from the Carltons', Frank Plowden tried to get the image of Sandy on a tombstone out of his mind. She stayed there, dancing through the vodka haze. Not a Sandy he knew now, or had ever known. The Sandy who danced on a tombstone didn't exist for him, for in those days he had been too tied up in Frank Plowden for anything to exist for him. Even Martha. Martha had existed all right, but as an adjutant of Frank Plowden, future M.D. Which was all right. It was what she had wanted. It was what she had got. He looked at the girl on the tombstone again and it was Layne, of course. Layne in the moonlight amid the gravestones. He reached out a hand and patted her thigh. "I love you, Layne-O," he said.

"I love you too, darling," she said, "but please watch the road. You're squiffed."

"I know."

Driving through the night like this, squiffed, as Layne so delicately put it, made him think of all the other nights, driving through the dark from that place to this one, from here to there, from now to later, from midnight to dawn. There hadn't been much of it. No time. Never enough time. In school the books and the labs and the lectures, the miles of memorization, the hours of microscope, the stacks of notes. Only during the time with Dixie had he let it pile up. Because he could, because Martha kept right on keeping the notes straight and the reference books open, and holding his head when he got sick. Then when he was interning and there was nothing but work and sneaking a cigarette sometimes in the hall, and Christine against him in the back elevator and the doctor's lounge and the times when his roommate had the duty. He got away with that too because Martha was keeping the budget straight and working and waiting and the doctor would eventually return.

Then, sure enough, there he was with a great big medical degree on the wall, and the patients came, and they built the house, and the money piled up, and the days went by. Then he started to get squiffed on Saturday nights and Sandy looked like a Botticelli. Dance with me, Sandy. Where did all of it go? He'd laughed himself out of that one. And Janice grew up and was a little bitch, even if she was his own daughter, and Martha went right on keeping the books straight.

Then because he was forty years old they sent him a birthday present for Christmas. Layne-O across a crowded room. He'd tried to laugh himself out of that one, too—for three years. But it isn't easy to laugh away the dream image you used to tote around in your sixteen-year-old mind. The one that gets a little battered with the years, but which, when you see it, even a long way up a worn-out road, is still as pristine as morning. Primavera, the figurehead on the old, old ship of fate. Scared, my God. Nothing to protect you anymore. Not even Martha this time. Not even Martha, because it came up from way back before Martha. It didn't matter that They'd waited too long to send it; it was here now and there just wasn't any making it go away.

You play the black and the red comes up, for all of life, so you learn to play it cautious. You learn to put only a little bit of it on the line. You learn that if They're going to rake it in, you're not going to have everything riding on the wheel. Then one day They let you know you've been kidding yourself. It's going to come up red this time, and you know it. Only you have to put it all out there for the chance at it. You've got this hunch that's as good and true as morning, but They're simply not going to let you play it safe anymore. If you want a chance on it you've got to lay every goddamned bit of it on that one little square. And what if you're just not constitutionally able to do it? What if you're a natural-born and cultivated coward? You want

135

to keep a little money in the poke. You want to copper it because you always have. Well, it makes for a hard three years.

"Why did you wait for me?" he said.

"I didn't have any choice," Layne said.

"That isn't true, honey. There's always a choice."

"It's truer, darling, than you'll ever understand."

She put her head on his shoulder and he put his arm around her. There was a lot of moonlight. They'd been saving it for a long time.

After she'd given in and driven the car home, Meredith knew she was hooked. It was like flying or sailing, only better. Better because she'd always thought automobiles were beautiful. She would have given everything she'd ever owned or ever would for a Stutz Bearcat. A car salesman had once told her there were only about five left in the world and they were worth so much even serious collectors couldn't buy them. So much for the Stutz. But an Aston Martin could do things too. It could win the Grand Prix and Meredith Green's heart. Screw you, Irving, she thought, shifting and hearing the sound of silk and satin meshing. Nobody buys me with an automobile. But after supper there it sat at the curb.

"I might just take it back around the block," she said.

Syd laughed. "Take it to Eutaw, honey. Drive it a little. I don't mind staying with the kids. I know you want to drive the thing alone."

"I am having an affair with an automobile," she said aloud when she put the key into the ignition. "I am truly in love with an automobile." We say a thing like that and laugh, she thought. But it is true. Love is an emotion inside yourself. What you put it on has nothing at all to do with it. You fall in love because something out there captures something in your soul. It is more trouble when it's another human being. Because they have a soul too, and maybe you capture it and maybe you don't. But an automobile doesn't care. You can love it all you want. Of course, just like people, it's potentially dangerous. It can kill you, just like people can. But one thing sure, it isn't going to love you

136

back. And maybe that's a relief. We weep because of unrequitement, but as long as we have it the love is all our own. We can hug it to us and enjoy it, even the sorrow. Nobody is going to mess with it because they just don't care. But let them start to care and you end up throwing away bottles of perfume and fighting the Jewish religion and producing children and God knows what else. They put it on you. They expect things. They insist on things. Damn Irving. But bless his automobile. She took it out on the highway and cut it loose.

Meredith and speed, the night going by out there and her in here and tomorrow the world. The first date she had with Syd they double-dated with Al Weisberg and Jo Griffith. They went over to the apartment in that ridiculous old house and cooked hamburgers and drank beer. Syd was thin in those days, all eyes behind his glasses. The damned most beautiful eyes she'd ever seen. Most near-sighted people did have beautiful eyes, but you only noticed it when they took off their glasses. Syd's were beautiful behind glass, like some watercolors. Blue, black-eyelash-fringed, deep as a well and 'twill serve. Only it was much later that she'd thought that, after she'd watched the pupils dilate when she looked into them.

The first time it was autumn, and they had a fire in the fireplace, like they had the night Evelyn and Burke had been there. Only there was nobody else there. Al and Jo were away somewhere and the old lady had disappeared into her inner sanctum. There had been a football game that day, but they hadn't gone. It was a snob thing with them not to attend ball games. They'd stayed at home and listened on the radio and got drunk alone, the four of them, Al and Jo and Syd and Meredith, supposedly studying, but actually just sitting in the chilly living room and drinking and being funny—always being funny. But a girl can't go on laughing all the time. So Al and Jo went away somewhere and they built the fire in the bedroom because it had the only fireplace that drew and besides the bedroom was close to the kitchen and besides . . . She had had on a blue sweater. Why did she remember that? Because it matched his eyes? They'd stood in front of the fireplace and she'd said, "Am I your girl?" And he'd said, "You're my girl." So she'd reached up and taken his glasses off.

Yes, it had been good therapy. It was the first time she'd ever taken all her clothes off. She remembered still the chill of the sheets and the warmth of his body and the strength of his arms, and at some moment her body had told her, This is love, and she'd quit trying to figure anything out at all. Because if like Al said it was all just an escape from reality this was most certainly the best way. Oh, yes, indeed. Unless you thought afterward, while the fire made patterns on the floor and you lay warm against him and he took your hand and kissed the palm, This is all the reality there is. There was that. It could be true.

It would all have been all right if she hadn't been his girl. That was what brought them down like the wolf on the fold. As long as Syd Green wanted to mess around with a little shikse, nobody cared. In fact, if they had known about it at all, they probably would have been glad. It saved him from any mistakes. It kept him contented while Irving was looking around for the right girl; somebody from a good solid Jewish family, not too orthodox, but not too lax. But she was his girl and he asked her to the Sammy Founder's Day Houseparty. He put her name down on the list on the bulletin board. There she was, Meredith Smith, right in the middle of all the Steins and Bergs and careful Greens. She could have been a careful Smith, but everybody knew better. The president of the fraternity knew better, Howard Gold, with the IQ calculated to calculate everything. He called Irving.

Even today it seemed crazy to her. She had been raised in a home that was really and honest-to-God prejudice-free. She hadn't known there was such a thing until they started talking about Germany. And even then she'd had to have it all explained. The only Jews she'd ever known ran a dry-goods store and went to the Methodist church and belonged to her mother's bridge club. So, only lately, had she known Jews were anybody different. Then they landed on her and she found out Meredith Smith was somebody different too.

Syd had called her at midnight on the pay phone in the hall because the desk was closed. She had stood there in her pajamas, expecting all the little half-caresses he put in his voice. "Hello, darling," she'd said.

"Meredith," he said.

And she thought, suddenly conscious of her bare feet on the tile floor, He's crying. My God, something awful must have happened. "What's the matter?" she said.

"I can't see you anymore," he said. Just like that.

All she could say—shivering now, feeling her teeth start to chatter, and the awful pain in her chest, and the old doubts rising up like a miasma—was, "But I'm your girl."

"Yes, darling," he said, "you're my girl. And I love you. But I'm never going to see you again."

"You can't do that," she said. She was crying now, but she was mad, too. Under the hurt there was a rage she hadn't even known she was capable of, a rage at the world that handed you something with one hand and waited until you were good and hooked before snatching it away with the other. "You just can't do that."

"I have to," he said. "Please don't make it harder for me, Meredith. I'm right on the edge now. Don't make it worse."

"Don't make it worse?" she said. "How can it be worse? You're telling me you're throwing me away and you're not even telling me why and you say don't make it worse? What in hell is the matter with you?"

"I'm a coward, Meredith. I'm not worth you loving anyway. So it's really better for you too."

"Why are you doing this to me when you know I can't get out of this house?" Meredith said. "That's not fair. That's not right. You ought to see me. You shouldn't tell me something like this over the telephone—" She stopped. "Is it some other girl?"

He laughed. He still sounded as though he were crying, but he laughed. "My God, Meredith," he said, "what do you think I am?"

"Well, you just told me you were worthless," she said. "That's usually what that means."

"No, honey," he said. "There's no girl. You're the girl.

139

Always. Now hang up and get some sleep and start forgetting about me."

"You're crazy."

"Good night. Please sleep well." He hung up the phone.

She stood there for what seemed forever before she called back. I'll probably get that stupid bitch of an old woman, she thought, and she won't even know who I'm talking about because she's too crazy to know the names of her renters. But she got Al. So quickly, she knew he'd been sitting by the phone.

"O.K., Meredith," he said cheerfully, "don't start blowing your top."

"If I could get out of this place I'd come over there and kill both of you," she said.

"Calm down, dear," Al said. "I'm not going to try to call Syd back to the phone. Making that call to you has just about destroyed him. He ain't in no condition to talk to you and you'll do nohing but torture each other if you try. Uncle Al is going to talk to you."

"What is going *on* over there?" Meredith said.

"Nothing now, but there has been. I will meet you for breakfast and explain everything, with my best couchside manner."

"Stop it, Al," she said. "I can't take this."

"You've already stopped crying," he said. "You're listening. He loves you. Do you love him?"

In that moment she knew exactly what he meant by what he said. Not just the words themselves, but all the permutations, all the connotations, all the unsaid thoughts. And she didn't know the answer. In that second she understood that love is an almost impossible and unheard of thing.

"You think about it, Meredith Smith," Al said. "You think very hard and in the morning we'll talk." He hung up the phone.

She met him for breakfast at a place a block from the sorority house. There was a lot of noise because a lot of people met there for breakfast dates. She sat in the booth, watching the signs swing on their cords across the top of the room: SODA, COKE, HAMBURGER, TOOTHPASTE, ASPIRIN,

KLEENEX, GLUE. Glue, she thought. Why glue? Is it something to do with the War? She didn't think of anything else at all.

Al came in the door, books in his hand, hurrying, as always.

"Morning, Meredith," he said. "Here I am. Feeling somewhat responsible, and very tired, due to a roommate who kept me up all night. How did you sleep, dear?"

"I didn't," Meredith said.

"That's three of us. Want to hear what happened?"

"No," Meredith said. "Naturally not. I'm just here because I love eating breakfast with fools."

"Stop it," Al said. "We'll order and we'll talk. Did you think?"

"I thought."

"Well. You've never met Irving," Al said.

"No."

"You've missed something. He is a suave and intelligent gentleman. And most most persuasive. You should have heard him come on last night."

"I thought he was in Miami," Meredith said.

"He was. Our friend Gold called him on the long distance to inform him that Syd was taking you to the Sammy do. He flew back up here."

"Flew?"

"Flew. He was probably bumping people like a general to get on a plane. Ruined his vacation you can bet."

"Because Syd was going to take me to the Founder's Day thing?"

"Yes, ma'm."

"That doesn't make any sense."

"It makes very good sense, Meredith. And I ask you again, do you love Syd?"

"I love him," she said.

"I mean enough for everything—not for hearts and flowers, nor even for sex, nor even for the cottage with roses. I mean enough to go to Hades and back to get him."

"I know what you mean."

141

"Commitment, that's what I mean. All the way, Meredith. No ifs and buts and maybes. On the line."

"Yes."

"Enough so that if you went through only the hell and he died before you even got him it would be worth it? Don't answer quick. Think about it. Enough so that if your family and his family were lost to you, enough so that it was only what you feel for him left for all your life? That much, Meredith?"

"Why are you getting so serious, Al? It isn't like you."

"No, but this is important. If you tell me yes I'll help you. I'll help you both. Otherwise, forget it. He's right. Don't ever see him again."

"I don't know," she said. "I think so, yes. But I don't know. How can you know that? Things change. Life isn't simple. I don't know."

Al looked at her very hard. "But you're willing to try?"

"Yes."

"All right. Maybe you're right. Maybe nobody's ever *that* sure. If we were it *would* all be simple. They gave him the business last night, baby. He had it. Please remember that and be gentle with him. Do not push him. He's had all the pushing he can take right now. Irving brought up everything from the prophets to the coming Messiah and you'd have thought Syd was in the personal business of trying to desecrate them all. He played on everything in Syd's life from the time he can remember. Hardly anybody can stand up under that, Meredith. So don't blame Syd too much."

"I'm not blaming him. I didn't. I don't. I don't run around expecting total commitment from people. I just told you. I'm not sure it's possible."

"Well, neither am I. It never has been for me. But I confess I'd like to see it. Maybe it would give an old cynic like me something to believe in. Maybe I want to see true love triumphant. Wouldn't that be a joke on Al Weisberg, the skeptic's choice? What the hell. Get up and come on."

"We didn't eat."

"Are you hungry?"

"No. But where are we going?"

142

"Over to the apartment. You might as well start using what ammunition you've got."

Meredith was almost twenty miles up the road from home now. She cut her speed and turned around on a dirt road and started back. "It's a beautiful car, Irving," she said aloud. "I thank you." She drove it home slowly, savoring the night.

When Martha came out of the movie theater it was wholly night. She had the displaced feeling she had always had as a child going into a dark world from sunlight, only to come out into the dark and neon and stars. She stood irresolute in front of the ticket booth, the harsh glare of the lights making her feel vulnerable and terribly alone. There was a long line at the ticket office, stretching down the block. She had the feeling none of the people in it were real. They stood there, robots, waiting to pay their money to watch other robots perform on a screen in front of them. Then they would come back out into the glare and go home and go to bed. Together, alone, it didn't matter. They would sleep and maybe dream and certainly wake up and face another day.

She hadn't liked the movie. It was one of those foreign films in which everyone did exactly as they pleased and it was supposed to be funny. That was never funny. Not to her. No sense of humor, she thought bitterly. It is not true. Some things are funny, some are not. I could never explain that to Frank. She walked away from the theater and went to her car and got in. Sex is not funny, she thought. All foreign filmmakers think sex is funny. Everybody thinks sex is funny. Everybody except me.

She put the key in the ignition and drove home. The stairs were long and the apartment was dark, but she went in and made herself a cheese sandwich and opened a Coke and had her solitary supper. She turned on the TV, but she really didn't want to watch it so she turned it off. She had a new magazine and she leafed through that, looking at the illustrations and the blurbs over the stories and articles and the more glaring of the ads. "Putting a baby in a wall isn't funny," she said. "That isn't funny, damn it. Not even

143

Frank would think that. Would he?" It terrified her because she didn't know.

She got up and made herself a drink. She was talking to herself again and she'd sworn she wouldn't do it. So she drank her drink and tried to think the things she needed to say aloud. She thought about Frank and sex and how it had always seemed more important to him than it had to her and yet she was more serious about it, and she didn't understand that. She wanted to say out loud, I don't understand that, but she didn't. Instead she remembered the first time, trying by seeing Martha and Frank a long time ago to understand what she had done wrong.

She had been in love before Frank. There was that. But so had he. Only hers had *meant* something. It just hadn't worked out. He had been too intense, a jealous, rigid personality, always making her defensive, giving her a lot more misery than happiness, so that finally when he had goaded her into slapping him once she knew he just simply wasn't the one. So she stopped it. She was always hearing the other girls talk about the men in their lives and how they had been hurt by them and betrayed by them, but it hadn't happened to her. *She'd* left. And really quite easily after the first month or so. She'd never wanted to go back; that had never occurred to her. It was over. Frank hadn't been that way at all. He'd had all sorts of romantic notions about this girl who was from his home town and obviously immature and not right for him at all. They'd give each other up and then go back together and all they did was fuss and fight. But that didn't seem to convince him she wasn't right for him. He seemed to think there was something important in that childish clash of personalities. So she had given in and slept with him herself. She had to show him the difference, that sex was merely an expression of love, that real love was forever. By that time she knew they were forever, Frank and Martha and med school and the future.

Then she did say aloud, "It was for his own good. He was wishy-washy." She turned up her glass and drained it and said, "He still is. I didn't win anything at all. It might as well still be that first damned girl I saved him from. Because I haven't saved him at all. He simply isn't mine anymore. He simply doesn't belong to me at all. So maybe he never did."

She got up and made herself another drink. But he had belonged to her. She had let him feel like he had planned it the first time. She'd been reasonably shy and gone with him to the apartment. It had been very good, even though he wasn't exactly the most experienced man in the world in spite of his girl friend back home. At any rate, it had been good enough to get rid of *her*—though later there was Dixie —and Trixie, and Wynken and Blynken and Nod. I must be getting tight, she thought. So what the hell. Even I need to get tight sometime. Even Martha. There isn't any store to watch anymore, so who cares?

But wasn't I right to watch the store? she thought. The doubt frightened her more than anything else she'd thought tonight. She'd always been certain of that even during the worst times. Frank would never have had the guts to get through med school without her, and certainly not the hell of interning. There was the time when he'd wanted to settle for a practice in his home town and she'd insisted they beg, borrow, or steal the money and buy this one here from old Dr. Lewis, and the time when he'd decided nothing was worth it and she'd insisted they both stop drinking and going out until it all settled down again. Of course, she'd been right. He was a good doctor and an asset to the world, even if he wasn't hers anymore.

She remembered an autumn afternoon. She'd gone out to the club to meet Frank after he came in off the greens. She'd walked down the hall to the Nineteenth Hole. There had been sunlight in stripes across the floor and the hall had seemed very empty and strange. She had felt happy, the way she used to when she smelled the first leaves burning in the fall. Just outside the door she had paused and in the stillness of autumn afternoon she heard Sandy's voice coming from the bar, clear, though low, amusement under the words. She was evidently answering somebody's statement. "You know," Sandy had said, "Martha is like God and fairies. I'm not sure whether I believe in her or not."

She had gone on into the room and Sandy had been sitting at the bar with Meredith Green. She hadn't looked embarrassed at seeing her at all. She'd smiled and said, "Hello, Martha. Isn't it the most beautiful day you've ever seen? When the men get in, let's all have a party." And they had.

Suddenly Martha couldn't stand the silence of her apartment. She stood up and went to the telephone and called Sandy. She never did anything on impulse, so she was certain it was the right thing to do. "What are you doing, Sandy?" she said.

"Watching the dullest TV program I've ever seen," Sandy said. "How about you?"

"I . . . I wondered . . . if you weren't busy . . . maybe I'd run over a minute."

"Fine," Sandy said. "We'll have a drink."

"Well, I don't want to . . ."

"Oh, hush," Sandy said. "We're all nervous as cats and you know it. Come on over. The monsters are in bed, Kurt's right in the middle of a new book, and I'd love to see you. Fifteen minutes?"

"All right," Martha said. "I'll be there."

All the way out to Sandy's she cursed herself. Am I begging for company? she thought. Not me. Surely not. Or is it that I want to ask her what she meant by that thing she said—like God and fairies—and now Frank's become an atheist. You see, you *are* funny, Martha. You're funny as hell.

Sandy put down the phone. "Which one of them was that?" Kurt said.

"Martha."

"She coming over?"

"Um-hmm. You want to retire to the bedroom or stay with us?"

"I'll go. If I get curious as to what you're talking about I can always come in for a drink."

Sandy grinned at him. "You could listen at the keyhole. Only doors don't have keyholes anymore. Ain't that something?"

"Gone," Kurt said. "Like five-cent candy bars and the drainboard on the sink."

"And God and fairies," Sandy said.

"What?"

"Just a thought I had."

"Are you making a pun?"

She giggled. "Maybe."

"I'll retire," Kurt said.

She went over to his chair and kissed him on the top of the head. "Have fun," she said.

"Sandy?"

"What, honey?"

"Do you love me?"

"Yes. That answer your question?"

He put his hand lightly on her back and drew her to him. He kissed her cheek, then pushed her away and stood up. "I guess so," he said.

She stood looking after him for a moment, then she frowned, sighed, and got out the bottle and glasses and emptied the ashtrays. "Men," she said under her breath, and smiled at herself. I sound just like Clarissa used to, she thought. The very tone.

She remembered a morning, early, with the sun just showing and the heat just beginning. She'd gotten up because it was too hot to sleep. That summer had started all the way back in February. No spring at all. It just got hot and stayed that way except for the cold spell for Easter. The sheets had felt like wet burlap, and she'd showered and gone down to the kitchen in her shorts. Clarissa had been putting the coffee on the stove. The kitchen was bare and clean and cool and she had suddenly felt absolutely wonderful for the first time in months. Clarissa had looked at her and said, "Hmmph. What you looking so sassy about this morning? You been moping around like a chicken with the dropsy."

She'd accepted the cup of old coffee because she didn't want to wait for the fresh and sat looking down into it and said, "Clarissa what's wrong with men anyway?"

147

"Don't get me started on that," Clarissa had said. "I got breakfast to get."

"No, really," Sandy had said. "What do they *want*?"

"Now you figure that out, honey, and we can all get some rest," Clarissa said.

"But I mean it," Sandy said. "Women want love and security in love. They're simple that way. Men do not. They say they do, but they do not. They can hate you worse for loving them than anything else in the whole wide world."

Clarissa looked at her, smiled, and shook her head. "You mighty young to be talking that way, baby," she said.

"Well, I don't want it to be that way," Sandy said, "but it is."

"What's the matter, honey?" Clarissa said. "That pretty little boy you run around with giving you a hard time?"

"No," Sandy said, "not him. Not ever him, not *that* kind of hard time. But then, it's nobody else, either, Clarissa. Not anymore. It's just I know it will be somebody else. It always is. And next time, next time I'd like to know what to do."

"Lord, child," Clarissa said. She poured herself a cup of coffee and stood propped against the sink, sipping it. "You ain't ever going to know that."

"But you ought to be able to know that," Sandy said stubbornly. "Life is so wonderful. Why do we all want to foul it up all the time?"

"You ain't gonna know that either."

"Clarissa, you're not helping me."

"Honey, you done got into the area where there ain't none."

"Sometimes," Sandy said pensively, "sometimes, later, after it's much too late, you know things you did wrong. But I don't believe you could have stopped doing them even if you knew sooner. And next time I bet you just do them all over again. You're like you are. That's the thing they don't like. They always want you to be somebody else. And the awful thing is, I don't think *they* even know who."

"Have some fresh coffee, baby," Clarissa said. "You ain't gonna solve it this morning."

148

Sandy stood up, almost upsetting her coffee cup. "You know what?" she said. "Men just simply don't understand how women *are*. They think there's some other kind."

"Well, I thought you were looking for something new," Clarissa said. "That is probably the best-known fact in the universe."

"But Clarissa," Sandy said, "some women, some girls, pretend they're another kind. Dammit, that's not fair. That's not cricket."

"Lord, don't start talking about no fair. Now you know better than that."

The doorbell rang and Sandy went to answer it, watching Martha's face as she came in, thinking, No, Martha. You don't think it was fair either, what life did to you. But I don't know. Maybe it was exactly fair, and that's what's so terrible about it.

"Well," Martha said apologetically, "I went to a silly Italian movie and then I just didn't want to sit in that apartment."

"Naturally not, after an Italian movie." Sandy tried to smile, but Martha winced.

"Sorry," Sandy said.

"Oh, all of you can't watch everything you say around me for the rest of my life," Martha said.

"I know it," Sandy said, "and we don't. I just felt a little callous there."

Martha sat down in the only straight chair in the room and crossed her legs.

"You want a drink?" Sandy said.

"I guess so . . . anything."

"You like scotch," Sandy said. "Why don't you just say so?"

"It doesn't really matter."

Sandy watched her perching stiffly on the edge of the chair, sighed, fixed her a scotch and water, and sat down across from her on the sofa.

Martha sipped at the drink. Finally she looked up, met Sandy's eyes and smiled tentatively. "Tell me something,

149

Sandy," she said. "You said something about me once that's been driving me nuts ever since."

"Oh?" Sandy said.

"You said I was like God and fairies," Martha said. "You said that. At the country club one day."

Sandy laughed in relief. "Lord, from the expression on your face I didn't know *what* I'd said or done."

"But what did you mean, Sandy? Exactly."

"Oh, Martha," Sandy said, "that deserves a decent answer and I'm really not sure I can explain it. It wasn't a kind thing to say, but it wasn't catty, either. I didn't mean it to be, anyway. I said that to Meredith Green once, and you know we both love you."

"Yes," Martha said. "I know you said it to Meredith Green. I heard you."

"Well," Sandy said. "God, I need a cigarette." She got up and went into the kitchen and took a pack of Kurt's out of the cabinet and tore open the pack and took one. She came back into the living room. "I'm trying to remember just what it was apropos of," she said, drawing hungrily on the cigarette.

"It was in the autumn," Martha said.

Sandy glanced at her quickly. "Yes," she said, "I guess it was. The autumn that I love above all else in the world. Maybe that was it. I was thinking about what autumn does to me, always has, still does, always will. You know . . . 'The autumn leaves. . . .' "

"What's that got to do with it?" Martha said.

"Oh, the difference in you and me," Sandy said. "I'm such a sentimental slob. I really am. I never forget anything and things go on being emotional to me long after they're dead and gone and over and done. I'm a kind of nut that way. You're not. You may be lonesome now, for instance, and you may miss Frank, but I'd be willing to bet you my new white shift that I—yes, *I*—have a more sentimental feeling about him than you do. That's what I meant about I'm not sure whether I believe in you or not. I've never figured out if you're really the way you seem and say or not. That's all."

150

Martha frowned at her. "Why should you feel sentimental about Frank?" she said.

She laughed. "Well, there you are," she said. "That's the normal question for any woman to deduce from what I just said, but I really didn't expect you to say it. You see, normally you wouldn't. It's only because of this crazy thing that's happened that you're being the way you are tonight. Normally you'd never call and come over here at night or say that to me about Frank. Now would you?"

"No," Martha said. "I guess not."

"But the way you're perching on that chair is normal. That's you right on. And not asking for scotch when you want it. And frowning at me for smoking this cigarette . . . which is delicious. Want one?"

Martha shook her head. "What *did* you mean about Frank?" she said.

Sandy laughed. "Good for you," she said. "Oh, I had a thing about him once, for a very little while, a very small thing."

"Really?" Martha said.

Sandy laughed again. "You see," she said. "You're not even surprised."

"Well, Frank is awfully attractive," Martha said.

Sandy really laughed then. She threw back her head and howled. "That's it, Martha. That's what I mean. Is it *really* that uninteresting to you?"

"Well, I know you," Martha said calmly. "You didn't *do* anything about it."

"No," Sandy said. "I didn't."

Martha shrugged. "I believe I'll have another drink," she said. "Aren't you drinking?"

"I wasn't," Sandy said, "but I believe I will now. This is some sort of an occasion. I think I'm beginning to understand you better than I have in twenty years." She fixed both of them a drink and brought them back. "But I'm still not sure whether I believe in you or not," she said.

Martha smiled. "Well, I believe in you, Sandy," she said. "You are a very attractive, honest, and nice girl."

151

"Why? Because I just told you I used to have a thing about your ex-husband?"

"No. Because you are my friend," Martha said quietly.

"Well, hell, Martha," Sandy said, "I told you I'm a sentimental slob. Don't go making me cry or something."

"No, really," Martha said. "I've always liked you. Remember when all that thing with Frank and Dixie what's-her-name was going on? I think all the rest of them thought it was funny. You didn't. You never did."

"I was having troubles of my own those days, Martha," Sandy said. "I could sympathize with somebody else's."

"No. It's just you," Martha said. "What you are. You see other people out there. Maybe that's what you mean about being sentimental. But I think it's just nice."

"Thank you," Sandy said.

"You're welcome."

They smiled at each other and were silent for a few moments.

"Say," Sandy said finally, "wasn't that funny about ole B.J. not knowing her boy friend was—how did you put it about Frank?—awfully attractive?"

"Yes," Martha said. "But that's just like her. We all have our ways of being unreal."

"Touché," Sandy said. "What's mine?"

Martha smiled. "Oh, you have them," she said. "Think of yourself dancing on Weldon Benson's grave, Sandy—in the moonlight."

"That ain't unreal, Martha," Sandy said. "That's as real as you can get. I only hope when I'm six feet under, somebody feeling just like I used to feel will dance on my grave in the moonlight. Then I wouldn't mind so much that the grave's a fine and private place. You know, I'd like to be buried in that old cemetery. It would almost guarantee that some student someday someway just might do it."

"It's a pretty graveyard," Martha said.

"Yes. It's one of the prettiest places in town. But it scares me that it's so close to the school. I can see dear E.K. Edwards thinking up ways and means to get them to move the dead and let him get the land for dormitories—him or

Oscar Ridley. You know, if those two ever really get together, we're lost."

"They couldn't move all those people, could they?" Martha said. "It's full of the best families in town. And there are so many pretty monuments and above-ground vaults. They wouldn't, would they?"

"Progress," Sandy said. "They'll do anything in that name. And it's such an oasis. It's right off that terrible highway and so near the school and the stadium, but it generates its own peace. And it's old enough to have weathered stone and trees and whispering grass. Oh, what the hell. They'll get it too. One of these days the whole country is going to be a gigantic parking lot cum housing development."

"Don't be a cynic," Martha said.

"O.K.," Sandy said. "I'll believe in you—and God and fairies—and the future of grass and trees. How's that?"

She and Lawson used to cut across the cemetery after class and read the names on the tombstones. Some of them were very old and mossgrown, the letters almost indistinguishable, the marble a rough and lovely dark gray memory. Others were newer, but somehow none of them ever looked raw. They all belonged and were so at peace that the occasional flowers someone left in tacky baskets and jars were an intrusion, as though the dead were saying, We have no need of flowers now. You could have brought them once and you never did. So leave us to the peace of earth and sky.

At night it was a different place. It couldn't always have been moonlit, but she always remembered it that way. In the center there had been a tall and graying monument, built like an arbor with seats inside. They'd sit in there and drink wine out of the bottle in the moonlight, she and Lawson and that Bob Allen that Edyth had gotten mixed up with. He was a real nut even then. They all used to talk about being crazy and neurotic and psychotic just like the kids still did nowadays, but Bob Allen really was, even though he talked less about it and acted more normal than the rest of them. He was really hung up and she had known

153

it. She would never have pushed Bob Allen, not about even a little argument, a tiny thing. There was something behind his eyes, something flat and quick and evil—so much for people who didn't believe in evil. She'd seen it, and that was one of the places, in Bob Allen's eyes. That's why she hadn't been surprised the time he'd tried to kill Edyth on the way back from Eutaw. She'd seen him sitting on the edge of a tombstone in the moonlight, and she knew.

She hadn't known at first that Weldon Benson was buried in that cemetery. It had been Bob Allen who had found it out and taken them to the grave. It was on the very edge of the cemetery, a plain marble slab on the ground giving the names and dates and calling him scholar and writer, giving no hint of that poetry that made you cry and laugh at yourself for crying, at that crazy far-out mind that saw the ridiculous in all its wild beauty and juxtaposed it in words to last forever, and that lay now, like all the rest of them, silent under the stars. So she got in the habit of dancing the Charleston on his grave. Because she thought he'd like that wherever he was. It was a pity he couldn't write a poem about it. He would have done it very well.

She knew something else about that cemetery, something she couldn't tell Martha, even now, because there was something evil in that too, though maybe not really evil, just amoral, premoral, something that smelled of Dionysian rites and blood baths and things so far back in the human race they left only a tiny trace of brass somewhere way back in the thalamic regions of the mind.

She had been to an extra ballet practice one afternoon with Carolyn Kent and they were walking home through the twilight, swinging their ballet shoes, and Carolyn said, "Are you signed out?"

"No," she'd said, "but I could get it done right quick."

"Well, do," Carolyn said. "I know where there's a good party going on."

They had stopped in the drugstore and she had called the house and gotten B.J. to sign her out. The party was at Al Weisberg's in that crazy old house where he and Syd Green lived. The old lady who owned it was just disappearing into the window when they went up the walk, and they'd stopped in the twilight and giggled about it. Then Syd had come down the steps and stopped to talk to them. She remembered the whole feel of that late afternoon with a sensual vividness. There had been a smell of pavement and grass and her own perfume and—oddly enough—Syd's flesh. He smelled clean and soapy and he'd said, "Seen Meredith?" She'd said, "Well, I reckon she's sitting at the Delta House waiting on some stupid guy named Green." He'd looked absolutely shiny. She remembered that especially because it was the first time it had ever occurred to her that a boy could love a girl like a girl could a boy, in a way that made him happy clear down to his toenails, with the all-gone feeling in his stomach and the here-it-is feeling in his chest, and all the happiness that made the world absolutely right. His eyes had looked like the kids' did now when you talked about Christmas. She'd wanted to hug him. She'd wanted to say, "Oh, thank you, thank you, thank you, Syd Green. It is all true."

He'd gone on off down the walk and she and Carolyn had gone up the rotting old wooden steps and across the porch and into the dark musty hall. They'd stood there in the darkness and hollered and Al had come out of the bedroom next to the kitchen and said, "Come on in, the water's fine."

The room had been full of people and they had all looked luckily beautiful in the last of the light. Jo Griffith was there, neat and practical, sitting cross-legged on the floor, talking to the Australian mathematician. His hair was rumpled and his glasses were crooked on his nose and he was telling a long story about a Turkish merchant marine who had tried to give him Turkish Delight. Bob Allen was there, looking like Mephistopheles in the last ray of sunlight from the window, and a half dozen other people she knew vaguely from class or the College Inn. The only surprise was Frank Plowden, already half-drunk, lying on the floor with his head in Dixie Smith's lap. He'd cut his eyes at her when she came into the room and put his finger

155

to his lips in an exaggerated gesture. "Shhh, Sandy," he said, "you do not see me."

"All right, Frank," she said, "I don't see you."

Al fixed them a drink and she and Carolyn sat down in the kitchen with a couple of med students. The sun went down outside, but nobody wanted to turn on any lights so they sat there at the old kitchen table with its scarred oilcloth and kept drinking the blended whiskey the med students had managed to get from somewhere. Then Bob Allen had walked into the room and whispered at her. That was exactly what he had done, whispered at her. "Hey, Sandy," he said, "we got a great ceremony to perform when it gets dark enough."

The hair had actually risen on the back of her neck. For a minute she honestly felt as though he was going to take her to a Black Mass. She made herself turn around and look at him in the half-dark. "Where is this rite going to take place?" she said.

"Did I say rite?" Bob said. "Maybe I did. Maybe it is a rite of passage. I like that phrase, don't you? Rite of passage. Yes, indeed." He went to the door into the bedroom and said, "Frank, bring out the sacrificial animal."

He had everyone's attention now. There was silence and then Sandy could hear Frank fumbling with paper. He came into the kitchen, Dixie hanging on his arm, and deposited a paper sack in the middle of the table. "We need a little light on the subject," he said. "Not much, just a little."

Al went to the hall and turned on the bulb out there. The light filtered in through the door, highlighting the table and nothing else. "O.K.," he said. "Unveil it, Frank. Is it something you sneaked out of the lab?"

"Well, I sneaked it out," Frank said, "but I do not believe you would call the place a lab. No, indeed. It is not in the nature of an experiment. Or is it? In that case perhaps *I* am the sacrificial animal."

Sandy had felt a terrible need to break the tension. "What the hell are you talking about Frank?" she said.

He shook his head, not seeing her. "I will now unveil the victim," he said. He reached over her shoulder and snatched at the paper bag, tearing it apart in a quick movement. They were all immobile, staring at the object in the middle of the table. Sandy didn't know whether she wanted to laugh or cry or scream, so she didn't do anything. She just stared at it like everybody else. Of course, she knew exactly what it was and maybe the others didn't, though Bob Allen did, and Dixie too, she was quite sure.

It was a huge red china piggy bank. It squatted there on the oilcloth looking absolutely obscene in its cuteness—pig snout curled into a grimace of joy, tail a-tilt over its rump, black spots on its hams, slit in its back. It belonged to Frank and Martha and they used it to save for the days of med school and interning when even pennies might be important. Martha had bought it in Newcastle and brought it back to school on the bus. It normally sat on the bureau in Frank's apartment.

Still nobody said anything. They all stared at the obscenely cute pig as though it really were a sacrificial animal. Finally Sandy managed to get her mouth open. "Is it a Poland China?" she said.

Everybody laughed except Frank. He was still staring intently at the pig. Suddenly he leaned over and gathered it up and deposited it in Dixie's arms. "We will now go and make the sacrifice," he said.

Nobody even asked him what he meant, they just all got up and trailed out the door behind Frank and Dixie. Somehow, Sandy knew where they were going. It was four blocks to the graveyard and for some reason they walked it in single file, Frank leading the way, Dixie behind him with the pig in her arms. Once Sandy said, "Have you got a knife?" But nobody paid any attention to her.

The moon was up by the time they got to the graveyard, a full one, of course. She was beginning to believe Frank had planned the whole thing ages ago. He walked confidently through the graveyard, avoiding tombstones and flowers. "I have the right one all picked out," he said.

"This is spooky," Carolyn whispered behind her. Then Bob Allen put his hand on her neck and she nearly screamed. "Edyth should be here," he whispered. "Ev-

157

eryone should be here. We are about to witness something."

Sandy fought her panic and turned on him in irritation. "Martha too?" she said.

"Of course," Bob said. "The final irony. But then, she is so terribly pragmatic she just might drive all the spirits away and ruin the whole thing."

Sandy wanted to say, "You're crazy," but she managed to stop herself. Frank had stopped in front of a tall, looming granite shaft, a memorial to a Civil War veteran. "This ought to do very well," he said. He swayed for a moment and Sandy was able to think, Oh, hell, he's just drunk. Everybody's just drunk. Then Frank took Dixie by the shoulders and marched her to the tombstone. "Will everyone please form a circle around Dixie," he said.

Sandy tried one more time. "Just like the Yankees?" she said. But nobody listened to her. They quite solemnly formed the circle around Dixie, and at Frank's signal she brought the pig up over her head and with both hands smashed it down on the monument.

It didn't make a very loud smash because it was really chalk inside, not china at all. But as the white dust rose into the air and the fragments fell, the faint tinkling of silver began. It seemed to go on forever in the moonlight, pennies, nickels, dimes, quarters, even a fifty-cent piece or two —you could recognize the thunk. He picked a tombstone with a slab under it, Sandy thought. He had the whole thing all planned out.

The last quarter spun away into silence. Then Bob Allen spoke again. She turned and looked at him this time and she felt she could almost see the horns. "Now somebody is going to want to pick it up," he said. "That's going to be the real test. If old Frank can avoid that he may be free for the devil."

They all stood there then, uncertainly in the moonlight, and Sandy thought, I wouldn't pick it up. I'm against this whole damned thing, but if I'd done it I'd have the guts to let the cash go with the credit. Then she saw Frank bend over and start picking silver up off the slab.

Dixie watched him for a moment, then she shrugged, said, "Oh, shit," and walked out of the cemetery.

Sandy walked out too. Bob Allen called, "Hey, I'll walk you home," but she kept going. When she passed Frank, on his knees now, she leaned over and said, "You're the damned pig."

"You can do better than that, Sandy," Bob said.

"It isn't worth the effort," she said.

Now she looked at Martha and thought, How did I ever get that crush on him that time, knowing how he looked picking that money up off that tombstone? He'd told Martha he'd dropped the bank. He could hardly explain dropping the money. Hardly anybody can ever explain that.

"A penny for your thoughts," Martha said.

"They're not worth it," Sandy said.

"Do you think he's happy?" Martha said.

Well, hell, Sandy thought. She set me up for that one. Honest Sandy has to tell the truth. "He's happy," she said, and hated herself.

"I've thought so too," Martha said. There wasn't any emotion in her voice. It was a flat statement of fact. "Why do you think he is?" she said.

Sandy thought about it. She knew why. He'd finally left the money lying at the base of the monument, but she couldn't very well say that. "Things happen," she said.

"There are always reasons," Martha said.

"No," Sandy said, "I don't think so. They happen. Look back on all of us. Remember Edyth and that insane Bob Allen? If he hadn't been insane, Miley and Edyth might never have gotten married. Or Meredith and Syd. If she hadn't got in there and fought he'd be married to some little Jewish gal with a lot of money and a mama to tell her what to do. Or B.J. What if she'd taken on the tennis player instead of waiting for J.D. of the Finch Paper Mill? Or me? God, or me?"

"It isn't the same thing," Martha said.

"Yes, it is," Sandy said. "There are a lot of different things for everybody. That's the mistake people make, believing it has to be just one way. Now, don't you make that mistake. There's going to be something else coming along for you one of these days, so don't ignore it."

"You're trying to be kind, Sandy, and I appreciate it. But you're just talking about a streetcar named you know what."

"O.K.," Sandy said. "I am. Wasn't that what you were talking about?"

"No, I don't think so. You're quite right. *That* isn't the important thing. It happens all the time. You even had a something about Frank yourself, but you didn't end up married to him. That's what I'm trying to figure out. What did I do wrong?"

Now that she had actually said the words out loud to another human being they startled her. Even though they were the words she'd been saying to herself for all the long months. They seemed to hang palpably in the air and she looked at them in faint astonishment.

Sandy looked astonished too. "Why are you sure you did anything wrong?" she said. "I've been trying to tell you. It's a chancy universe."

"No. You have to be wrong about that. You're talking that no-God stuff—no plan, no reason—existentialism. No. I won't buy that. I can't buy it and live." She finished her drink. "That's the way Janice talks," she said. "I don't like it."

"It's better than the other way," Sandy said.

"What do you mean?"

Sandy sighed. "That it's all your fault," she said. "You don't want that, do you?"

"I don't know," Martha said.

"Well, if you do it's just sheer self-indulgence," Sandy said. "It isn't all your fault. You didn't call Layne up like with an incantation, did you? She came along."

"From out of nowhere?" Martha said.

Sandy laughed. "O.K. Blame yourself. Blame Frank. Blame Layne. Blame me. If I'd gotten him she couldn't have. How about that?"

Martha laughed too. "O.K.," she said. "It was what is known as a concatenation of circumstance."

"That's right," Sandy said. "That is precisely right. Now don't start asking me if the concatenation was preordained or not because I do not know and I have always been weak in philosophy. I almost flunked Religion 101 because I wouldn't spell he with a capital. Bill Friday used to say I believed absolutely everything and would and could argue any side of anything. He was right."

"I wonder what Bill would have thought about our scandal?" Martha said.

Sandy looked into her glass. "He would have thought it was life, which is what it is. He would have laughed and wept inside and wondered how it would affect all of us. And he'd have written a poem about it . . . no matter who it turned out to be."

"That sounds so ruthless."

"No. It's being a writer. I used to think of it as ruthless, but it isn't. Not half so ruthless as living in the midst of things and being so involved you never see them. A writer sees it and uses it. That's a hell of a lot better than most of us manage."

"I ought to go home," Martha said.

"Oh, have another drink," Sandy said. "You can always go home."

"Not again," Martha said.

"I'm not even sure about that."

"Well," Joan said, "I guess you children have somewhere you want to go."

Dylan looked at her. "No," he said. "We're happy. You going anywhere?"

"No. I thought I'd have supper here and then tackle some of your father's papers. I keep meaning to get to it."

"We'll help you," Dylan said.

"Yes," Miranda said.

"It would be nice," Joan said. "We have a casserole and I'll open some wine. I keep meaning to get to those . . ."

"We are going to do it, Mother, so now let's all have a drink and eat whatever that is that smells so good and light in. I'll drag out the boxes and you go through and Miranda can make separate stacks of things."

161

"All right," Joan said. "You've destroyed all my excuses."

After supper they went into the study and Dylan put the first box in the middle of the floor. Joan stared at it, then sighed and took out the first handful of papers. "Miranda," she said, "let's have one stack of bluebooks. There seem to be an awful lot of them. I get the idea Bill saved every halfway decent paper he ever got."

"He'd say that wasn't many, I bet," Dylan said.

"Well, when you average out the years and the number in each class and the number of exams it isn't many," Joan said. "But here in my house tonight it looks like a lot of bluebooks. So one stack, bluebooks, one, term papers, another poetry—yours and Bill's. Notes, letters, miscellaneous. That ought to get us started. The trouble is, you always stop and start reading everything and then you end up just cramming it all back into the boxes."

"We won't let you," Dylan said.

Joan opened the first bluebook. It was hers, the one she'd looked at that afternoon. She didn't read any of it but handed it to Miranda. She sorted through the box and took out all of them, stopping only to glance at the names on the covers.

Miranda stacked them neatly in a pile. Suddenly she laughed.

"What is it?" Joan said.

"They all seem to be girls," Miranda said. "Didn't any boys ever take poetry classes?"

Joan smiled. "Bill always said that he'd taught more bright boys than girls, but that when you *did* get a bright girl she was far and away beyond the bright boys." She picked up the stack of bluebooks. There were quite a few of Sandy's, there were some of Meredith's, one of B.J.'s even. There was only the one of hers. "I wasn't one of the bright girls," she said.

Miranda looked at her. "Here's one of your bluebooks," she said.

"It belongs in the funny category," Joan said. "He saved some for that reason too."

"Do you want me to separate them out that way?" Miranda said.

Joan glanced at her, but her face looked perfectly innocent.

"No," Joan said. "I think I'm just going to throw the whole bunch out. Bill may have had the idea of doing a book using some of them. I don't know. But I haven't got any use for them."

"Isn't that some sort of plagiarism?" Miranda said. "Or do you mean a funny book?"

"I don't know," Joan said. An edge of exasperation had gotten in to her voice.

Miranda was scanning through the bluebooks. "He could have done either one," she said. "There are some good things in this Sandy MacPherson's stuff."

"Yes. Sandy was one of the bright ones," Joan said.

"She was funny, too," Miranda said. "But deliberately. She makes great puns."

"Throw them all out," Joan said.

"Yes, ma'm," Miranda said. "The poem too?"

"What poem?" Joan said.

"There's one bluebook here that has just a poem in it. It's a good poem." She looked at the front of the bluebook. "There's no name on it, but it's this Sandy's handwriting."

"Lemme see," Dylan said. "I didn't know she ever wrote poetry."

"Oh, everybody does sometime or other," Miranda said. "Even me."

"You never show it to me."

"It isn't your kind of poetry," Miranda said. "It's what you'd call archaic, sentimental, and in very poor taste. You'd probably tell me to try to get it into the *Ladies' Home Journal*."

"Well, well," Dylan said. "Are you accusing me of being too intellectual?"

"No," Miranda said. "I was accusing you of being just a tiny bit cold."

"Me and Ciardi?" Dylan said.

"Don't overestimate yourself," Miranda said.

163

"What kind of poem is it that Sandy wrote?" Joan said.

Dylan took the book out of Miranda's hand and read it. "It's good," he said.

"Yes, and it isn't the least bit avant garde or plagued with logic, either," Miranda said.

"What kind of poem is it?" Joan said.

"It's a love poem," Dylan said. "That's the only kind girls ever write. It's good though. I'll read it."

"It's called 'The Lesser Dane,'" Miranda said.

"What does that mean?" Joan said.

"It means she thinks the fellow's a second-rate Hamlet," Dylan said.

"Oh," Joan said.

"'The Lesser Dane,'" Dylan read. He stood up and read the poem out loud:

I had a lichened liking for you once,
Watching you in that self-erected tomb,
Playing the adage cat, matching your stride
To all the Dane-like gestures you've assumed.
Until I glimpsed behind the stately spate
Of words, words, words, you uttered there was not
A depth of soul, but only posturings.
And even those, it seems, are plagiarized.
Although I recognize the green-gray picture
Of wild-haired nymph gone mad for love,
I shan't strew flowers with a spent abandon,
Nor mouth the shroud songs of the maudlin dove.
There's some motley spirit in me that would rather
Cry apples to the groundlings than indulge
In my own pratfall. Too much drama dulls.
Not that I had no need of rue, I wore it rather
Conspicuously . . . and always on the sleeve,
As some rich ornament of glad dark hours
With you. I had no need for watered weeds
To prove a sort of anguished permanence.
My rue was green . . . There was the difference.

"What does it mean?" Joan said.

"Oh, Mother," Dylan said.

"Well, what does it?"

"It's all done with things from Shakespeare," Dylan said. "She did it to impress Dad, and get an A, I imagine. I bet she got it, too."

"She's saying she's not Ophelia," Miranda said. "Even her sorrow is part of life for her. She ain't gonna drown herself for love. Damn, she sounds like a nice girl."

Joan laughed. "That's Sandy's poem all right," she said. "She sure wouldn't ever have drowned herself for love. She'd have been too interested in her own reactions."

"Why don't you show me your poetry?" Dylan said suddenly.

"I told you," Miranda said. "You wouldn't like it."

"I like this one of Sandy's. I bet I'd like yours."

Miranda shook her head until her long hair looked like a waterfall. "I've read enough of yours to know," she said. "You don't like poems that say things."

"That's unfair," Dylan said, "and you know it. I don't like crap about baby shoes and Mother's Day and the flag and somebody's little cheeild. That doesn't mean I don't like poetry to mean something, for God sakes."

"I think there are some of your first poems in here, Dylan," Joan said.

"God, don't get them out. For all I remember they may have been about baby shoes and Mother's Day."

"Not bloody likely," Miranda said.

"Why not?" Dylan said. "Everybody has been a baby and had a mother."

"Yeah," Miranda said. "And 'it takes a heap o' livin' in a house t' make it home.' "

"Your father wrote very good poems," Joan said, "and they always meant something. I couldn't always understand them, but they meant something. The only ones in this junk are the unpublished ones or duplicates. I guess we ought to go through them. The duplicates of the published things can go to the library, I guess. I don't know what to do with the unpublished ones."

"Maybe we ought to try getting out another book," Dylan said.

165

"I don't think there are enough of them. That quarterly that used to do his stuff might want them."

"Maybe he wouldn't want them published," Miranda said. "Maybe he thought they were rejects."

"Well, I'll just put all of them in a folder right now," Joan said. "We'll have to decide something eventually. I've promised the letters to the library. Every time I see E.K. Edwards he says something about it. That really ought to be the first order of business. I could leave them his lecture notes too. That would take care of most of it, wouldn't it? We throw out the bluebooks and give the personal papers to the library. Maybe they'd want the term papers too."

"Gee, here's a term paper on Housman called 'Bright Flesh,'" Dylan said. "I bet that one's old Sandy's too."

"There were other girls with ideas like that," Joan said.

"Why, Mother, dear," Dylan said.

"Dylan, dear," Joan said, "college professors are in the class with doctors and writers, and my particular one was also a poet. There were a lot of girls with bright ideas."

"Aren't there always?" Miranda said.

Yes, Joan thought. There always are. There always were. But they didn't mean anything, not ever. Bill fell in love with her and they got married and all the rest of them were nothing to him after that. Only sometimes that very fact bothered her. She knew that made no sense; she should feel happy and smug and proud because Bill had thought she was the only woman in the world. But there was a part of her that couldn't help wondering why on earth he did. He was so terribly bright, and she just wasn't, and she knew it. It used to make her wonder if Bill had ever really seen her at all. She'd lived with him almost twenty years and had borne his son and been his wife in every way. But sometimes she thought of the way he looked at her on the deck on *The Lady of Shalott* and she wondered if she wasn't *really* the Lady of Shalott to Bill Friday, not Joan Holmes at all. Not the Joan Holmes who used to act in the Players and have to have help studying for exams and who wore blue because she didn't have the nerve to wear red. That Joan Holmes had simply disappeared when Bill Friday de-

166

cided to fall in love with her. She might have thought she had never existed at all except that some of the girls still saw her. Martha did, and Sandy, and even B.J. sometimes, even though B.J. couldn't really be depended on to see anything. She'd certainly never seen Clark Kent and the various things he was up to. Not Clark Kent, she told herself disgustedly, Clark Davidson. Well, *he'd* seen Joan Holmes all right, very clearly the one time she'd been with him. She guessed nobody else had ever seen her exactly the way he had. What on earth made me do that? she thought. And after all this time she still didn't know.

She had had the lead in *Dream Girl*, and she'd had a terrible time remembering all the lines. She'd had to wear a slip all during the first act and she'd had one made special, a beautiful yellow silk one with lace all down the front and around the hem, thick enough so she wouldn't show through in front of the footlights. She'd been so nervous opening night; they'd had a full house and the smell of grease paint in the awful little cubby hole they gave them to dress in had been making her sick at her stomach. So she'd put the slip on backward and there simply wasn't anything she could do about it after she got out on the stage. So there she was saying all those interminable lines and trying to keep one eye on the prompter and feeling like an absolute ass with all the beautiful lace down her back instead of in front where it belonged, until finally Sandy had got her off the stage and changed the slip around and shoved her back on.

So she'd had a headache, something she hardly ever had, and she went out of the stage door into the big parking lot outside. The fresh air had felt wonderful on her flushed face and Clark Davidson had been standing there. He'd been leaning up against the side of the building. There wasn't anybody else around because everybody had gone back-stage from the front of the auditorium and the cast was all inside being congratulated and getting ready for the back-stage party. She'd just meant to come out and breathe good once and go back in.

"Come on," he'd said.

"Come on where?" she said.

"With me," he said.

"Why?"

"Because you want to."

She'd never wanted to go anywhere with Clark Davidson. She thought he was something to look at like every other girl on the campus. He was. You'd have to be blind not to see that. But she didn't like tennis players and that seemed to be the only thing he did. He and B.J. were so disgustingly wholesome about that whole tennis bit, dashing out before daylight. But now she looked at him and she knew she did want to go with him. Just like that. So she did.

He'd had a car parked out there behind the building, and she had said, "Where in the world did you get that?" and he'd said, "From a girl I know." Then he'd driven straight to a gas station and used a C stamp to get gas and she'd said, "Where did you get that?" and he said, "From another girl I know." He was really completely awful and impossible and she knew it every minute of the time. But she could no more have stopped herself from going with him than she could have stood up on that stage and changed her slip around the right way.

He didn't tell her she was pretty or that he wanted her or that he loved her. In fact, he didn't say much of anything. They drove out to Druid Creek and parked and he took her. It hurt like hell, just like everybody always warned you it would, and he smiled at her and said, "I figured that," and after a while he took her again and that was better. The third time was almost what she wanted it to be.

Then he took her back to the house and walked her to the door and kissed her cheek and said, "O.K., Miss Holmes. Put the slip on the right way tomorrow night."

The next time she saw him she looked very carefully just past his eyes. He said, "Hello, Joan," but she didn't speak to him. She never spoke to him again. And he never called her or tried to see her or acted as though he'd ever had anything to do with her at all.

But he knew me, she thought now. Even though I haven't thought about that in fifteen years and I am simply not ever going to think about it again, because it couldn't have happened. Still, he knew me. And he knew I wasn't the Lady of Shalott at all.

She looked up at Dylan and Miranda. They were absorbed in a term paper, their arms touching on the chair arm between them. It was only a tentative touch, but it seemed to charge the air like the beginning of an electrical storm. She sighed and picked up the bluebooks and found her own. "Lancelot was really the innocent party," she read. And dammit, Bill, she thought. He was.

Mary Alice carried the plans with her when she went over to baby-sit for Shari and Bill. She spread them out carefully on the coffee table and looked at them for a long time. It was a very beautiful house. It had everything she'd ever wanted. For years she'd cut pictures out of magazines and put them neatly in folders. There had been house plans, room plans, detail drawings. But each of them was something special and right for Mary Alice Cross's dream house. So here it was. "I hate the damned thing," she said.

Nobody answered her because there was nobody there but a three-month-old grandchild sound asleep in a crib in a rented bedroom. He didn't care what kind of room he slept in and why should she?

She'd bought the lot three years ago when Oscar had first put the country club estates into operation. It was one of the best lots in the development, toward the back of the tract, bordering on the one creek he hadn't been able to cancel out, not a real tract plot at all. She had long ago given up the idea of having a place out from town. Once she'd thought of buying from Joan Friday, but it was too far from both her and Lew's work and the price Joan wanted was just too much. If she paid it she'd never get the house on it, and at that time she'd needed that house. It meant something, it meant everything. So what had happened to it? She didn't know. Maybe it was Oscar. How could the bloom stay on any rose around Oscar? But she didn't believe that. Miley was going to supervise this house and Miley was good. Miley was the one smart thing in Oscar's life as far as Mary Alice was concerned. He simply refused to let Oscar cut the corners too far, and that was the real reason Oscar got the prestige trade whether he knew it or not. Miley was for real. He wasn't like the architects some firms hired to keep the customer happy. She knew one of those in Newcastle; the snow-job artist, she called him. He went in while the head architect was drawing up the plans and kept the lady of the house happy. He had a really great technique. He was like the good guy the police and insurance companies use to offset the bad guy. He told the little lady what an artist he was and how the two of them had to get together and keep the crass old architect from ruining all *her* good ideas. One of these days Oscar was probably going to have to have a guy just like that. But if he was smart he'd keep Miley. Miley was for people who didn't snow.

She remembered Miley from all those years ago, how he'd gone overseas and left Edyth bawling and all those V-mail letters he used to write and the picture on Edyth's desk that she'd sit and stare at after she started running around with Bob Allen. But never a Dear John. Not Edyth. She had admired her for it, because the temptation to write them was exquisite. Mary Alice thought that no man had ever understood that phenomenon. The lavishly presented guilt: Dear John, I'm sorry. There was this man. It was like going to a priest and scourging yourself at the same time. Masochism and sadism in perfect combination. How many men came home from World War II with a scar from it that never quit aching when it rained? But not Edyth. She suffered it and she never put it on Miley. And, Jesus God, Mary Alice thought, that is probably going to come out now too. All of us have been made to remember too much and it's hit us at the wrong time in our lives. How does it feel to get a Dear John letter twenty years after the fact? Especially when you were the guy who started the whole damned thing.

She rolled up the house plans and went into the kitchen. The kitchen was dirty, so she spent a few minutes wiping off the counters. She couldn't help it. She always swore she wasn't going to do it, but some part of her simply couldn't

170

stand not doing it. She washed the few dishes and put them away and looked inside the refrigerator and then firmly shut the door. No, she told herself. I will not get into that. It would take me all night and I'm tired. She did put some new aluminum foil under the stove burners though, because it was actually dangerous the way it was. She thought about the stove she was going to have that would clean its own oven, but even that didn't tempt her tonight. Hell, I'm tired of cooking anyway, she thought.

She went back to the living room. Maybe I'm just tired period, she thought. Maybe that's all it is. All the years of building the business and keeping it going, getting Shari grown and married and keeping Lew happy. Maybe now that it's all starting to go right I just simply want to sit down and rest. Only I never have. Why should I now? I don't. I'd be miserable sitting. So maybe that's it. If I build the house, what else is there? What's to work and plan and hope and dream for then? I can sit in it and look at it and there it will be. And I still got a long, long time to live.

She saw the years stretching away down a corridor, work in the morning, dinner at night, another grandchild eventually, another vacation in the Caribbean maybe. "It's not enough," she said. "It's not enough."

She remembered the night Edyth had come into the dorm after that maniac had tried to kill her. She'd walked in as calm as a cucumber. It had been twilight, the faint haze of summer dust in the air, the faint hope of a breeze. She'd been sitting on the bed and Edyth had looked in the door, said, "Hi," walked in and taken a cigarette out of her pack and lit it. She'd sat down on the bed, smiled at her and gone all to pieces. Mary Alice had never seen anybody do that in quite that way before or since. Edyth just started shaking, as though she were literally going to fall apart, and then she'd started trying to cry and couldn't—just gasping and making strange little noises as though she couldn't get her breath, and all the time shaking like that. Jesus. She'd had to go down the hall and get a Coke and a wet rag and talk soothingly about absolutely nothing for thirty minutes before the shaking stopped and Edyth started looking

171

around and saying, "What the hell did I do with my cigarette? I'm probably burning the house down."

But then for the longest time Edyth had been *alive*. That was what she really remembered, not the fear or shock of seeing her like that, but what it did to her afterward. She'd wake up at daylight and try to get all the rest of them up to watch the sunrise, she'd iron a dress as though the very act of ironing were a beautiful and wonderful privilege, she'd eat as though every bite were ambrosia, she'd walk as though the ground made love to her feet.

Maybe every once in a while we all ought to know the shock of our own mortality, Mary Alice thought. Maybe then we wouldn't need a house, or hate the moment when it ceases to mean anything.

She and Lew had been married secretly for a whole year without anybody knowing about it. It was easy in those days. The men were all at camp anyway and for the few passes he managed to get she could always sign out for somewhere to spend the weekend with a girl friend. The night they'd gotten married they'd gone to a hotel in Newcastle carrying a bottle and a bought wedding cake in a white bakery box. They'd sat on the bed and drunk out of toothbrush glasses and eaten the really terrible sugarless cake and giggled like a couple of teenage girls. The really silly thing was that nobody knew it even yet. When Lew had finally gotten his discharge they'd simply gone home and gotten married all over again in a nice little ceremony in her mother's parlor. So she was a twice-married woman and nobody knew it. How silly, she said out loud. I think I will tell somebody. I'll tell Shari. She'll think it's funny. Maybe it is.

The baby woke up. She could hear the faint stirring noises he made and she waited, knowing almost to the second when he would start to cry. He whimpered once, then howled. She got up and went into the bedroom, changed him, and picked him up, balancing him neatly in the crook of her left arm so she'd have the other one free to fix the bottle. She made small clucking sounds at him as she got the bottle out of the refrigerator and unscrewed the cap and threw the seal into the pan of water on the back eye of the stove, and pushed the nipple through and stuck the bottle into the pan. The series of familiar operations comforted her. For a moment it was Shari she held and Shari's bottle she negotiated so mechanically and neatly with one hand. She could remember doing it so near asleep she wouldn't know she'd done it, waking later in the dark wondering why Shari hadn't wanted her two-o'clock bottle. The water began to boil and she took the bottle out and tested the milk on her wrist. The baby was really beginning to cry now. He had stopped when she started walking him around the kitchen, but now his impatience had gotten the best of his curiosity. She took him into the living room and sat down and put the nipple in his mouth, watching the random greed that made him push the nipple away until he suddenly latched on and began to eat.

"Maybe this is really the only important thing, sonny boy," she told him. "Maybe just getting the nipple into the greedy mouth is the best thing a woman can do in this world. But if that's so I've really cheated myself, having only Shari, and a share in you. But look at B.J. She's got five, she'll probably have a dozen. And she is happy. You can not deny that she's happier than all the rest of us. But then B.J. is B.J. I'm not. I needed that store and those endless accounts and the choices I have to make so that I buy six months ahead of time what they want six months later. I needed the trips to New York and Dallas to market." She pulled the bottle out of the baby's mouth and held him on her shoulder and burped him. He gave a nice resounding belch immediately and she put him down and gave him back his bottle. Shari had been almost impossible to burp. It took patting and back-rubbing and sometimes holding her over your knee—and if you didn't get it up she'd throw up the whole bottle ten minutes later, whoosh, all over herself and the crib and her teddy bear.

"But that's just it, sonny boy," Mary Alice said. "That's it. It was the job I needed, not the money to buy a house."

The baby sucked on, eyes crossed blissfully. "You won't ever have that problem," she told him. "Enjoy. Eat hearty.

Grow up for tomorrow. Because the world expects you to find your work in it. It is only the girl babies that there's any doubt about."

He'd gone to sleep with the nipple still in his mouth. She looked at him, completely relaxed, limp, comatose, utterly asleep as only a three-month-old boy can ever be. More so than a girl three-month-old is. Girl babies' nerves are closer to the surface. I don't give a damn what doctors say, she thought. They say babies don't run a fever when they cut teeth, too, but I know better. Even I, who wasn't cut out for the maternal role, know a thing or two. She changed his diaper and he didn't even stir. She put him back in his crib and drew the blue blanket around the mattress and pinned it securely and smiled at him.

"So what's the matter with your mama, buster?" she said. "Why is it my daughter doesn't feel the need of some work in the world?" Maybe she just hasn't found it yet, but I don't know. Can the winner of a beauty contest ever feel she needs to be anything except a woman? Was the face nature endowed her with a seal on her fate? It really isn't beauty that ruins you, it's a certain kind of beauty. It's a deep and devious thing, the thing that made the doctor say, "What a pretty little girl," the moment Shari was born. And everybody else say it and keep saying it right on for the rest of her life. So that she didn't have to do anything or think anything or be anything. "What long eyelashes," they used to say when I took her to the grocery store in her stroller. "This is a pretty one," the men used to say, picking her up and throwing her into the air. What does it mean? I don't know. Well, it got you here, buster. It did that. Though God knows that isn't such a feat. You sure as hell don't have to be beautiful to reproduce your kind.

She leaned over and kissed the baby on the top of his head. They were so damned irresistible. Nature simply *does* that to us, she thought. A baby is really a strange and grotesque thing. It is an uncoordinated bundle of twitches and greeds and needs. It is a food machine. Put it in one end, clean up the other. Yet we see it as something soft, cuddly, vulnerable, warm, and wonderful. And that is sim-

174

ply so we will put the food in one end and clean up the other. And that is one of the ways life is.

So how does anybody put one into an airshaft? But then how could anybody have called poor stupid old Mrs. Cowan, the half-witted housemother, and said, "I just had a baby. We've got to bury it." Jesus. Could any teenage girl manage to do that? Hell, none of them could even stand to face the old fool when they were ten minutes late getting in at night. And each other? Could they have helped each other? She didn't know. She couldn't remember enough about what any of them had been to know. They were all so wrapped up in themselves and their loves and their hopes and dreams and fantasies. Could any of them really have stood that kind of reality? Could they yet?

She went back into the living room and picked up a magazine and leafed through it, looking at all the ads for all the bright new things. Well, she thought wryly, at least I know something about me now. I know it's the job and always has been, and I'll still be working at it when they get ready to shovel me under. She put the magazine down and picked up her house plans. They looked pretty good to her again. She was even able to smile at the little square that was going to be a terrace in the sun. Now that she knew she really didn't need it she might be able to enjoy it after all.

"*Aren't you going to put the car up?*" Oscar Ridley's wife said. She was already halfway up the walk, and she didn't even turn, just said it in a flat voice.

"I've got to go back to the office for a while," Oscar said.

"Good night, then," she said, and kept walking. At the door she paused, took her key out of her purse, and turned toward him. "Did it go all right tonight?"

"It went fine. It always does when I've got you in there pitching."

"That's good," she said. She put her key in the lock and went inside and shut the door behind her.

Oscar sat under the wheel for a moment, watching the lights go out downstairs, then the upstairs lights come on. He unwrapped a cigar, lit it, and backed out of the driveway. He drove downtown to his office, went inside, and turned a light on and left it burning. Then he came back out and drove across town to the neat brick bungalow he'd built three years ago for Thelma. There was a light on over the side door so he got his key out and let himself in. Thelma was in the kitchen, wearing an old bathrobe and with her hair up in curlers.

"My God, Oscar," she said, "I didn't expect you tonight." She disappeared for a few minutes. When she came back her hair was brushed and she had on a rose silk robe. She sat down across from him.

"How is everything?" she said.

"Fine," Oscar said. "Real fine. I think Dr. Edwards and I just may come up with a deal."

"I wouldn't trust him too far, honey," Thelma said. "I believe under all that pretty talk and big smile he's a shrewd, slick man."

"That's right," Oscar said. "That he is. And that is exactly why I've got him by the short hairs. He's got a picture of himself as a really big wheel somewhere really big, and that don't go with being the college president that couldn't even hush up a little case of bones in the wall."

"You were telling the truth about that, weren't you, Oscar? That airshaft really was open only the one summer?"

"Of course it's the truth," Oscar said. "What good would a lie like that do? They'd just find it out. No, all that bunch of society matrons were all by themselves in that house that summer. I remember them all right, all running around that house half-naked, and us trying to get an honest day's work done."

"Still and all, it's a pity."

"My God, Thelma. What ain't?"

She shrugged. "You're not a woman," she said. "I guess I can't expect you to see it."

"I see it to the tune of a million bucks, Thelma," he said. "In the long run how's it really going to hurt any of them? They're all in the catbird seat as near as I can tell. They got money, they got husbands, they got a good life. If one of them pulled a stupid thing all that time ago, well, she did. It damned sure wasn't all of them, and whoever it was is a long way from it now. Besides, it happened. I didn't do it. If things work out I'm going to save somebody's hide. Don't you see that? I'm gonna end up with that land I been wanting for ten years, E. K. Edwards is going to end up with his prestige intact, the women are going to end up freed from suspicion. If it wasn't that summer people are going to blame it on the younger generation. You know that. They always do."

Thelma shook her head. "Well, I'm just glad I'm not having to sit here tonight thinking about it," she said.

"Thelma," Oscar said, "your heart's as big as your head."

"Seems to me I've heard you say that before."

"Most likely."

"You hungry?" Thelma asked.

"Nope. Ate out at the country club tonight. Steak. I like that place, always have. It's a pity about the new one."

Thelma laughed. "Oscar," she said, "you invented the new one. How can you say that?"

"Of course, I can say it," Oscar said. "That deal made me money, too. But that don't mean I don't sort of regret it. You always act as though I'm not human just because I'm in business. But you know it's not so. I sort of hated to see those trees go out near the rubber plant, too. But they had to. That's the way things are. Somebody is going to make the money off doing these things. It might as well be me. This town was ripe for a new country club estate and I saw it first, that's all."

"How's the membership coming along?"

"Pretty good, pretty good," Oscar said. "I'm going to have every last one of those lots sold by the end of the year, and half the town's going to belong to that club. Tell you the truth, that sort of surprised me. I guess it was the restriction clause. I really wouldn't have thought those people would go for that. I really think it's sort of disillusioned me."

"Poor Oscar," Thelma said.

"What you mean, poor Oscar? Don't you start getting

sarcastic with me, Thelma. I get enough of that from Miley."

"I believe I'll fry me an egg," Thelma said. "I wasn't very hungry at supper."

"Well, go on and make me an egg sandwich, too," Oscar said. "I reckon I could use a bite."

Thelma got up and put a pan on the stove. "Oscar," she said, with her back to him, "what about Edyth and Miley?"

"What about them?" Oscar said.

"You know what I'm talking about," Thelma said. "She was in that house."

"Well, she never did really belong with that crowd anyway," Oscar said.

"That doesn't make any difference," Thelma said. "She was there. And they are your friends. Miley is the best friend you've got, with the possible exception of yours truly."

"O.K., Thelma. If it was Edyth, I'm saving her neck. Look. There's something you don't seem to understand about all this. *I* didn't find that baby in the wall. Miley did. Miley himself, because he can't keep his hands off the work. I've let Miley surpervise for me for years. He don't have to do anything but stand around and watch and tell a bunch of stupid bastards what to do. But Miley has to work. He wants to climb up and get into the lathes himself. He wouldn't miss topping out a building for all the money you could give him. And he couldn't miss taking out the really difficult part of this job. He's about work like I am money, Thelma. Different people are hung up on different things; everybody's got his own kick going. And this time Miley got hung up on his. He should have let the bulldozer do the rest of that job. But, no, he wanted it torn down *right*. There might be some damn two by four he could salvage by climbing up and doing it by hand, so that's what he had to do—play Jack and the beanstalk. So this time it backfired on him. That ain't my fault."

Thelma finished frying the eggs and put them on buttered bread. She brought the sandwiches to the table.

"What do you think the law's actually going to *do*?" she said.

"Hold a hearing in private chambers most likely. What else can they do? They've got to do something. Everybody in town knows about it and Gus is coming up for re-election. I hope he makes it. He's been a damned good sheriff and he's had enough troubles, what with the Supreme Court and all that without this ruining him. He's had to walk a line so thin it's a wonder to me it hasn't cut the soles of his feet right through to the bone, but he's been making it without too much hoopla and too much hate and too much national publicity. They don't want to reckon with him—either side—so they don't push him too far. But this thing could ruin him. Handle it one way and he loses the whole damned upper-middle-class vote, handle it another and he loses the rest of the county. He's got problems. I'm going to help *him* out too. Now, come on Thelma, why do you begrudge me my million bucks?"

"Oscar," Thelma said, "if you hadn't mentioned it nobody would have known about the airshaft only being open one summer."

"Somebody would have thought of it," Oscar said. "That's what I keep trying to get to you. It's like the new country club. Somebody would have thought of that. Why does it bother you it's me?"

"Well, it's you so often," Thelma said.

"Thelma," Oscar said, "I didn't come over here to get into an argument."

"Yes, you did," Thelma said. "That's why you have me."

Oscar laughed. "Fix me another egg sandwich, woman," he said.

He knew it was true. Thelma was a good-looking woman and she was more than adequate in bed, but in his heart Oscar really preferred sleeping with his wife and he knew it. Often he never got to bed with Thelma when he came over, but he always got into a conversation with her and more often than not an argument. He thought about it, watching her busy over the stove again. He wondered if Thelma were, in some weird way, his conscience. That

179

seemed pretentious. But there was no getting around the fact that only she and Miley out of all the world ever jumped on Oscar.

Betty did not jump on Oscar; Betty didn't have to. She was always one jump ahead of him. He thought about Betty, cool, elegant, beautiful, and in love. Not with Oscar, but with money, just like Oscar was. That was the thing that held them together, a mutual love, not for each other, but for the same thing in life. That and sex, which had been and was something really and truly special between them, a stripping away of all the cool hard elegance to find what? A tiger sounded pretty trite, but that was what Betty Ridley minus clothes turned out to be.

Yet Oscar had a mistress. And had had for years and would have for the rest of his life, he guessed, unless Thelma suddenly turned an argument into a real argument and went away. He didn't want to think about that. Because she could go away. There had already been one man who wanted to marry her. And what if one day she just married somebody? It was, like all things, within the realm of the possible. Because Thelma really and truly didn't care anything about money. She was perfectly capable of marrying some farmer and cooking three meals a day and scrubbing floors for the rest of her life. She hadn't even wanted the house. He'd had to build it and insist she move into it if she wanted to see him again. The really awful thing was that Thelma loved him, Oscar Ridley. Every once in a while that scared him to death.

"Thelma," Oscar said, "could you ever have put a baby in an airshaft?"

Thelma turned from the stove and looked at him. "That's a straight question that hasn't got a straight answer," she said. "I don't think so, to tell you the truth, but I don't know. If it was dead, never had been alive, never had even been a baby to you; if you were a kid alone with the world ready to gobble you up, if the man you loved just hadn't given a damn and gone away—if all that—I don't know, maybe. Then, too, there's the fact that I'm not a sorority girl and never was. With my kind of people there's usually somebody to turn to, somebody that won't condemn and censure and click their tongue. With that kind of girl there most likely isn't. Leastways they can't be sure of it. But I don't know—your baby, Oscar, a part of you and me—I don't know . . ."

And as usual, you're right, baby, Oscar thought. Miss Betty might do it. It'd be a hell of a lot harder for you. So what makes a lady? The coldness? The veneer? Or is it that what we've all grown accustomed to thinking of as a lady really isn't? Maybe a lady is you standing over that stove fixing my fried-egg sandwich and loving me even if I'm not worth it and never have been and never will be.

He remembered a story his mother used to tell when he'd been just a little boy. It was a secret scandal concerning one of the oldest and most well-to-do families in town. They had a touch of the tarbrush. When he'd first heard it he hadn't believed it. Mr. Corey was a staid and respectable businessman, and while he might have black hair and did have a thick nose, he looked pretty Anglo-Saxon to Oscar. But it was the fact of Mrs. Corey that made Oscar incredulous. She was a tall, cool, lovely woman, who belonged to the book club and the garden club, who took baskets to the poor, who worked in her roses in gloves and a huge sunhat, and who had once given Oscar Ridley a brownie when he was passing her house and she'd just set them out to cool. What must it have meant to her when she found it out? Because being a woman she must have. If even the Ridleys knew it, sooner or later she must have known it too. She came from another town, another state, and she had met Mr. Corey at a party somewhere else in another world. She knew him as a man with money and prestige from another small town somewhere. What must have been unbelievable tragedy had happened to her for no reason of her own. But to this day the image of lady brought her to Oscar's mind. She was one, even though she had the veneer and the silence, the ramrod stiffness that took her through a long life in a town where the impossible was whispered. But underneath it, Oscar knew now, had been the love. Nothing less would have carried her with that seeming serenity

181

through thirty years of it. Nothing less would have let her have two children, who by the time they were grown had almost completely lived the old rumor down. That tall lady with the haunted eyes had brought it off. Oscar was probably the only person in town who even remembered the old rumor anymore and he only because the image of lady was forever connected with Mrs. Corey in his mind.

So maybe it took both things to make a lady, and maybe for a man like Oscar it took two women—Betty's façade and Thelma's soul. Because there just plain weren't many Mrs. Coreys in the world, and who the hell could expect Oscar Ridley to have gotten one?

"Oscar," Thelma said, "do you want to go to bed?"

"After a while maybe, Thelma," Oscar said. "Right now I'd just as soon talk some more."

"All right," Thelma said.

"Thelma?"

"Hmmm?"

"Can you make brownies?"

"Of course I can make brownies. I thought you didn't like sweets."

"Make me some brownies tomorrow," Oscar said. "I haven't had any since I was a kid."

"Miley," Edyth said, "why won't you talk to me?"

"I'm tired," Miley said.

"No, that's not it. You're always tired and we always talk. You're mad."

"I'm not mad."

"Yes, you are. You came home mad. You ate supper without saying a word. I'm tired too, but I'm not mad at you. What did I do?"

"You didn't do anything. I told you, I'm not mad."

"Miley," Edyth said, "if we ever stop talking we're lost. Why can't I explain that to you? You're thinking about that damned baby in the wall."

"O.K., I'm thinking about a baby in the wall. What are you thinking about?"

"You."

"Yeah, sure."

182

"Yeah, sure. Forget it, Miley."

"There's nothing to forget."

She tried one more time. "Miley, I didn't put that baby in that airshaft."

"But you could have."

"Why do you say that?"

"Oh, hell, Edyth, I know it. I've always known it. There was somebody else while I was overseas, wasn't there? Come on, what's the use of denying it now?"

"What's the use of talking about it now?"

"I believe you were the one who said if we ever stopped talking we were lost."

"All right, all right. There was somebody else. Are you happy?"

"Sure, kid. I'm happy. I'm ready to turn cartwheels with happiness. How many of them were there?"

"Oh, for God's sake, Miley. There was one. And he was crazy and is now in an insane asylum."

"You sure showed good taste."

"Miley, what the hell is it you want me to *do*?"

"There isn't anything you can do, is there? It was your mistake."

"Miley, it's been twenty years. He was a nice kid. But crazy. It happened. I was sorry. There was never really anybody but you. Surely to God you ought to know that by now."

"I know I've been a damned fool for twenty years."

"That's ridiculous."

"No, it isn't. If you could do it then you could do it now. For all I know you have. God knows you have plenty of opportunity in that shop all day long."

"Opportunity? God, that's a laugh. I work like a damned slave in that shop, and you know it. You're just talking nonsense."

"Well, I'm talking. That's what you wanted, wasn't it?"

"You're talking, but you're not communicating."

"Well, that's because I don't have the advantage of a college education, honey. I was fighting a war while some people we know were busy learning how to communicate."

183

"Oh, stop it, stop it, stop it."

"I didn't start it."

"Oh, didn't you?"

"Well, I did find the baby in the wall. That is quite true. But I didn't put it there."

"Neither did I."

"Prove it."

"Miley, how can I prove it? If what I am and have been for all our life together doesn't prove it, what could?"

"Nothing, I guess."

"My God."

"You're just upset because you got caught out," Miley said. "I don't think you really care at all."

"Miley, I love you. I always did. I always have. And, dammit, you know it."

"You had a funny way of proving it."

"Miley, I was a kid. I was lonely and unhappy and afraid. I was a lot of things."

"So was I, baby. And believe it or not I was true to you the whole goddamned bitched-up war. What about that? Who do you think was lonelier and unhappier and scareder, Edyth? Who do you think was?"

"O.K. So you're a better person than I am. I've always known that, but I've done the best I could—always. And it was only then and only a little while and never again."

"You sound like Oscar trying to talk his way out of one of his shady deals."

"Oh, Miley, that's unforgivable."

"Good. Then you know what unforgivable means."

"All right, Miley. So what are you going to do? Leave me?"

"I don't know yet. I have to think about it. And quit crying. That isn't going to move me."

"I didn't mean for it to. I don't cry for reasons. I'm not that kind of person. Jesus! Don't you know what kind of person I am?"

"I'm finding out."

"Miley!"

"There's no point in discussing it any more, Edyth."

"But what do you want me to *do*?"

"I told you. There isn't anything you can do. Let's go to bed."

"I'm not sleepy."

"Well, I am. I've got a hard day's work to do tomorrow. Just why, I'm not sure, but it's a habit I've gotten into."

"I love you, Miley."

"Don't make me laugh."

"*Miranda*," Dylan said. "*Don't you like my poetry?*"

"I like your poetry," Miranda said. "I only said you wouldn't like mine."

"We both liked that one of Sandy's, didn't we?"

"It was terribly clever, Dylan. You'd have to be a little dumb not to like it, especially if you're an English major. It doesn't change the facts about our kind of poetry. You think all the old ones are nice but archaic. I still like them. I even get a bang out of Swinburne. I even like Keats."

"So do I, Miranda," Dylan said. He stopped driving toward Miranda's house and parked in the moonlight on the side of the road. "I only say you have to put them in a sort of perspective. They were perfect in their time, but not today."

"Is love dead too, then?" Miranda said. "Like God is? Or would be if Billy Graham hadn't talked to him this morning. Hasn't anybody talked to Eros lately? Or is Eros only the name of a magazine that backfired on Ralph Ginsburg?"

"Oh hell, Miranda," Dylan said.

"I'm not trying to be difficult, Dylan," Miranda said. "I really want to know. Does Hugh Hefner know more about love than Byron? Does Helen Gurley Brown know more about it than Elizabeth Barrett Browning? I don't know, Dylan. I'm asking you."

"We all have to live in our own time, Miranda."

"I will tell you something, Dylan," Miranda said. "I wasn't going to tell you, but I will. I love you, Dylan. I love you like in all the books. I'm not being bright or clever or modern tonight. You are my love, the way it's always been."

185

Dylan didn't say anything. He looked at the moonlight and it was most certainly there. It was the way it had always been, too. My God, Miranda, he thought. I just can't say it.

But she was still watching him, her face solemn and dear in the moonlight. After a minute she reached over and touched his hand. "It's all right, Dylan," she said. "You don't have to say it. I know it anyway."

"Yes, damn you," he thought. "I guess you do."

Clarissa lay in her bed watching the moonlight. It was very late and neither of the children was home, and she knew there wasn't anything she could do about it. I failed them somewhere, she thought. But what was I to do? They didn't have no daddy, and if they had, if Jackson had stayed around, it wouldn't have been any better. I had to work. And even if I hadn't, would it have been any better? She knew the thoughts were the same old thoughts and that she wouldn't come to anything with them. She got up and got a cigarette out of her almost-empty pack and lit it with a kitchen match and stood looking at the moonlight. "Lord," she said, "you've made us a funny kind of world to live in. Lord, you've given women a hell of a row to hoe. I could stand here and blame it all on being black, like I do sometimes, but here's Miss Joan Friday coming to me with a need and a fear in her as sad as any of mine. So what does it all mean? Do I start now blaming it all on being a woman, white *or* black? Lord, I don't know. Maybe nobody gets much of a chance at it whatever they are. All my babies that summer, as pretty and young and innocent as my own two babies used to be, and tonight in all this moonlight every one of them scared and anxious and worried and maybe one of them living through a hell as bad as a black woman's—maybe worse, for all I know. Maybe whatever we do it ain't going to come out right. Maybe we have to reach a point of not wanting it to anymore. Just learning to live with the trying, maybe that's got to be enough. And, Lord, you know I've done my share of that."

A dog barked somewhere outside and she listened, but there was no car coming, nothing in the empty street. She picked up her alarm clock and looked at the hands. It was two-thirty. "And I got to go over and help out Miss Sandy tomorrow," she said. "I reckon neither of them children are going to get into this house all night long. Maybe I ought to be just as glad they don't. They may come toting a bale of trouble when they come." She smoked the cigarette down to the last quarter inch and put it out and got back into bed.

"Old moon shines right on," she said "Right on, no matter what."

After a while she turned over in the bed and made herself go to sleep.

Sandy woke up. The room was full of moonlight—and gardenias again. She sat bolt upright in bed this time, not trying to fight it. "Oh, shit," she said. Kurt stirred beside her and she patted his shoulder gently and eased out of bed. The room was so bright it made her feel unreal. She tiptoed out to the kitchen and walked to the window and looked out at the back yard bathed in a steady white-gold light. The barbecue grill looked like an alien object on the shining grass. "But not the stars," Sandy said. "The stars came otherwise." Victorian poetry. Yes. Now I have to think about that too. She put her head down on the window ledge and cried for a minute. "Oh, Bill," she said, "you've been dead a long time now. I don't see why it still has to hurt me so. You're under the grass now, for such a long time. But never before or again anything like you. And never is such a hell of a long, long time."

Eyes locked across the crowded classroom, pretending it wasn't so. Because he was a professor and older—oh, yes, that. Scribbling notes inside the covers of the big green book; the poetry, to take home at night. Then one day she knew she was maneuvering to pass him in the doorway and their arms had brushed and it was like being touched with a white hot—at that age, what else?—star. Heloise and Abelard. Oh, yes, she really used to think of that. Think of it and weep. And that night on the porch at·Philip Carlton's —watching him, watching his hands moving the glass to his

187

lips, quite clearly in his mind had said to her, "My dearest dear. Don't start it. It wasn't ever meant to be."

But it was, Bill, Sandy said to the moonlight. You just weren't man enough. You knew it. You were scared of me. You had to love Joan Holmes who had nothing, nothing, nothing behind the pretty face. Because you wanted to love only yourself, and if you'd dared love me you couldn't have sustained it. Someday, someway, you'd have had to admit that I was not just the object of your lovely mind but a human being with a mind of my own. Not Elaine, or the Lady of Shalott, but me. Me with a temper and a Charleston on a tombstone, me with the moonlight and the stars up there.

"Don't play games with me, Sandy," he'd said.

"I don't know how to play games, darling," she'd told him back.

She hadn't known. She still didn't. She'd only wanted him to want her. Well, she'd had that. And she'd always wished she hadn't. Because that was when she knew she'd really lost. If she never had pushed it maybe the rest of her life she could have said, It wasn't meant to be, the way he'd said it. But not. She'd had to push it all the way, make him want her and love her and have her with all the beauty that turned out to be. And still lose him, lose him still. Not because it wasn't enough, but because it was too much. What was the really awful thing he'd said?

"You're like a liqueur, darling—a little in a very small glass after dinner. A man has to live on bread and jam."

"Oh, screw your bread and jam," Sandy said to the moonlight. "And screw the fact that it never even gave you indigestion. And screw me for loving a man that wasn't man enough, and for loving him still, dead and underground like Weldon Benson. And buried where I can't even dance on his tombstone. And yes, my love, the grave's a fine and private place."

She knelt in the window, feeling the hard tile of the floor on her knees with satisfaction. "I'd never have made it without Lawson," she said, "never in this world. But he believed in all the beauty, or said he did. And he believed I

188

was part of it, not its enemy. So he saved me, saved me for Kurt. Who *is* a man, who is *my* man, who wants me the way I am. It's only a tiny part of me that's still vulnerable to the weak ones—only that little part that answered Frank that time. And maybe soon even that little part will all be gone and I can look at moonlight without even remembering Bill's face. And when that happens I will know. Know what, Sandy? Know that you are dead? Dead and under but alive in a dusty statue somewhere and in a poem a poet wrote me once. And in two children in there, don't forget them. They are there. Just as Dylan is. She felt herself smiling. Dylan is going to make it, she thought. That little Miranda is going to make him care. What about that, Bill? she told the moonlight. Your bread-and-jam-begot son is not going to live on bread and jam.

∞
Part
Two
∞

On Wednesday morning it rained. Gus Thurgood, sheriff of Druid County, forty-two years old and feeling every day of it, sat at his desk and looked out the window at Main Street, black with rain, slick with rain, empty because of rain. I was just plain born at the wrong time, he told himself morosely, and I might as well face it.

"Did you say something, Gus?" Jimmy Lou Allbright said.

"Nothing, Jimmy Lou," he said. "Just grousing, I guess."

"You need some more coffee," she said practically, and got up and poured from the pot she kept going in the back of the office.

"Thanks," he said. "Have some more yourself."

"I think I will."

He watched her pour the coffee and walk back to her desk. Jimmy Lou held the sheriff's office together. She was a local girl who had come home after her World War II marriage had gone to pieces on her, bringing two little girls but no chip on her shoulder. She hadn't even moved in with her parents but had gotten a job in Lawrence's department store and gone to secretarial school at night, living in a garage apartment, hiring a girl to look after the kids. Now, at forty, she had both the girls almost grown, a house of her own, a new car, and, he suspected, a good-sized savings account. They were good girls, too, Lou and Carrie. Both in the high school band and honor students. In the ten years Jimmy Lou had been holding up the sheriff's office he'd never once heard her complain, whine, sigh, or argue. Quite a woman.

For a while he and his wife had tried to matchmake for Jimmy Lou. She was a good-looking girl and it seemed a shame for her just to give up on marriage because she'd made a mistake while she was still a teenager. But none of it ever seemed to take and they'd finally given up on her. Gus suspected her of having a boy friend somewhere, but if she did he was the most discreet boy friend in creation. Still, she didn't look like she was about to dry up and blow away and neither had he ever seen her cast an eye at anybody in the office. She was friendly, efficient, cheerful, and worth her weight in file copies.

Gus wondered what she thought about this thing that had been dropped in his lap. He'd end up discussing it with her, he always did, just as he ended up discussing things with his wife. Gus liked to talk and he had long ago faced the fact that he was going to do it, even if it wasn't always discreet. The best he'd been able to manage was to learn not to talk to the wrong people. Neither Jimmy Lou nor Beatrice was likely ever to repeat anything Gus Thurgood said in a talky mood, and to have two women like that in your world was more good luck than any man ought to have, born at the wrong time or not.

If he hadn't been able to talk the first time they hit him with the demonstrations he might not have gotten through it. But it had worked out. He'd just, by God, told them all, white and black, they could walk all they pleased, but nobody was going to do any shoving, hitting, pushing, throwing, or yelling. That seemed simple enough, but it took him two days to convince them he meant it. He'd

194

done it though, without a single deputy hitting a single demonstrator or observer. He'd had the jail pretty full—of both factions—for a day. After that most of the observers went on back to wherever the hell they'd come from in the first place and the marches went on quietly. Then they were over and all *those* people went back to wherever they'd come from. They'd gotten a couple of token Negroes in the college and a couple into stores in town. And it was quiet till the next time. He'd almost begun to think it was going to stay quiet past next election anyway, though there were times when he wondered why he wanted to *be* in the next election. Beatrice and Jimmy Lou both laughed when he said that. "You know, Gus," Beatrice had said, "you aren't about to let some slob like Myron Benson get into the sheriff's office and tear this town in two and you might as well face it." "Don't kid yourself, Gus," Jimmy Lou had said. "You're toting responsibility whether you like to admit it or not."

So, sure he was probably going to run again. So why the hell did Miley have to pull a bunch of bones out of an airshaft?

"Jimmy Lou," he said.

She stopped typing. "O.K., Gus," she said. "Talk about it."

He laughed. "This time there isn't much to say."

"Ho, ho," she said. "That's what you always say."

"O.K.," he said. "What am I going to do? We got to hold a hearing. I plain don't see any way out of it."

"Hearings don't mean anything," Jimmy Lou said. "It'll be a closed one and in front of Judge Palmer, and we'll all damned well keep our mouths shut about the time. We'll manage all right."

"What I can't figure," he said, "is why the hell Oscar wanted to blow this thing open by telling about that airshaft. That's what's caused the whole trouble. Oh, it would have been a scandal, whatever; but it wouldn't have been like this. This pinpointing it is about the worse damned thing I've ever run up against. Surely to God Oscar hasn't got it in mind to show up at the hearing with that tale. Has

195

he? He can't want to pin a murder rap on some middle-aged housewife."

"No," Jimmy Lou said. "You know Oscar well enough to know that he's up to something. But that isn't it."

"Well, what could he be up to? What in hell could it be to him?"

"I don't know," Jimmy Lou said. "But it's something to do with a profit for Oscar. Maybe it's some sort of blackmail. I don't know."

"Oh, he wouldn't go *that* far."

"Gus, you're a nice guy . . ."

"But . . .?"

"That's right. Oscar's plain ole up to something that'll end up by profiting Oscar. I don't think for a minute he plans to show up at any hearing. If anybody were to ask him he'd say he didn't know what the hell they were talking about, he never said anything about the airshaft."

"But I heard him," Gus said. "*I* have to take it into consideration."

"Gus," Jimmy Lou said, "you sound like a gal talking herself into writing a Dear John letter. You do not have to take it into consideration. What good can it possibly do anybody? Pretend you didn't hear it. For God sakes, don't let your puritan conscience turn you into the prick of the year."

"Jimmy Lou."

"Sorry," she said. She smiled sheepishly. "I'm afraid I couldn't find another word."

"You think we just ought to hold the hearing, get this thing declared death by misadventure or something like that and forget it?"

"Nobody's going to forget it, Gus. The damage is done. But I think that's the best you can do with it. Yes."

"If I can just keep the hearing from turning into a damned circus," he said. "Why is it everything I touch turns into a damned circus?"

"I don't think it's going to turn into a circus. Nobody that's supposedly concerned is going to show up at that hearing. Would you? No, the circus is going on all right, but it's going on behind closed doors with each different act taking its turn in the center ring."

"But folks are going to say I held off because it was the people it is," Gus said.

"Oh, they'll say it," Jimmy Lou said, "but I don't think they really want you to light out to arrest J. D. Finch's wife or Sandy Mackintosh or Meredith Green or anybody else."

"Well, I see you know who they all are."

"Dear God, Gus, I have lived in this town since I was born. That sorority has been the local sorority ever since Old Lady Carmichael gave the money to have it established beaucoup years ago. Of course I know. Everybody in town knows."

"Jesus," Gus said.

"My mother sat down and figured it all out the minute she heard about it, and she had heard about it before I got home from work Monday. The phone was ringing when I went in the door. Of course she knew damned well she wasn't going to get anything about it out of me, but she didn't have to. She had it all worked out to a fare-thee-well. You should have heard her, Gus. 'I hear from Mrs. Cloud who runs the bakery next to sorority row that they found a baby in the walls of that Delta House. Well, I'll tell you! When I heard it I called Mrs. Burke who does work over at ADPi House and she told me she was right outside the kitchen when it happened. Saw Miley come down off that house like a crazy man, saw Gus come up, and Oscar drive up in his latest new car. Heard what he said, too, only one summer in the world that airshaft was open. You know, Jimmy Lou, I've thought on that summer and I have reason to remember it. It was the summer you took off like a crazy person and married that smart-ass buck private that left you with two fatherless little girls. I know practically every child who was in that house that summer. Reason I know I was doing sewing for folks, trying to take my mind off my own child making a fool of herself because of the war. The war! What an excuse that gave all of you. Well, I did a bit of sewing around the campus and I did a good bit of it for Mrs. Carlton. Used to see that bunch of girls over there.

Did some sewing, too, for Joan Holmes—she was one of them. That's what's called it all to mind for me. I made a fuchsia cape, a cape yet. Awful color, glad it never has come back in. She and that pretty little Sandy and B.J. and Meredith Smith. Why on earth *that* child married Syd Green, I'll never know.' Etc., etc. You cannot hush this sort of thing up, Gus. Not in a town this size. And that's just Mother. Think how many others there are just like her. Still and all, I don't think it's going to lose you any votes in the long run. People love to talk and they love to talk maliciously, but I don't think there's a voter in this county who really wants to see some poor middle-aged woman ruined because of something she did twenty years ago in a moment of desperation. I just plain don't believe it."

"Now who's being the optimist?"

"Guilty. In the short run I'm the biggest cynic on earth. In the long run I believe in people." Her voice softened. "Heaven knows, people in the town have all been good to me."

"You've been good to them, Jimmy Lou," Gus said. "It ain't exactly hard not to hit somebody that ain't ever hit first."

"Nonsense," Jimmy Lou said. "I hated everybody in the world for a whole year once."

"Not so much as anybody could tell it," Gus said.

"Oh, shut up, Gus, and start setting up that damned hearing," Jimmy Lou said. "You've already talked yourself through and off the subject."

"I wish to hell it'd quit raining," Gus said.

Clarissa shook the rain out of her old black rain hat and opened Sandy's back door with the key from her ring. The eaves dripped dismally around her, but the smell of wet grass was sweet in the early morning. She hung her raincoat inside the kitchen door and went directly to the stove, surprised to find the coffeepot full and hot. She poured herself a cup and leaned against the sink to drink it. The house was still and she wondered why the boys weren't up yet. She went down the hall and looked into their room.

Both lay curled in their beds. She listened at Sandy's door but heard nothing. She went back to the kitchen and started on the cabinets which she'd promised to get done today. Might as well light in if nobody wanted breakfast.

She worked for thirty minutes before she heard the sound of bare foot on the floor and Mark looked in at her. "Mama's still asleep," he said. "Daddy said not to wake her."

"You want an egg, Mark?"

He shook his head. "Pancakes."

"All right. Sit down over there and stay clear and I'll mix 'em in a minute."

"Kim's still sleeping too."

"You boys up late?"

"No, but it's so quiet when Mama doesn't get up."

"And unusual," Clarissa said shortly.

"That's so," Mark said. "But Daddy said, 'No classes till eleven. Let Mama sleep.' "

"You done been up once, boy?" Clarissa said suspiciously.

"Yep. Had egg with Daddy. Now pancakes."

"You gonna get fat."

He shook his head.

"You better get Kim up, you boys gonna make school."

"He's up. He's dressing." Mark made a face. "He wants to be all ready. I wanted pancakes."

"O.K., O.K.," Clarissa said. "Give me a stopping place." She took down the mix and made pancakes and put six on the grill. Mark watched with satisfaction.

"I'll go dress now. Quick," he said, and disappeared.

Clarissa shook her head and turned the pancakes. She'd left her two both sound asleep. God knew what time they'd gotten in. But she was surprised to find Sandy Mackintosh asleep. She never had in all the years she'd worked for her part time. Or back when I knew her in that sorority house, either, she thought.

She fed the boys, made them brush their hair, and saw them off to the bus stop. Watching them go down the street she thought that it was funny Sandy had such young children. Course, she and B.J. were the youngest of that bunch, but still and all their friends had grown ones and B.J.'s were all ages and there would probably be more. But Sandy had waited longer than any of them to get married and start a family. Too interested in everything else, I reckon, Clarissa thought while she swabbed away at the cabinets. She was always getting up early to look at dew and suns coming up and all that stuff, and staying up all night to look at stars and moons. "Hmmmp," she said out loud. "I wonder if that's what's the matter with her this morning. Stayed up last night to look at all that moonlight. Most likely is. When you get on you can't look at moons all night and sunrises in the morning. Got to pick and choose. Got to sleep sometime. Rain out there probably sent just to help her out with it."

She finished the cabinets and mopped the floor before Sandy came into the kitchen.

She looked at Clarissa accusingly. "Why'd you let me sleep like that, Clarissa?" she said.

"Had orders from headquarters," Clarissa said. "Mr. Kurt told the younguns and they told me. Said you didn't have no class till eleven, let you sleep."

"But I feel awful when I do this." She went to the stove and poured coffee.

"You want some breakfast?" Clarissa said.

"I don't know yet. God, what time is it?"

"Ain't but nine-thirty."

Sandy sat down at the table and looked at the rain outside. "Know what this reminds me of?" she said.

"Nope."

"Mornings in the sorority house when I used to come down and talk to you before anybody was awake. I was thinking about that just yesterday. Everything was always so new and tentative and wonderful before everybody else got up."

"Can't ever remember it raining much, though," Clarissa said. "That's funny, isn't it? Must a-been a lot of rainy mornings, but don't seem to remember them atall. Seems like the sun shone all the time."

"Oh, it rained all right," Sandy said. "It was raining that morning you sneaked me back in the house."

"Um-hmm," Clarissa said. "Looked like a drowned cat. Couldn't hardly do anything else. That wasn't summer, though."

"No," Sandy said, "that wasn't summer. That was a cold rainy winter day with the trees all black and weird."

"You ate three eggs," Clarissa said. "Want me to fix you some now?"

"I guess so," Sandy said. "I need some fortification if I'm going to teach ballet at eleven this morning."

Clarissa looked at her. There were circles under her eyes and her mouth looked drawn. "Why don't you get Mr. Kurt's sister to take over for you?"

"I can't start doing that," Sandy said.

"Why not? She likes to do it."

"No, not today," Sandy said. "I need to put in my public appearance."

"Um-hmm," Clarissa said.

"You've heard about it, haven't you, Clarissa?"

"Naturally I've heard about it. Lord, child, everybody in town's heard about it."

"What do you think they'll do about it."

"Nothing. White folks protect their own just like black folks. They ain't gonna do nothing about it. Mr. Gus is a good man. He'll handle it all right."

"Have they bothered you about it, Clarissa? Said anything to you?"

"The Law? Lord, no, honey. They still pretending what that Mr. Oscar Ridley said ain't even so. That what they'll do. Have to."

"Why do you suppose he said it, Clarissa? Is there one of us he hates?"

"Mr. Oscar? No, baby. Mr. Oscar ain't got time to hate. He just up to something."

"Oh," Sandy said. "But that's worse, isn't it? Look what he's doing to everybody. How could he do that without even hating? That's a really terrible thing."

"There you go," Clarissa said. "Ain't you always been

201

this way? Trying to figure out. Ain't no figuring out, honey. Things is."

Sandy laughed. "That's exactly what I was trying to tell Martha Plowden last night," she said. "Now here you are trying to tell it to me. I guess we always think it's different when we're the one involved."

"Yes. Got to try to make sense out of it someway for ourselves," Clarissa said. "Do it myself. Did it last night, waiting on them children to get in."

"How are they, Clarissa?"

"Same as always. Sassy and up to no good. I was hoping when they got into them demonstrations last year they'd meet up with some nice young folks from other places. There was some here, but it didn't take. They weren't really interested in no demonstrations. Just wanted to make a lot of hoorah."

"Maybe not, Clarissa. They're awfully young. Maybe in the long run it will work out."

"Yessum," Clarissa said.

"Don't yessum me," Sandy said. "I'm Sandy Mackintosh. Remember me?"

Clarissa's shoulders relaxed. "Oh, they both just like Jackson," she said. "Not much use in hoping otherwise."

"Whatever happened to Jackson, Clarissa?"

"Got himself killed in a razor fight," Clarissa said. "What else? I heard about it last year from Mr. Frank Plowden. He'd heard it from some doctor friend of his up in Newcastle. And he remembered who he was from Miss Martha likely, and told me."

"Didn't you ever hear from him after he left?" Sandy said.

"Oh, sometimes. He'd come by. Just out of nowhere like every four or five years maybe. Come in drunk and say he wanted to see them younguns. Stay just long enough to make me start thinking about him again and go away."

Sandy smiled gently at Clarissa. "Men!" she said.

Clarissa smiled back at her. "That's right. That's what I always told you. Must of took, though. You got you a good one when you finally settled down and got."

"That's right," Sandy said. "He is very special. Whatever happened to my eggs?"

"You the one got me started talking."

"I know it . . . Clarissa?"

She turned from the stove where she was busying herself. "Hmmm?"

"Did you ever quit loving Jackson? Have you yet?"

"He gone, Miss Sandy."

"Nobody's ever gone," Sandy said.

"There you go," Clarissa said. "Hush up and let me fix your eggs."

But all the way to work down the rain-swept street, walking because she had the feeling she wanted to walk in the rain, had almost forgotten what it was like to walk in the rain, Sandy was thinking about *Prufrock*, remembering bits and snatches of the poem, knowing she'd never known what it meant before; Knew now. Once she stopped in the middle of the sidewalk and started to go back to the house and get her copy of *The Collected Poems* and read it. But she didn't. She walked on through the drizzle, feeling it on her face and knowing she would never have to worry about the voices in the other room, never have to dare a peach, never have to doubt the mermaids singing. They had sung to her. And always would. Poor old Bill, she said to the dripping trees and the yellow buttercups in the studio yard. Poor old Bill. And for the first time in twenty years she meant it.

Meredith Green was sitting in her car in front of the studio, her daughter beside her. Sandy waved and they got out of the car and waited for her to open the door.

"What are you doing walking in this mess?" Meredith said.

"Smelling the grass," Sandy said.

"Let's have a cigarette before I have to get to the store," Meredith said.

"O.K."

Candace went into the dressing room to change and she and Meredith sat down in the crowded little front room that served as an office. Sandy picked up a brochure lying on her desk and said, "Have you ordered extra shoes?"

Meredith nodded.

"I don't know why none of them ever manages to make them last till recital time," Sandy said. "But they don't. Right about this time of year they start wearing right through them, especially the little ones. I hate for them to have to buy new ones so late and then paint them up for the recital and throw them away this summer."

Meredith shrugged.

"You're mighty quiet this morning," Sandy said.

"Talked out, I guess," Meredith said. "We've all worried this thing to death and what is there left to talk about? It's still on all our minds."

"Not really," Sandy said. "What's on all our minds is what used to be or almost was or wasn't. It's been like being subjected to a time machine."

"I know," Meredith said. "I've been through the whole thing with Syd. Remembered things I'd forgotten completely. You know what I did this morning? I wrote to Al Weisberg and his wife. I haven't written them except for the note on the Christmas card in years. I asked them to come see us."

"That'd be fun," Sandy said. "We'll have to throw a party at the club."

"Which one?" Meredith said, and grinned.

"I'm not joining the new one," Sandy said.

"No?"

"No."

"That puts you in a minority, doesn't it?"

Sandy winked at her. "Some of us choose that," she said.

"Yeah," Meredith said. "Me and Sammy Davis."

They both started laughing.

"What's so funny?" Candace said, coming into the room, looking lumpy in her leotard and tights.

"Life, baby," Sandy said. "Go practice your tours."

They watched her, standing in front of the wide wall mirror, arms raised, body straightening, acquiring a sudden grace.

"I never believe it," Meredith said. "She bangs around the house like a clumsy ox, she knocks over tables, she can stand up and fall down right in the middle of a perfectly bare floor. Yet when she starts to dance she turns into grace and rhythm and beauty. It's plain weird."

"It happens sometimes," Sandy said. "Not often. Not enough to encourage all the mothers who bring me their awkward ones, but it does happen. What you're looking at is the woman Candace is going to be. It comes out when she dances, that's all. You can be very proud. She's going to be quite a gal."

Meredith put her cigarette out. "I reckon I'd better go to work," she said. "Can't seem to get started this morning." She got up. "I drove that damned car last night," she said.

"How was it?" Sandy said.

"Like great," Meredith said.

"I walk in the rain, you drive automobiles," Sandy said. *"De gustibus."*

"They're going to hold the hearing tomorrow," Meredith said.

"I hadn't heard that."

"Irving heard it downtown. He hears everything. I don't think it's common knowledge yet."

"Oh, I don't know," Sandy said. "It all sounds pretty common to me."

"Idiot."

"It's a nice day," Sandy said. "Enjoy."

"You sound like Irving."

"It ain't no bad way to sound."

"No," Meredith said. "Maybe not."

The phone woke Frank Plowden. He turned over in bed, groaned, and reached for it. Beside him Layne stirred, reached a hand out for her cigarettes and lighter and went halfway back to sleep again, holding them in her hand. Then she hoisted herself up, lit a cigarette and lay back down, watching the rain outside the windows. Frank finished talking and put the phone down.

"They're holding the hearing tomorrow," he said.

"Umm."

205

"I hope it doesn't get out. Surely they'll try to talk to Holcomb at the paper, but hell, newspapers. I guess they're right, too. The public has a right to know . . . all that stuff."

"I suppose you have to testify?"

"Yes. Medical evidence. I examined these bones and found them to be those of an infant, or some such crap. They want to keep the whole thing short and sweet."

"You want me to go?"

"Hell, no. What for?"

"I don't know. Moral support, maybe. Maybe just to let everybody know I did go."

"I don't see the need, honey."

"Dear one, there are some people in this town who might think, with some reason, that it was your little mistake in that airshaft."

"It wasn't."

"I said some people might think . . . they always do."

"I've never known that to bother you."

"Oh?"

"I was not sniping at you, honey, and you know it."

"I know."

He leaned over and kissed her neck, sighed, snuggled against her. "Oh, God," he said peacefully.

"We did that," she said. "Last night."

"Are you averse to doing it again?"

"No."

He took her, still drowsy, kissing her with long slow morning kisses, feeling her warm soft body turn urgent and demanding against him, experiencing the climax, as always with her, as something completely new and different and for the first time in the universe.

They lay together quietly in the warmth of tangled bed-clothes listening to the coziness of the rain.

"I love you," she said.

"Why?"

"I haven't the faintest idea," she said. "Have you? Perhaps it is purely and simply because of the way your hair grows on the back of your neck. Or maybe this mole on your shoulder, or maybe this funny little place right at the corner of your mouth that makes you look as though you are going to smile."

He sighed and rolled away from her and got cigarettes for both of them. "I should quit smoking," he said. "I tell my patients to."

She took her cigarette and smiled at him.

"That's why *I* love *you*," he said.

"How's that?"

"You didn't say, Yes, you ought to."

"I don't think it's any of my business," she said.

"I know," he said.

"Oh, hell, if you came in here and told me that, in your medical opinion, you were going to have a coronary tomorrow if you didn't stop, I'd feel like I had to help you stop. Sure. But you don't think that yourself or you would stop. Right?"

He didn't say anything, just looked at her tangled hair. He picked up a strand of it and blew through it.

"The only reason you say it is to hear me refrain from agreeing with you," she said.

"Caught."

She hugged him to her suddenly and fiercely and he could feel tears on her face.

"Hey," he said, tilting her face back and looking at her. "You never cry."

"I know. It's because it was so beautifully right this morning. Sweet. Forever. That kind. I guess it scares me a little when it's like that. I can't really believe we have each other. Even now. I always think how close it came to never happening at all."

He looked at her. "Why did it happen?" he said.

"You've never asked me that," she said.

"No. Maybe I've been a little afraid it would all go away myself. But it's true. You know we'd given each other up, and then something happened—to you, not to me. Something happened that made you go after me. Isn't that true, Mrs. Plowden? Isn't that the God's truth? I know you women are never supposed to admit that. We men are

207

never supposed to admit that. But we know, love, don't we? I didn't have the plain old nerve and you gave up on me. Then one day something in Layne changed and she said, I'm going to give him the nerve. Isn't that right?"

She smiled at him and got out of bed and picked her nightgown up off the floor. She slung it over her shoulder and started toward the bathroom. "It is *not* right, darling," she said. "You changed your mind, that's all. You couldn't do without me after all." She winked at him and went into the bathroom and shut the door.

He lay looking after her, smiling a little, enjoying the sound of the shower running, imagining her under the needle spray. Hell, what difference does it make who couldn't stay away from whom? he thought. I get the feeling it was all pretty mutual there somewhere.

Layne stood under the shower, watching the water cascade over her body, remembering.

There had been something between them the minute she'd met him at that horrible Christmas party. But it wasn't anything she had to think about or consider at all, because Frank Plowden simply was not her kind of man. She'd seen that when he came in with "Mama" beside him, that regal look to her the mama ones always have. She recognized it because of her own mother, always seeming to tower over her father though he was a foot taller than she was. Queen Victoria and Albert. Who wanted a prince consort? Well, a lot of women evidently did. After watching her father be one for all her life she recognized the type fairly easily and there were plenty of marriages around like that. It didn't even take marriage sometimes. There were girls who were already dragging boy friends around that way. An ornament for my sleeve? A Knight of the Garter? *Honi soit qui mal y pense?*

Two more parties that Christmas season, "Albert" amusing himself with the local ladies and "Victoria" smiling tolerantly. A tolerant smile, Layne had thought, is the nastiest thing on God's green earth. Six months later she came back to Druid City to take a summer job at the university.

An August afternoon, sitting on the edge of the country

club pool with the Bernhams, barbecue night. And there he was, looking at her—just looking. She'd thought, Oh, hell, "Albert," go away. You are making one big mistake. I do not play games with prince consorts.

And "Victoria" watching, eyes saying, "We are not amused." Go back to your gin bottle, "Victoria." Only "Victoria" decided to take her up. "I'm sorry, Martha, I don't go to parties much. Thank you so much, Martha, but I have a date." *Screw you, Madam. You ain't gonna sneak me up the back stairs.*

Sitting in the shoe store, talking to Syd and Meredith Green, buying a pair of pink shoes, silly damned thing, pink shoes. He came in with Janice. "Are you coming to the party Saturday night?"

So she went to that one—everybody in Druid City, drinking and eating, cocktails and buffet, yackety-yack. Holding hands suddenly under the table. Never even knew how it happened. Never would. Just suddenly had a hand to hold. Couldn't have let go if the Prime Minister had walked in. Too many martinis. What else? *"I love you, Layne."* *"You're drunk, Albert."*

Christmas again. "It's been a year." "Stop it, Frank." "Of course. We have to." And that wasn't what he was supposed to say at all.

She started dating a guy that Philip and Cassie Carlton knew. He was a very nice guy, a lawyer from Newcastle. They went dancing a lot, and ate at all the decent restaurants they could find. She started to hate her job—really hate it. And then it was Christmas again. A party at Sandy Mackintosh's house, Sandy watching her with amused eyes. She sat down by Sandy, and Martha came over. "Where do you keep yourself, Layne? You're so decorative. You ought to come to more parties. We're having one tomorrow night . . ."

That one had been a gasser. Her nice steady lawyer had gotten looped to the gills and gone off with Kurt Mackintosh and J.D. Finch to shoot craps in the kitchen. "All the men are being kosher," Martha said. "Excuse me, Meredith."

"It is very drunk out, Martha," Meredith said, with appropriate drunken dignity.

"Speaking of kosher, I'm hungry," B.J. Finch said. "What's to eat?"

"I'll have it ready in a minute," Martha said. "There are last-minute things in the oven."

"We're all drinking too much," Joan Friday said.

"I'll see about it," Martha said. They ate.

"I never want to see another thing to eat or drink," Mary Alice Cross said.

"Where's Frank?" Martha said.

"Where is he always?" Frank said. "Right here." He was sitting on the sofa in the living room, three empty glasses lined up in front of him, looking very drunk.

"Maybe you ought to have some coffee, Frank," Joan said. "What if you get a call?"

"Martha can go," Frank said. He didn't smile.

"Victoria" cased him. "You sound sullen," she said.

"As is my wont," Frank said.

"He's drinking too much," Martha said to all of them.

"I heard that," Frank said.

"Heard what?" Martha said. Tolerant smile.

"I have to get home," Layne had said. "Where's my wandering solon?"

"I'll take you home," Frank said.

"Yes, why don't you, honey?" Martha said.

"We've got to go too," Sandy said. "Go with us."

"I didn't mean to ruin the party," Layne said.

She didn't go to the other Christmas parties. She ran into him one afternoon at the country club. It was just beginning to be spring in late February. He was coming in off the golf course, red and blustery and cold, and she was sitting cozily in the bar with Cassie, having a beer and a hamburger. When he walked in there wasn't any kidding herself about it anymore because she'd felt he was walking in to her. It was just for a moment, but it was enough. He came over and sat down and she said, "I'm quitting my job and going back home next week."

"You haven't said boo to me about that," Cassie said

—then looked at Frank, looked back at her—eye flicker, nothing else. "I need to get home," she said. "Bye, Layne. Bye, Frank."

They were alone in the little bar, sunlight on the floor. "Don't go," he said.

Loving him enough to hate him by then. "Why the hell not?" she said.

Holding her hand again, hard. "Don't go."

"I said, Why not?"

"All right," he said. "Maybe it's better."

She could have killed him. But what the hell? It was probably some fatal flaw that made her want him anyway, he being everything she hated.

Joan Friday came in. They didn't quit holding hands quick enough. Who could be quick enough for Joan Friday?

So next day Martha called her at the office and asked her to lunch. But then she'd already turned in her notice and didn't care. She went. Back to the good old club with the quiet waiters and the quiet sun that didn't dare shine too harshly on the members, and the salad and the two bloody marys beforehand.

She wanted to say, Will you pour? to the Queen, but she didn't. She watched her eyes, watched her eyes saying, Off with her head.

And her mouth saying absolutely nothing, nothing pertinent, nothing you could put your finger on and say, I am being warned off. Nothing at all. Only in the sunlight, harsh enough for that, all right, she could see the Queen's pupils, shrunk to a pinpoint, letting nothing in, concentrating on inner visions, planning, working, enacting. Mouth said, "At so many places things go on among the country club crowd, but not here." Mouth saying, "I don't really think things go on anywhere. Not as many men have affairs as people think they do. They get flattered, but they don't follow through." Eyes saying, "Poor Frank, incapable, you know."

Layne smiled politely. And ate. And watched the eyes, and after a while she knew exactly what they were saying. Not really "Off with her head," but "Let the game go on. Keep hitting the balls with the mallet. Play the game *my*

211

way with hedgehogs and flamingos. And I will just hang on long enough and he will die and I will have won."

Layne had a moment of the most intense blinding anger she'd ever had in her life, followed by something she didn't know she was capable of, an all-consuming love for the unloved one, a fierce protective feeling that made her even madder, because, for God's sake, she didn't want to take him on and make him hers like he was this one's. She wanted to cut the goddamned ropes and let him breathe.

And all the time a cold hard part of her mind, as cold and hard maybe as the one across the table from her, was saying, He isn't worth it. He got himself into this mess. Why the hell do you want to get him out? But she did. Christ, she thought. I've got a Messiah complex.

The voice across the table was going on. It had switched to housekeeping in long minute detail, describing the hard job she had with the "slob" in the house.

Layne had almost quit listening to her. She had gotten the message and she was just beginning not to give a damn —about either of them, the Red Queen or her White Rabbit —and then her mind made a shocked recognition of what the voice had just said.

She sat very still, part of her shrieking, She didn't say it, she didn't say *that*. I don't believe it. Nobody does that to anybody else. Another part of her hearing it all over again in disbelieving clarity.

"I have a thing about the bathroom," Martha had said. "I simply can't stand it if the bathroom isn't *spotless*. And there was this time when it kept being wet around the john. I put up with it a long time. I got down and scrubbed it up. But finally I just *told* Frank, I hate you when I have to *do* that." She paused, then threw the last sentence across the table like the hedgehog croquet ball it was.

"I don't have that trouble anymore. He sits down now."

After a long moment of looking at the table, across the room, anywhere but at Martha, she managed to say, "Do you think I could have another bloody mary?"

Then the voice across the table said, "I hear you're leaving town."

"I can't imagine where you heard that," she said, meeting the pinpointed pupils across the table. "I love it here."

And she had thought, Martha Plowden had just made the first mistake of her long and happy life. She just told the wrong person that the emperor has no clothes.

The shower was running colder and she turned it off and got out.

"I thought you were going to stay in there all day," Frank said from the bedroom.

"I didn't steam it up any," she said. "I didn't have it on hot enough."

"I might even forgive you if you had," he said.

"I doubt it, so I didn't."

She powdered and dabbed on cologne and deodorant and put on her clean underwear. She looked at her face in the mirror; it looked a hell of a lot younger than it was. She opened the door and went out.

"I think I will go with you tomorrow all the same," she said. "Unless you'd rather I wouldn't."

"I don't know," he said. "I really don't think it makes any difference either way."

"Frank, do you know whose it was?" she said.

He shook his head.

"In a way I don't guess it matters," she said. "It will change everybody. I've just been thinking. It takes such little things sometimes to change big things, and this isn't a little thing. It's something that has to affect all of them, whether they want it or not. Do you believe in fate?"

"Naturally."

"I don't know whether I do or not. Sometimes it seems as though things just happen, then you look at them another way and some person is responsible for it all. One act leads to another and so on ad infinitum."

"But that, honey, is what fate is."

"Ah."

"Yes, ah. What are you going to do today?" he said.

"For one thing I'm going to have lunch with Cassie. She asked me last night."

"Come here," Frank said.

"Why?"

"Oh, I don't know. There's this little spot, right on your shoulder, that I seem to have the oddest desire to kiss."

"Pervert," Layne said.

Martha sat at her desk in the newspaper office looking at the front page of the morning paper. She felt very strange today. It was because she'd gone to Sandy's last night. She shouldn't have. It had made her look vulnerable, as though she needed somebody. And she didn't. Never had, never would. She took yesterday's paper out of the desk drawer and looked at that too. They'd been as discreet as you can be discreet about a thing like this. The first notice had been halfway down the front page. It had said simply: Bones found in demolished sorority house. Miley Innes, local contractor, discovered a cache of bones in an old airshaft in the Delta House, which was being demolished to make way for a new one. Sheriff Thurgood is investigating.

But the Newcastle papers had had no nice friendly town editor to edit. She picked up yesterday's Newcastle *Banner* and looked at that. There were black headlines: INFANT'S REMAINS FOUND IN DELTA HOUSE IN DRUID CITY. There was a two-column cut picturing the demolished house and a lead story describing everything from the way Miley looked to a statement by E.K. Edwards. A very politic statement, of course, saying nothing. She made a disgusted noise and shoved the papers into the wastebasket.

She was still smarting over what had happened to her this morning. The City Editor had clled her in and asked her if she wanted a couple of days off. She'd never felt so insulted in her life.

"I can think of no reason why I should want any time off," she told him, and he'd at least had the grace to look away. The truth was she would have liked some time off. Not because of this mess, but to think. To think about why she was hearing the damned presses again, to figure out what had made her call Sandy last night. She didn't like to do untypical things. People who started that ended up having nervous breakdowns. She certainly wasn't ever

214

going to fall into that category. That was the sort of thing Frank would do—not her.

Of course men were by nature weaker than women. She remembered that Allen boy of Edyth's. He'd just gone right over the edge. Of course they should all have known that would happen after he tried to drive Edyth off the road in his car that time. Hardly an act of a stable person.

She looked at her assignment sheet again. Nothing interesting. PTAs, bowling, welfare office. She took Janice's letter out of her purse and read that. Dear Mother: French exam this week. Ugh. Up half the night studying. No real news but not long till Easter vacation now. Bought a new yellow outfit that ought to knock everybody's eye out. Take care, will try more next time. I'm bushed. Love, Janice. Hardly worth wasting the stamp for.

She stood up and went to the window and looked down on Main Street. It was still raining, but not hard now. She saw Dylan Friday and his girl cross the street and run, laughing, toward his car. What were they doing downtown at this hour of the morning? The girl had taken her shoes off and was carrying them, her bare feet throwing up water from the pavement as she ran. Her long hair whipped around her face and Dylan kept tugging at her hand, but she was laughing so hard she couldn't keep up with him. They reached the car and got in and slammed the doors. Are any of us really ever that young? Martha thought. I don't believe I was. She turned away from the window and went back to her desk. Order your life, her father had always said, and nothing from outside can ever get in to harm you. She began to type up the PTA minutes.

"*You're going to make me cut right out of school, Dylan,*" *Miranda said.* "I can't go to class. Look at me. I'm soaked. Besides, I simply do not want to go."

"Of course not. You want to go out to the house with me and do something terribly cozy like playing chess."

"There isn't anything cozy about chess."

"Of course there is."

Miranda shook her head. "It is not at all cozy. It is steel and swords and helmets, it is a horse, a horse, my kingdom

215

for a horse, it is the Middle Ages and up with the portcullis. Or, if you are whimsical, which you, Dylan, are, it is the Red Queen running as hard as she can to stay in the same place. It might even be sea horses or Shakespeare. But cozy it is not."

"I stand checked."

"No, I just swapped you a pawn."

"And exposed my queen."

"Naturally."

"You're very lovely with a wet face, Miranda," Dylan said.

"Thank you."

"Now, come on. We've got the wine for tonight and enough money left for food. Let's forget school and go out to the house."

"Your mother's getting tired of me."

"No," Dylan said thoughtfully. "I get the feeling she wants the company. Let's go and help her get the rest of those papers sorted out."

"I really am sorry for all of them," Miranda said.

"It is a hell of a silly thing to happen," Dylan said.

"It isn't silly, Dylan, not really, and we know it. It's tragic. For somebody. Maybe for everybody. Let's go see your mother."

They drove through the rain-soaked streets and onto the highway. The rain had stopped, but there was still a thin drizzle and water dripped from the tree branches. The dirt road was slick with red mud and Dylan geared down. The house looked quiet and empty and sad in the gray morning light. They went in through the back door.

Joan was sitting in front of the fireplace, hunched forward uncharacteristically. She had an old sweater around her shoulders and her face looked pinched.

"You're making Miranda cut class. I can tell by your expression," she said when they came in. "You're both wringing wet, too. My heavens, go get a hot shower." She pushed Dylan toward the stairs and led Miranda into her bedroom. "Right in there," she said. "Plenty of hot water now. I'll find you something to put on."

"We're being too much trouble," Miranda said.

"No . . . no . . . I . . ." She stopped and stared at the girl in surprise. "I guess I was lonesome," she said haltingly. "It gives me something to do to fuss over you."

She was irritated with herself and she turned abruptly and went out of the room, leaving Miranda in the whiteness of furniture, rug, and curtain. Miranda stood still for a moment, looking at the room she'd never been in, the careful French provincial appointments, the neatness, the cleanness, the smell of a very, very good perfume. Then she tiptoed into the bathroom, all white and gold too, with crystal jars of bath salts and acres of thick towels and white carpet. "Well, la-di-da, Miranda," she said, "today you are Queen of the May." She stepped out of her wet clothes and put them carefully over the edge of the lavatory. She looked over her shoulder and saw a full-length mirror in the door reflecting Miranda, pink and white and terribly naked. Her small pink nipples contracted in surprise. "Heavens," she said, "is that you, girl?" She looked away, embarrassed by her own body, the revealed intricacy of all the parts of it, each fitting into the other to make a perfect wholeness. Miranda: face, neck, arms, breasts, belly, legs, feet, hands —all of a piece. Her mother always said that. *You're no beauty, Miranda. You never will be, but you're all of a piece. It's a rare and unusual thing and it serves better than beauty. It will be there all your life.*

She turned on the shower and stepped into the tub. Dylan is all of a piece too, she thought. It is very strange. What is it that makes that, what combination of genes? Or is it that it happens when just the right little sperm wins out and gets to the egg and says, "Um-hmm, this is just what was intended all along"? Because there are seldom more than one all-of-a-piece people to a family, so it isn't simply combination or heredity. It must be that specially eager little sperm. She giggled. I'm a real nut. One day they'll come after me in their white coats.

She got out and dried on a huge fluffy towel and put it around her and tucked it together under her arm and went out into the bedroom. Joan had laid out a skirt and sweater

217

and a set of underwear. She dressed, feeling unaccountably guilty. The skirt was too long, but the clothes fitted otherwise. She went out to the kitchen.

"My shoes won't do," Joan said. "I'm afraid it's these or nothing." She handed her a pair of Dylan's bedroom slippers.

Miranda laughed and put them on. "Are we going to finish up the scut work on your papers today?" she asked Joan.

"We might as well," Joan said. "A day like this . . . it's right for it."

They went into the den and by the time Dylan joined them they were already sorting. He stood in the doorway looking at them, Miranda in his mother's clothes, his mother, looking not much older than Miranda. Two women, waiting for him to change the odds. But of what use is a jack in a two-queen hand? It isn't even worth holding for a kicker. He went on into the room.

"The ace of spades arrives," he said.

Miranda looked up at him. "You're not an ace, Dylan," she said.

"I know it," he said.

By noon they had most of the papers separated. There was only one small stack to go through. "Let's finish it," Joan said, "then I'll get some lunch." She picked up a stack of papers and put them in her lap. At the bottom of the pile she came on a yellowed paper with a poem on it. It was a carbon and she had to squint to make out the faded print.

"What's that, Mother?" Dylan said.

She shook her head at him impatiently and went on reading. After a moment she gave a small gasp. Dylan and Miranda were both watching her and she was conscious of it. She read on, trying to keep her face from changing, knowing it was changing.

"Mother?" Dylan said.

"It's nothing," she said. "An old duplicate." To her horror she burst out crying.

Dylan got up and took the paper out of her hand. He read it and handed it silently to Miranda.

Joan dabbed ineffectually at her eyes. "I feel such a fool," she said. "But he wasn't like that. Not ever. Not Bill. It must be somebody else's."

"It's Dad's," Dylan said. "Surely to God you recognize the rhythms. It's a damned fine poem. A little erotic. But not for the present day."

"It's so . . . so damned graphic," Joan said.

"Oh, hell, Mother. You didn't get me out of a Cracker Jack box," Dylan said.

Joan looked at him, at Miranda reading the poem. "You children are so sophisticated," she said. "I'm sorry, but I guess I'm old-fashioned. It seems crude to me, like those things everybody used to be reading when we were in school by—what was his name? Walter Benton? It isn't like your father."

Dylan smiled. "Evidently it is," he said. "He wrote it. To tell you the truth, it makes me sort of happy for the old boy. I always thought he was too much of a romantic for his own good."

"Well," Joan said, "do you think it should go into the hold folder?"

"By all means," Dylan said. "I wonder where the original is."

Joan looked at him, but his face was completely innocent. She knew where it most probably was, and maybe it was that, more than the shock of the poem that had made her cry now years after she'd given up crying. But she guessed Dylan didn't know enough about how an eighteen-year-old Sandy had looked to connect her with the girl on the paper. When was it? she thought. Before me? Of course before me, it had to be. But the thought didn't comfort her. She had a strange sense of loss, of having been cheated, of complete and utter despair. It made no sense. She had married Bill, loved him, been loved back, had a good marriage even though she had lost him sooner than she should have. Why then this sense of desolation, of the utter hopelessness of life? So Bill had had an affair with Sandy. Did it matter? Could it matter . . . now? But she knew it did, and the upsetting and unbelievable thing was that what gave
219

her the sense of loss was not that Bill had had Sandy before her, but that he could have felt like that about her and left her. It told her something, not about Sandy, but about Bill. She simply didn't like what it told her. It surprised her that she felt that way. She should have been glad he'd gotten over adolescence, become a stable, staid man in an ordered world. But she wasn't. She wished desperately that he were here so she could castigate him for it, tell him that feeling that way about someone's legs was worth something, tell him that when something is written in the stars it is written, and that you do not escape by throwing it away.

"Mother, are you all right?" Dylan said.

She looked at him, and at Miranda, both looking at her out of the innocent faces of youth in spite of all their sophistication and knowledgeableness of sex. Sex, hell, she wanted to tell them. That isn't it. You miss the whole point if you think it is. Then Miranda met her eyes and smiled. And she knew she didn't have to tell her anything. Two women looked at each other over the twenty years' gap between them and said everything there was to say. She didn't have to say, Miranda, I never felt that way about anybody. Ever. Miranda knew it. Because Miranda did feel that way. For Miranda, Dylan was written in the stars.

"I'll go fix some lunch," Joan said. "No. No help, please." She went into the kitchen and busied herself as she had for all the years with washing lettuce and buttering bread, and all the things that have to be done all the same.

Tell me about it, Miley said.

"Miley, for God sakes," Edyth said.

He stood at the window watching the rain.

"Why not?" he said. "I've got a nice long day ahead of me. We can't do anything outside on a day like this, and none of the inside jobs need me. Tell me about it."

"Let it come down," Edyth said.

"What's that supposed to mean?"

"Macbeth," Edyth said.

"Oh, shit," Miley said. "Now you're trying to make me out the villain of the piece. Just as in that play, dear. The lady was the moving force."

"Yes," Edyth said. "Eve too. None of you is ever going to forgive any of us for intruding on that all-male paradise."

"Bitch."

"Miley, please." She got up and poured herself another cup of coffee. Drink coffee and smoke cigarettes . . . something to do . . . stay alive. Don't ask why. "I have to go to work," she said.

"Call in."

"Why? So I can stay here and listen to you call me names?"

"So you can explain to me why you feel so self-righteous about this. You keep acting as though I'm at fault somehow. I didn't do anything."

"Miley, I just cannot see what good it does to go over and over it like this. We have to live. Either you stay and we live with it, or you go and we live with it separately. That's it. That's all. What possible good can it do to go on and on beating each other to death?"

"I want you to tell me if you put that baby in that wall."

"I told you I didn't."

"How can I believe that?"

"If you can't, you can't. I cannot do anything but tell you the truth. If you won't believe it, that's that."

"That's that, huh? Twenty years?"

"You are the one who is ruining everything."

"I didn't do anything."

"I'm going to work, Miley. This just isn't accomplishing anything."

"Jesus, how can you be so calm about it?"

"Calm? Oh, my God. It's because I simply cannot stand another minute of it that I've got to go to work."

"Is that why we couldn't ever have a baby?"

Well, that's done it, she thought. That's torn it. He's finally gotten around to saying the one thing that makes it impossible for us ever to have any sort of marrige anymore. He's made it.

She got up and put on her raincoat and went out of the house into the morning drizzle. All the way to work she thought that she ought to take the damned car off the road

221

like Bob had tried to do that time, but she knew she wouldn't. She knew it as well as she knew her own misery. Suicide never comes from misery anyway. It comes from despair. Despair is not pain, it is absence, absence of everything, even pain. As long as the pain is there, there is the hope that it will cease. When even the pain has gone, along with the joy, then the possibility of ending it exists. It takes a certain sort of person to reach that sort of despair. She wasn't one.

My God, how she'd fought Bob Allen off that wheel, the dead weight of him—the strength of desperation. It was true, you could do things you were incapable of when the provocation was there. She was a girl who had wanted to live enough to move almost two hundred pounds of dead-weight male with the hands and wrists that rested now on this steering wheel. She wasn't about to throw away that life she'd saved which had been her own.

But what was it going to be worth without Miley? She looked ahead into a corridor of empty days and nights, working, sleeping, eating, staying alive. It seemed impossible. Like an alcoholic she knew she'd have to learn to do it one day at a time. Even the thought of one of those days seemed a weight too heavy to carry. He was too much a part of her, been too long the life she lived. She couldn't see it without him, wouldn't see it without him. He'd just have to take her back, have to learn to live with life as it is and was. Otherwise, what? That corner of her mind she couldn't see around. But she knew the dangers there, all of them, including the unbearable one that if he goaded her long enough and far enough she might actually quit loving him and accomplish what he thought was already fact. A part of him must want that, she thought. He must, without knowing it, want me to quit loving him. Why else would he be driving me toward that?

It rained.

At ten o'clock J. D. Finch quit watching the rain outside his office window and went home. All morning he had been thinking about marrying B.J. in that God-awful week-long wedding. At least that was how it seemed to him now, looking back on it. There had been parties and rehearsals, and food and liquor and enough champagne to float the *Queen Mary*, and through it all B.J. had laughed and joked and acted as though the whole thing were happening to somebody else, not them. In a way it was. Weddings were really for the parents. Certainly neither of them had wanted one, not one that elaborate or expensive or exhausting. Hell, by the time they'd gotten to a hotel they'd been too tired to want to do anything. Thinking that, he knew he wanted to do something, right now. So he got up and put his hat and raincoat on, and went home.

B.J. was in her room, two children with her. He ran them both out to the kitchen and shut the door and flipped the lock.

B.J. watched him, grinning. "Why didn't you just stay home today?" she said.

"It isn't good for the character."

They lay in bed in the dim room washed with rain light, comfortable, a little sleepy, talking.

"I really came home because I want to tell you something, B.J." J.D. said.

"All right."

"But, I don't know. Maybe I just told you."

"Yes. I think so."

"Well, I'm going to try to say it anyway. I love you."

"Yes. You said that."

He laughed. "I mean . . . really."

B.J. pushed herself up in bed and looked at him. "I know."

"Well, hell. The years pile up and the kids come and most of the time you're awfully involved with them. That's the kind of person you are, B.J. You like kids. Most people really don't, you know. They can stand their own, if there aren't too many of them. Other people's they can do without. And a hell of a lot of the time they could do without their own. But you really like them—they're people to you. So they take a lot of you, but you don't cheat about it. There's plenty of you for me, too. So I wanted to tell you, this morning while it's raining and I ought to be at work,

223

that I think it's all worth it. Even when I *don't* think it, even when I'm tired and I bitch at you and the kids, even when I get the mully grubs and wish to God I'd stayed a bachelor or at least gotten out of the old man's business and gone to Europe or painted a picture or any damned thing. Even then, underneath the irritation and the mad, I think it's been worth it . . . life, I mean."

"But . . ."

"I know. I don't say it when I get that kind of mully grubs. But I get them just like everybody else. The cut-and-run days, the where-and-why days. But underneath, where it counts, I know they're just that, days in a lifetime. And the lifetime has added up."

"Even though the choices are gone."

"Yes. Even though the choices are gone."

"I thank you."

"I thank you. B.J., it's mainly that you don't run us."

"Heavens, how could I?"

"Easy. But you don't. You see every kid as a person. You see me as one too."

"I should hope . . ."

"It's a rare and unusual talent, Mrs. Finch."

"No. Everybody tries that . . . don't they? Sure, we're all hung up on ourselves, but we all try."

He shook his head. "Not true, honey. When you have to try, it ain't there."

"J.D.," B.J. said, "you haven't ever been a big fat little girl."

"No."

"It changes you. It makes you see the big fat little girl in everybody in the world, forever."

"It makes some people bitter."

"Well, there's always that, but it ought to give you something else too."

"Compassion's the word you're hunting."

"Yes, I guess so. Now I want to tell you something. I wasn't going to talk about it, but if you're going to tell me you've wanted to cut and run and haven't and won't I

224

ought to tell you this. You see, there was this boy, in college."

"Your tennis player."

"Yes. Well, you see, I found out yesterday at Joan's that all the girls had a crush on him. They thought he was some sort of sexy object, some dreamboat, you know. Well, this was all news to me. Isn't that funny as hell? You see, being me, being B.J., gawky, funny B.J., I couldn't imagine that anybody that *I* had, that was *my* boy friend, could be anything special to anybody else. I liked him. I loved him, I guess. But it just never occurred to me that anybody else did. And finding out they did, I don't know, it's changed me. It's made me feel different, about myself, about everything. It's like something a woman told me once. She said she'd had a backache all her life, been to dozens of doctors. None of them could do or find anything. Then she moved to this new town and went to this doctor and he put her at a certain slant on a table and it went away . . . just like that. He said her kidney was displaced and he fixed it. She told me if she'd had a million dollars he could have it. All those years, all that pain, and suddenly it was gone . . . forever. I feel like that. Do you understand?"

"But darling, you are a beautiful, wonderful woman."

"But I never felt like it. I told you, you've never been a big fat little girl." She leaned over and kissed him. "Jesus, I've made it sound as though I didn't think *you* were a catch. I did. But to tell you the truth there was always this little sneaking doubt that it wasn't just *me*, that part of it was my family and the money and the fact that your old man liked me, that I was the proper wife for the Finch Paper Mill heir. Today, I don't feel that way anymore. Today I feel like it might have been just me."

"It's always been you," J.D. said. "Have you forgotten? Don't you remember the first time we went swimming out at Hatter's Lake and I looked at you in the moonlight? My God, women, were you blind?"

"In a way . . . yes."

"B.J., you are not fat, you are not big, you are not a little girl. You are my love, my great love, my woman."

225

"Yes."

"And I will tell you something else. There is a part of me that has thought about that baby in the wall. I have wondered, and then I told myself that it could not be you to whom all the children are people. But I will say one more thing about it and nothing else, ever. Even if it was you, which I don't believe, but even if it was, it does not matter. If you did it you would have had a reason and you would have had to. Do you understand?"

"I . . ."

"Don't say anything else. I mean it. I know you did not. But I tell you again. If you had, it wouldn't matter."

"Why don't you take me out to lunch?" B.J. said. "We haven't done that since Jim was born."

"I'd love to take you to lunch. We'll go to the club and eat something terribly fattening and have a couple of drinks and watch the rain on the greens."

She looked at the man beside her, older now, like they all were, but still handsome, still flat-bellied, with black hair and gentle hands and full of a quiet capable energy. He ran a paper mill. Maybe it was not the most romantic job in the world, but it was his job and he was her man.

"When you feel those cut-and-run days," she said, "why don't you ever cut and run and take me with you?"

He laughed. "Where would we go, dear heart?"

"Who knows? Tahiti? Bangor, Maine?"

"Well, for now, let's go to lunch."

She got up and went into the bathroom, leaving the door open to call back to him. "Do you ever remember, J.D., that when you were little you thought grown people had it made?" she said. "Can you remember that? Thinking that if you just got grown all your troubles would be over?"

"I can remember."

"Jesus," B.J. said. She took a quick shower and stuck her head back around the door. "I keep thinking about poor old Martha."

"Why?"

"Well, she's having to face this thing and be reminded of everything like all of us and she hasn't got anybody to help

226

her with it. Joan at least has Dylan. But Martha hasn't got anybody."

"Nobody's got anybody in the dark places, B.J.," J.D. said. "That's what we've just been telling each other. No matter how much love, how much closeness, we come and go alone, and in between we have the lonely days."

"But we *have* each other."

"And we are lucky. We have work, too. Martha has that. You'd be surprised what a job of work can do for the human soul."

"That's true," B.J. said. "Remember the old joke about the woman with all the kids whose friends kept having nervous breakdowns and her doctor said to her one day, 'Mary, why don't you have a nervous breakdown?' And she said, 'Doctor, I just don't have time.'? I understand that woman."

"Yes, love, I suspect you do."

There was no one in the bar at the club, so they sat together at a corner table and had a drink and went on into the almost-empty dining room. Two sides of the room were glass with a view across the greens toward the river. All the grass looked new-washed and brilliant in the gray light.

"I can almost smell it," B.J. said.

They had another drink and ordered shrimp. Layne Plowden and Cassie Carlton came in and stopped at their table. "What? Not working?" Cassie said.

"You ruined us last night," J.D. said.

"You aren't hung?"

"No, but I am conscious of my head. It isn't doing anything, but It Is There."

"Ah," Cassie said. "Me too."

"Join us?" B.J. said.

Cassie shook her head. "You look like two people who want to be together. We'll see you. Soon." She went away, Layne behind her, both of them trailing smells of good perfume.

"I'm thinking," B.J. said.

"That's good."

"No. I'm thinking that people get what they want. That

227

sounds so silly when you say it out like that. But it's an important truth all the same. They don't think they do. They're always complaining and whining and bitching, but everybody I know really got what they wanted. I thought that, looking at Layne and Cassie. When we were all in school together and Martha and Frank were so obviously going to get married, if I had seen Layne walking around I'd have said, That is the girl for Frank, but not now. He wanted to have Martha for all the growing-up years and then he wanted Layne . . . That sounds callous."

"Well, it's obviously true."

"It's almost as though he needed Mother and then didn't anymore. And Philip. He used to run around with every girl in town, but here he is married to Cassie, who could have been picked for him from the cradle."

"And here we are, and that is precisely what my father knew when he met you."

"So? Maybe everybody was right back in the days when parents used to arrange marriages. Maybe we all just do what they'd have done for us anyway. Joan wanted to be the professor's wife. Of course she didn't want to be his widow, but if you marry someone that much older that's in the cards too. And Kurt and Sandy. Heavens, they're so exactly right. I don't think even Sandy knows how right. Of course Martha hasn't got what she wants, has she? Or has she? There's no getting around that martyr streak. She never wanted the kind of Frank that Layne wants. The shrimp is delicious."

"So are you."

"I am one thousand and one years old and the kids all need new tennis shoes."

"Mañana."

"O.K."

"Well, B.J. looks blooming this morning," Cassie said. "I don't think she's hung."

"I can't imagine B.J. with a hangover," Layne said.

"Oh, she's had them," Cassie said. "I remember one real lulu of a party we threw when Philip and I first came back to live in the old house. Jesus! Everybody was hung."

Layne lit a cigarette. "B.J. doesn't look worried," she said.

"Hell, B.J. didn't put any baby in an airshaft."

"Everybody puts babies in airshafts," Layne said.

"What do you mean by that?"

"I don't know. Everybody's noticed it though. This thing has had everybody connected with it in a tizzy and obviously everybody didn't do it. But somehow everybody feels as though they did. It's like when they used to call us into assembly at school and make some sort of announcement about somebody stealing something. I always used to get the feeling I ought to go up and confess. Did you?"

"Yes."

"This is the same thing. Everybody has something hidden in the wall. No, don't give me that look. I don't mean skeletons in closets, yack, yack. I mean in your own head."

"Well, your skeleton rattles around town busily enough."

"Martha's not my skeleton. She's not in my head, either. Frank's maybe. Not mine."

"I don't see why she doesn't go somewhere else."

"Don't you?"

"No. I never have. She could go where Janice is in school, work there."

Layne shook her head. "Here is where everybody is sorry for Martha," she said. "Here is where I remain the villain of the piece. No pun intended."

"Does it bother you?"

"No. I made my decision a long time ago. Just like she did hers. I do not feel guilty. Not about Martha. My guilt, when I have it, is that maybe I'm running him the way she used to. I don't think so, but sometimes it worries me."

"You're not."

"I try not. Maybe that's the best we can do." And she thought, Well, at least he can stand up in the bathroom.

"Well, well, there's Oscar and E.K.," Cassie said.

"What is that evil man up to, anyway?" Layne said. "He started this whole mess."

"What is everybody up to?" Cassie said. "A little room for me, me, me."

229

"I bet he's got enough babies in walls to populate the world," Layne said.

"Oscar?"

"Um-hmm. E. K. Edwards too, for that matter. When I start thinking about the troubles of being a doctor's wife I can always say, You ain't stuck with a politician, kid, ain't that great?"

"E.K.'s a college president."

"He's a politician."

"Yeah, I guess he is."

The two men sat down at a table in a corner. They nodded toward Layne and Cassie and toward B.J. and J.D. B.J. made a face behind Oscar's back. Cassie laughed. "Tomorrow, the world," she said.

"Next week, *East Lynne*," Layne said.

"And meantime," Cassie said, "Little Eva and Eliza and all the ice, ice, ice."

"Which reminds me," Layne said. "Let's have another drink."

"Did you bring the papers?" Oscar said.

"A preliminary contract," E.K. said. "Yes."

Oscar lit a cigar and picked up the paper E.K. put on the table. "A hundred-year lease," he said. "That ought to do."

"Yep," E.K. said. "The first hundred years are the hardest."

"I was refraining from saying that, Doctor," Oscar said.

"Just a little joke," E.K. said.

"Whereas, whereas," Oscar said. "This looks good to me. Of course I'll have to have my lawyer look it over."

"Yes," E.K. said. "I figured that."

Oscar looked up at him. "We're going to do a class job with this, Dr. Edwards," he said. "You don't have to worry about that. You know I can do class work. You've seen it."

"Oh, yes," E.K. said.

Oscar sighed, leaned back in his chair and blew smoke across the dining room. He felt magnanimous and a little sorry for E. K. Edwards. "We'll leave the trees next to the river," he said.

E.K. Edwards felt sad. He could not have defined why.

He believed Oscar. He would give him a class job because he could afford to and because he felt so triumphant about finally getting his hands on university property. He probably *would* leave the trees, a few of them, anyway. By the terms of the contract the school would profit—there was no doubt of that, either. Why then this feeling of grayness, failure, old, old age creeping across the golf links? From where he sat he could see the flag on the eighteenth green; it flapped dismally in the damp air above the brilliance of poisonous green grass.

"Are you joining the new club?" Oscar said.

E.K. came back a long way and looked at the man across the table from him. He was a very ordinary, even attractive, man. He did not smell of brimstone. "That'll be up to Mrs. Edwards," he said.

"We're going to have a great golf course out there," Oscar said. "It'll take time for it to settle in, of course, but eventually . . ."

"Yes, time," E.K. said.

"Maybe you won't be here by then, huh, Doc?" Oscar said.

"I plan to stay here indefinitely," E.K. said.

Oscar winked at him. "Unless something better comes along," he said.

"This is a pretty fine institution," E.K. said.

"I believe you need a drink," Oscar said. "You sound peaked this morning, but no wonder. I wouldn't want your responsibilities."

"Just tomato juice for me," E.K. said.

"Oh, hell, with a tiny little bit of vodka in the bottom of it," Oscar said.

"Well, all right," E.K. said.

A small breeze had stirred outside and the flag was flapping against the pole, Beyond it lay the fourteenth hole on the back nine with its truly great ravine, ringed by a tangle of oak and wisteria. He'd never gotten below par on that hole. Hardly anybody did. That was why they had placed the fountain and the rain shack just beyond it. So that when you climbed up after losing at least one ball and

231

wishing your handicap was higher you could pretend you
were thirsty or there was a rock in your shoe and sit down
and look back over the way you'd come and plan how you
were going to play that hole next time so that you could
avoid the low branches of the trees and the treachery of the
vines and the trap of the water. Then next time, you'd play
it the same way again.

"We'll only be able to open the first nine holes right at
first," Oscar was saying, "but by next year we'll get the
second nine going. Have you seen the model of the club-
house?"

"Yes," E.K. said. He had seen it. It was displayed promi-
nently in a bank downtown. It was a lovely model in all its
details, and to E.K. it looked exactly like a synagogue. He'd
told his wife that and she hadn't thought it was funny. She
said it looked like an airline terminal to her. "You miss the
point, dear," he'd said.

And she'd said, "That really isn't your kind of humor,
dear."

"Say," Oscar said. "Have you heard the one about . . .?"

And that, of course, most definitely was.

*Kurt Mackintosh was waiting until his secretary came
back from lunch before leaving for his own.* The fluorescent
lights in his office gave a glow of unreality to the walnut
desk and the file cabinets and the neat leather chairs. To
the papers on his desk too. There was the new policy for
one hundred thousand dollars that he'd gotten written for
the guy who'd had the coronary a couple of years ago. That
had to be delivered personally and he put it into his brief-
case to carry with him. He was proud of that policy. He'd
fought long and hard for it and it gave him a hell of a kick
to be able to take it out there this afternoon and tell the
guy he could sleep easy nights even if his premiums were
going to be sky high. The policy was also going to win the
district salesman contest for him, but that was only inciden-
tal. The real kick came from getting a hard one through.
There was a chain letter on his desk that had come in this
morning. It looked like a good gimmick because it was all
done with checks and it depended on your own buddy not

232

screwing you up. He left a note for his secretary to type it up and send it on. It would be nice if a little money came through on it. He'd buy Sandy a new cigarette lighter, just for the hell of it, because he knew she was secretly smoking again. He thought about Sandy, lying curled in sleep when he'd left this morning. It wasn't like her so he assumed she'd been up half the night. This damned baby in the wall. It was tearing them all up. Even Martha Plowden had had to have company last night. He thought about Sandy as she must have been at eighteen and he wondered about her, but he didn't want to think too closely about it. Not yet.

Marybelle came in, shaking rain out of her umbrella, and he gave her instructions for the afternoon. She looked at him and behind the clear gray eyes there was a look of . . . what? Not exactly speculation, commiseration maybe. She was a good girl. He guessed they'd all just have to get used to that look for a while. At least until the damned thing was old news and something else came along to engage their interest. He thought briefly and ironically about the war in Viet Nam and he knew it didn't have one-tenth the emotional value this thing did, not for anybody in town. A Buddhist burns himself, but it is far, far away across the ocean. Push the button and the Chinese die and you get the million bucks.

"Is there anything the matter, Mr. Mackintosh?" Marybelle said.

"No," he said. "How hard is it raining out there?"

"Not hard, but steady."

"Thanks. I guess I'd better get my hat and coat."

He put them on and went out into the gray street. There were a lot of cars parked around the block, but few people on the sidewalks. The air smelled fresh and clean and it cheered him. Hell, we'll get through this too, he told himself. The human animal gets through everything. He remembered the time he'd been afraid Sandy was interested in Frank Plowden and the sheer black precipice that had put him on. But it had ended, stopped, gone away. He never even thought about it anymore. Not often, anyway. He remembered a Saturday when he'd sat all alone in the office, a dark day like this one, listening to the rain, pretending he was working, doing nothing but wondering if they ought to end it all, get divorced, forget trying to forge a viable relationship out of the frailties of human possibilities. He remembered too that finally at long last, with dark coming on, the rage had left him and he'd known he was hungry and had to eat and the thought in his mind had been, We'll get through this. We have to. It was as simple, after all, as that. We have to. Whatever the hell it is.

As he got into his car Irving Green came out of the shoe store and along the street toward him. He waved and Irving motioned to him to wait a moment. He nodded and watched him come across the street toward him, looking dapper and cheerful even in the rain.

Irving got in the car on the other side. "Hi, Kurt," he said. "Heard some things you might be interested in."

"I don't doubt it," Kurt said. "Have a cigarette?"

He took out the pack, damp from his walk to the car. Irving took one and lit it with a silver lighter. "They're holding the hearing tomorrow," he said.

"Just what do you think they plan to do?" Kurt said.

"Nothing. But I thought I'd tell you. As soon as it's over all of us can settle down and start being people again. It's waiting around for it that's got everybody in a tizzy."

"Yes," Kurt said. "I guess so."

Irving looked at him. "I'll tell you like I told Syd," he said. "The only thing to do about it is try to forget it."

Kurt laughed shortly. "Come on, Irving," he said.

"I mean it," Irving said. "You think I don't know that for six out of seven of us it would be better if it all did come out and they proved who did it? Sure it would. But life isn't like that. Job never did know till his dying day why Yahweh took out after him. He just had to live with it. This thing is going to be the same way. We are all going to have to have a little faith. Pardon me if I sound like the rabbi. But I mean it. Now, enough of that. I have some more news of interest to impart. E. K. Edwards is going to give Oscar Ridley a lease on that river land to put his damned high-rise apartments on."

234

"Oh, shit."

"Yes, indeed, my boy. Oh, crap. But it is true. Now you know why we are all being tried and tested. Not by Yahweh, but by Oscar Ridley. And that, I'm afraid, calls for even more faith. If Oscar, not God, sent us this problem involving our loved ones, how in hell did God manage to send us Oscar?" He winked at Kurt.

"Hell, Irving," Kurt said. "But it figures."

"Yes. Just thought you might be interested in knowing. Don't ask me where I found it out. I got friends, here and there. Give my love to Miss Sandy, the beautiful."

Irving paused with his hand on the door handle. "You know something, Kurt?" he said. "When God sent me a little shikse to take my son away from me I felt like Job. For a sophisticated man I made a lot of old-fashioned noises. You might say I tore the lapels a little. And do you know something? Our Meredith is about the best thing that ever happened to the Green family. I don't know whether she's ever figured that out or not. But I have. I remember her standing under the canopy becoming one of us for pure and simple love of my son and you know something, I knew then and I know now I couldn't have done it. Hell, when Syd broke the glass I wanted to stand up and cheer."

"Meaning, Irving?"

"Meaning, love exists, boy. And where love is, there God is also. Oscar Ridley and murder-will-out be damned."

"O.K., Irving," Kurt said. "We'll all make out."

Irving got out of the car, then leaned back in. "Job never did know what Yahweh was mad about," he said. "But Job won. He beat the Old Boy at his own game. He never questioned him. Not one damned time."

"Irving," Kurt said, "you forgot to put on your cap."

"I know. I sound like an ass, but I figured if I was going to tell you the good news about Oscar and Edwards I ought to say something to counteract it. You aren't interested in my Aston Martin."

"What the hell are you talking about?" Kurt said.

"I'm getting wet," Irving said. "Take care." He walked rapidly back across the street and into the store.

Kurt looked after him, smiling. Then he backed out and drove toward the dance studio.

He parked behind the building and sat watching the kids come out and get into the family cars, short little girls, tall little girls, gawky little girls, graceful little girls, all trying to learn to dance, all glad to be released for the moment from the effort. He thought about Irving and grinned. He'd always liked Irving. The store was close to his office and they had coffee together a lot of mornings. In a way he knew Irving better than Syd. He realized suddenly that Irving was simply a good man. It is strange, he thought, how seldom we're ever able to say that about somebody, that they are a good man. The world isn't over-populated with them, that's all.

The last mama drove away with the last little girl and Sandy came out of the back door of the studio wearing her black raincoat, waving at him across the parking lot. He watched her move toward him, loving the grace of her, thinking, Here I am, Yahweh, Old Boy, an ordinary man, crowding forty, not too handsome, getting just a little bald, wondering if I'm not going to have to start to wear glasses pretty soon now, sporting a crooked nose from a futile attempt to play football once, an insurance salesman with a degree in Business Administration. I get hemorrhoids on occasion and I've lost two of my very own teeth, and the sacktime I put in is not what it was at twenty-five. But there comes my wife, and she is beautiful, and she moves like a goddamned dryad over the wet grass. To all is something granted, Oh, Lord. Bless you, Irving. He leaned over and opened the door for her.

Clarissa had made salmon croquettes and green beans and cornbread with iced tea. Sandy laughed when she saw the table. "Clarissa is comforting me," she said. "This is the kind of meal we used to have for lunch at home when I was a kid and I've talked about it enough for her to know it comforts me. How nice."

"Well, I got a little item for you that isn't going to comfort you," Kurt said.

236

"Oh, Jesus, Kurt. What now?"

"Well, it's not that bad. But Irving told me that E.K. is signing that river plot over to Oscar."

"That makes me sick," Sandy said, but she went on eating.

"You don't sound very surprised."

"No. No, I'm not. I was telling Martha last night the whole country's going to be a gigantic parking lot and housing development someday. And we all knew Oscar was up to something. No, no surprises for me in this one. Maybe I'm past being surprised anymore, anyway. She says grandly."

"Um-hmm. The hearing's tomorrow."

"I know. Meredith told me. But I'm not going to worry about that either. I thought last night. I thought about a lot of things. Maybe I grew up a notch or two, who knows?"

"Don't grow up too far," Kurt said. "I rather like you the way you are. Pass the bread, please."

"What way I are?" Sandy said.

"Interested. Alive. Hell, Sandy, things happen to you. They always have and they always will. I married you knowing that. Even if I don't remember it all the time."

"I'm a romantic ass," Sandy said. "That's what I figured out last night."

"So be it," Kurt said. "Consider the picture you give the kids who come to be taught to dance. Think on it, love. You are beautiful. You make them beautiful. It is a good way to be."

"I believe salmon croquettes comfort you too," Sandy said.

But she thought about it. About Bill and Lawson and Frank and Kurt and her railroad man, about all the books and all the music and all the moonlight and the stars that came otherwise. All of them were part of her and made her what she was, and what she was was the lady who taught ballet to children. And, who knew, without the dancing on Weldon Benson's grave or the heart breaking for Bill the unworthy maybe she wouldn't be able to teach first position to a future ballerina. Maybe it *was* a teleological

237

universe. Just maybe, hopefully, on a rainy dreary morning, it was.

There had been so many of them, the hopeful open faces, little girls, all vulnerable, even the bitchy ones, all bearing the stigmata of woman, all going to win and lose and suffer someday, no matter how vulnerable the soft necks, the grubby hands, the recalcitrant feet.

She remembered the nightmare of the first recital the first year she taught. At that time it was still an adventure to her and one she wasn't sure she was going to survive. She had felt helpless in the face of the awkwardness of children, in trying to train into them what either came naturally or not at all. She had felt the recital would break her on the rack and that all the mamas would rise up to demand their money back. Because she didn't seem to have taught a single one of them anything, not one step, not one gesture of grace.

She had had no alternative but to concentrate on the staging of chaos. And how she had worked on that! She'd made up a ballet herself, scorning the tried and true little numbers you could find in the dance magazines, that you remembered from your own recital days. She worked like a fiend on it, trying to fit in each child according to her abilities, to give a small solo, if only a few steps, to every one.

She'd designed the costumes herself, drawing them on file cards, painting them with watercolors, even sprinkling them with diamond dust to indicate the way they would really look. Jimmy Lou Allbright's mother, old Mrs. Lewis, had agreed to take on the job of making them, but her fees were so exorbitant they frightened Sandy to death. She had planned to have at least two costumes apiece for the children, but when she heard the cost she cut it to one.

She rehearsed each child desperately in front of her brand-new floor-length mirror, and at night she crawled into bed so tired she would be asleep before Kurt turned out his reading light.

At just about that time all their ballet shoes started wearing out. She was used to it now, but that first year it had panicked her. There were only the few weeks to the recital and she'd thought they could all spray-paint the shoes, old as they were, and discard them. But it didn't work that way. More and more of them kept arriving in new shoes, new shoes their mothers had just bought and paid for and that she was going to demand be painted and ruined. One night she wept about it and Kurt had laughed and kissed her and said, "My dearest Sandy. They'd be too little next year anyway. You aren't going to ruin anything by having them painted." She'd looked at him gratefully and fallen into sleep like a pole-axed steer.

Gradually the ballet had begun to take shape. She actually began to believe the children were going to make it. They were all trying so hard and something like real dances were beginning to emerge. Then the mothers began. The phone would ring. "Mrs. Mackintosh, I can't understand why Estelle is doing only three steps. I talked to Madge Winston yesterday and her child has a whole little dance." "Sandy *dear*, I know assigning costumes for as many students as you have is a terrible problem. But couldn't you do something about Susie wearing purple? It just isn't her color. She looks absolutely awful in it." "Mrs. Mackintosh, you don't know me, but I'm the twins' mother. We've never let them dress alike. We believe in giving them their individuality. Couldn't you dress them differently for this?" "Sandy? Mrs. Lewis says she can't get Cindy's costume done before week after next and her grandparents are coming and we wanted them to see Cindy in her costume and take moving pictures. Couldn't you get her to take us first?"

"Quit worrying about it, child," Mrs. Lewis said. "I've been sewing for people for thirty years and they carry on at you all the time. When they walk out with the new dress or whatever, they love you and they come back next time. You worry too much. You're going to be sick."

By the time for dress rehearsal she'd lost six pounds.

She'd arranged to rent the auditorium of the junior high school for the recital and she arrived the morning of the dress rehearsal feeling as though she were on her way to the guillotine. Kurt's sister was helping her or she'd never have made it. She put her in charge of the new record, the rehearsal one being by now ground to static, and she kept thinking wildly, What if this one breaks? The stage looked huge and ugly and bare, and the auditorium smelled of staleness.

The first group began arriving at ten. Some of the mothers brought them and stayed, others dumped them and left. The behind-the-stage scene was chaos. They were all costumed and their hair was curled and their faces made up, but they were still little girls, and they were excited, wriggling, squirming, screaming, running little girls. She tried for a time to settle them down, then gave up, and compromised on attending to each one just before she stepped onto the stage. It was boiling hot and the only relief came from two fans high in the back of the auditorium that only barely stirred the air. All the mamas were smoking and there was a ground haze in the auditorium. Six ribbons broke on ballet shoes, three headpieces disintegrated, two girls ran head on into each other and raised bumps on their heads. Naturally these two were ones whose mothers had left. And through it all, with a detachment that made her want to throttle him, a proud daddy stood just below the stage taking pictures. He didn't miss a scene.

The entire dress rehearsal was a blur of forgotten steps, untied shoes, and moiling mothers. She began to take a perverse delight in knowing how impossible it all was. At five o'clock she went home, took three aspirin, drank a bourbon on the rocks, and told Kurt she was through as a dancing teacher.

Of course, because life is like that, the recital had been fine. Oh, some of them forgot, and some shoes came untied, but nobody cared. Every mama thought her child was beautiful and perfect and danced better than every other child, and every child, in spite of Mama and the pressure of being pushed and the thousand eyes of audience, pasted a terrible smile on the rouged mouth and tried like hell.

Standing there on the stage with the bouquet of roses they'd all contributed their quarter apiece for and which, that first year, had really surprised her, she'd cried. And when they all came backstage to hug her and bring the little presents, wrapped with care as awkward as their dance steps, she'd known something. She'd known she wasn't in the business of staging a professional ballet and she'd known it didn't make much difference whether she ever taught a real dancer in her life. It hurt her, but it cleansed her. Because in spite of the mamas, wanting only show and display, wanting only to push cute little whosis into a proper marriage X years hence, in spite of herself who wanted some sort of perfection and the chance at teaching the one who might make it, there were all those little girls, each one human and real and full of the potential of a life to be lived. And by getting them through this, by letting them know they could stand up there and perform in their aloneness, she'd given every one of them something that would outlast their remembrance of Mama's pushing or of her classical ballet. She'd never considered quitting teaching again.

"What are you thinking so solemnly about?" Kurt said.

"Oh, nothing. Just that a job of work ain't no bad thing to have in this world."

"Well, if you're through eating I'll do mine then," Clarissa said from the kitchen door.

"Oh, sure, Clarissa. You can clear off. It was a great lunch. Just what I wanted."

"I believe you've done pertened up some," Clarissa said.

"Oh, I always do, sooner or later," Sandy said.

"I heard what you said about Mr. Oscar," Clarissa said.

"That's right," Sandy said. "Now we know. You were right. He was just after a piece of land, as usual. But I'm damned if I'm going to let it spoil my day."

"Gonna ruin that pretty place by the river," Clarissa said.

"Yes," Sandy said.

"Make everybody miserable," Clarissa said.

"Yes," Kurt said. "And that's what I can't forgive him for. I guess we all blink at the spoilers until they get at us personally."

241

Clarissa backed through the swinging door, hands full. "*His* job of work, I reckon," she said.

Sandy laughed. "She's right, you know. Oscar's machinations are to him what your policies and my dancing are to us. If we're going to believe in a teleological universe we have to believe that the bad has a place with the good, or maybe even that we don't really know the difference. That's what bugs me sometimes. My good is somebody else's bad. Do you ever think about that, Kurt, when you take the check to the widow?"

"That's everybody's bad, honey. The widow lost, the insuree lost, the company lost. It's when it rides on forever that everybody wins. Maybe that's what I like about the insurance business. As long as the insured remains, everybody wins. I've yet ever to find a widow who really wanted the check. Oh, there may be some. We've all ready *Double Indemnity*, but I've never run into one, which gives me a little more faith in the human race maybe than the average guy."

The phone rang and Sandy went to answer it. She was gone a long time and she came back looking puzzled.

"Who was that?" Kurt said.

"Joan. And I'm damned if I can figure out what she wanted," Sandy said. "Sometimes I think I just don't track with the rest of the world. Or maybe I try to assign motives and reasons all the time when there just aren't any for most people."

"What did she *say* she wanted?"

"Well, to talk. I never believe that. Why would anybody call you on the phone just to talk? I never do that. If I want to talk to somebody I go to see them."

"What did she talk about?"

"Nothing. Don't look at me like that. I mean it. Nothing. She rambled on about Dylan and Miranda and the rain and some old papers of Bill's she's sorting out and asking me about people we used to know a million years ago."

"She just wants company," Kurt said.

"Well, I asked her to come in this afternoon and she wouldn't hear of it. Said she was busy."

242

"Why don't you go out and see her?"

"I've got classes this afternoon. Oh, she did say something about calling that other girl who was in the house with us —Kat Hodges. But she has her address. She keeps up with everybody, being the alumni head. I don't know, maybe you're right. Maybe she's just lonely. Dylan seems to be spending a lot of time with the little Miranda, and let's face it, Joan doesn't have any resources. I don't even think she likes to read. That must be hell. I don't see how anybody can get through the rough places if they don't like to read."

"I'd have to agree with you."

"I know. Well, back to the salt mines. You ready?"

"Yes. I'll drop you and make a couple of calls before I go back to the office. The rain's let up."

"Yes," Sandy said. "So it has."

Joan didn't know why she'd called Sandy. She just had. She called B.J. too, but she wasn't at home. She didn't want to bother Martha at the office or Mary Alice at the shop or she would have called them too. She sat at her white desk with her white telephone book open in front of her, and finally she dialed the operator and got Kat Hodges Wright in Newcastle.

"This is Joan Friday," she said.

"My God, Joan. What is all this about bones in the sorority house?" Kat said.

"I meant to call you sooner," Joan said, "but we've all been busy here. I gather you haven't heard the really good part."

"Good part? Are you nuts?"

"Well . . . bad part. It seems, according to our local contractor, one Oscar Ridley, that the only time the place where they found it was accessible was the summer of 1944 . . . Mean anything to you?"

"Are you kidding? That was that weird year when they let us stay in the closed house."

"Yes, dear."

"Oh, good Christ."

"Be glad you don't live in Druid City, dear," Joan said.

"Oh, Joan, really. What are they going to do?"

243

"Hold a hearing. We all hope this thing about the time won't come out."

"Hope? We'd better be seeing that it doesn't. Can't we do something?"

"You have any ideas?"

"No."

"Well, I had to tell you in case that hearing does turn into a three-ring circus. You were there too, you know."

"Should I come down there?"

"Lord, no."

"You know something really weird?" Kat said.

"What?"

"I ran into that damned Clark Davidson last week. You remember? The tennis bum? The one who looked like Richard Burton?"

"Where?" Joan said. "With Elizabeth Taylor?" She suddenly felt better.

"Silly. He was at a party we went to with some of Bob's clients. And this is what'll kill you. Everybody always hopes those types will get fat and bald and ugly way before the rest of us. It only seems fair, you know. But he looks just the way he always did. Oh, his hair's getting gray, but that just makes him look better. I could cheerfully have killed him."

"What's he doing now?" Joan said.

"Well, I never did find out. But he was dressed well, and he was alone. Wouldn't you know? It was one of those mob scenes, a lot to drink, huge buffet, a 'paying back' party. I saw people I hadn't seen in months and by the time I tried to talk to him a minute he was gone."

"It *is* funny him turning up just now," Joan said.

"Oh, life is one damned coincidence after another," Kat said. "I've given up trying to avoid them. But this thing is pretty gruesome."

"Yes. It's made everybody . . . well, not exactly unhappy . . ."

"I know," Kat said. "I was already remembering school again when I first read about the thing and I didn't know it was any particular time."

"Maybe it wasn't," Joan said. "Maybe Oscar just thought that, or said it."

"No," Kat said. "It's nice to think so, but you remember all that building was going on."

"I remember."

"Well, what the hell. There really isn't anything to be done about it, is there?"

"I guess not."

"You still planning on sending Dylan to Europe?" Kat said.

"No. He enrolled in school here, for the next semester anyway. I had planned on sending him this summer. I may still."

"You sound doubtful. Has he got a girl?"

"Why do you say that?"

"ESP maybe. No. The sound of your voice. Everybody has a girl, Joan."

"They're too young to get married."

"How old were you?"

"That was different."

"Oh, come on."

"Look, we're using up money. I'll write you."

"Get up soon. We'll have a shopping day and lunch. It's been forever."

"O.K., Kat. I'll let you know about the hearing."

"They won't do anything . . . will they?"

"I don't think so, no. Kat . . . ?"

"No, Joan, I haven't the faintest idea who it could have been."

"I'll see you."

"Ciao."

Joan put down the phone and sat looking at it for a moment. Then she got up and put on her raincoat and went down the slick wet path of pine needles to the boathouse. Dylan had taken Miranda back to school after lunch at her urging and the house was silent, the woods silent, the lake under its burden of rain, silent. She walked across the wet planking and sat down on the edge of the dock. My God, she thought, my joints creak. It was actually an effort to sit down here, and I used to do it so automatically. One day you probably look into the mirror and you're an old woman. A really old one, like Grandma used to be. Now there are the bad days, the days when all the lines and all the sags and all the living shows, but there are also the good ones when you can look without flinching. And the face is still recognizable. It is *you* looking out of the glass, even if you are a little the worse for wear. But one day you'll see an old lady looking at you, not you at all. And how will you feel on that day? And why should you care? She thought of Miranda's face, and the idea of it ever being old or wrinkled seemed absurd. But of course it will be, she thought.

Across the lake a tree leaned out from the opposite bank, black branches trailing almost to the water. She watched it, wondering if it were dead or if the root system still managed to maintain itself on the precarious perch. She wasn't close enough to see if it had buds. One of the lines from Bill's poem to Sandy came into her head: *Your legs like summer in a winter world.* Martha is lonely too, she thought. If all the religionists and psychologists were right I'd call her and we'd get together and give each other company. But the truth is I don't want to see Martha. She was here the other night and when she left she left and that was that. I will not put the legs like summer in my world against the legs like summer in her world and let us comfort one another like two old bags who've been cheated out of something. Because that really isn't the way it is, and indulging in that sort of thought is self-pity, and I was the prettiest one of them, so what the hell?

She got up and went back to the house and into her bathroom. Miranda had left it very neat and clean. Only a faintly damp towel on the rack showed there had been an occupant. She thought about Miranda, bathing and dressing in her white private world. Lee Benson's daughter drying on her monogrammed towels. I will send Dylan to Europe this summer, she thought. That will stop it. "Absence makes the heart grow fonder" is simply not true for children of that age. He will meet someone and she will meet someone and they will forget all about each other. Even if it is written in the stars. The stars are always writing something. And the damned things are dead before we see the light from them anyway. To the nagging corner of her mind that kept saying, It does matter, she said very firmly, It does not.

After Kurt and Sandy left, Clarissa washed dishes slowly. She had to stay till Sandy got in from her three-o'clock class. She'd do up the bedrooms good during that spell. Having the vacuum out would give her time to think. She had to make up her mind about it, had to see all the way through to the other side to know what to do. It did seem unfair to have this on her now. She had enough troubles of her own without taking in washing. But what was she going to do? She loved them all, especially Sandy, had a special place in her heart for every one of them, even Joan Friday who didn't know how to ask for anything and Martha Plowden who didn't even know she had anything to ask for. Maybe it all had to do with it being the first summer she'd let Jackson go in her heart, even though she didn't quit loving and wanting him—never had, never would. But that summer she'd made up her mind, faced the fact he was no good in this world to her, and there had been the kitchen and the girls like flowers always asking her things and telling her things and keeping her alive when she'd thought she didn't want to be anymore. So maybe she owed them all something. Maybe that was the Lord's truth. There was one other white child she felt a fondness for, but that was Lady Lane she'd raised from a tiny baby to a big girl ready for college while her mother was sick and couldn't do it. She'd watched Lady grow up, washed her, combed her, even bought things for her and given her birthday parties. To this day Lady came to see her when she got into town. But the reason for that was plain. Lady was her baby. These girls weren't. They'd already been grown and on the edge of being women themselves. Still, they were like Lady to her. She kept all their wedding announcements and birth announcements and pieces from the paper about them in her scrapbook along with the things about Lady. It was a thing she could no more have explained to her children or even most of the grownups she knew nowadays than she could spit. Things weren't that way anymore. She had enough sense to know they were better the way they were now, even if she was old-fashioned enough to miss some of the old ways. It was just she'd been caught between things, born at a bad time, too old to change enough, too young not to understand the change. There just wasn't any point in trying to say she owed nothing to any white person. Because inside where it counted she did. She could take all the fears and all the outrages and all the hate and balance it against nothing but a few girls in a summer kitchen and the equation still came out the same way.

She remembered the time Lady's mother had forgotten her birthday. It was the year Lady was seven, an important year, because she'd started to school and made friends. Mrs. Lane had been having an especially bad time then. They'd got her onto four shots a day and she couldn't get off and she didn't know Lady half the time. So Clarissa did it, did it all, because children can't help what's going on in the world, can't fight it, can't go anywhere. Somebody has to care. Mr. Lane might have, but he wasn't there, out working to pay for the doctors and the shots and for Clarissa's salary. Lord, she could still see Lady's seven-year-old face, brown eyes looking at her from where she sat on the kitchen stool where she stayed most of the time after school in the afternoon. "It's time for my birthday, Clarissa."

"Lord, when, baby?"

"Anytime now. Remember? It's always in November."

She'd stretched her mind and couldn't remember and asked Mrs. Lane, who couldn't remember, and finally dug out the old baby book and found it . . . three days away.

"I'd like to have a party, Clarissa, but Mama couldn't stand a party, could she?"

"Shoot, baby," she'd said, "I reckon your mama don't care. Clarissa'll give you a party. We'll have one all right."

They had had it, the two of them. Lady had told her names and she'd called the mamas. They'd gone downtown to the five and dime and bought the favors, those pink

248

poppers they used to have that in those days had a hat and a fortune and a little bitty silver-looking prize—dogs and horses and umbrellas. They'd had a good loud bang to them, too; they didn't anymore. They'd made a big pink cake with pink icing and she'd left batter in the bottom of the bowl because Lady really liked the batter better than the cake, and she'd borrowed a freezer and made ice cream.

All the children came, too, and brought presents for Lady. Clarissa had had a real bad moment just when it was time for the party to start. Lady had been sitting all dressed in a pink dress with starched ruffles that Clarissa had been an hour ironing and with a big pink bow in her hair, and she'd thought, None of them will come. Their mamas are going to be afraid of Mrs. Lane doing something or that I can't handle it all by myself. But they did come. It didn't happen bad, and Lady had a fine party. After that she gave her one every year.

Clarissa realized she'd stripped and remade all the beds and cleaned the bedrooms without even knowing she'd done it. "Probably left dirt everywhere like some low-life," she said and went around and inspected what she'd done. It was clean, but it was a wonder. She sure hadn't been here when she'd done it. Do something so long it gets plumb automatic and you could do it in your sleep probably. Poor little old Lady. But she turned out real well—went off to school and married a nice man and still came back to see her. And Mrs. Lane still alive and still half-dead—and probably would live to bury them all. But Lady had had her birthdays and got sent to school clean and learned to cook sitting on a kitchen stool watching. All these other girls had sat in her kitchen too, just as lost, just as big-eyed as Lady, wanting just as many pink poppers and cakes and batter in the bowls. So she had it to do and she might as well quit worrying it around in her mind.

When the boys came in from school she fixed them a snack and made them change out of their good clothes and gave the kitchen floor one more going over. Then she put on her coat and old black hat and put out the garbage. By that time Sandy was there.

"I made the boys a cake," she said while she waited for Sandy to write her check. "Not much of one, a little sweet cake. It's cooling on the drainboard."

"Thanks, Clarissa," Sandy said. She looked at her. "Something the matter?"

"No'm, I'm just tired. I'll see you next week."

"All right," Sandy said. "Take care." She watched her go down the driveway and out along the sidewalk to the bus stop. Clarissa's old, she thought. It's funny, I've never noticed it before. I guess it's something about the way she's walking today.

Clarissa walked down to the corner where the green bench with the advertisements for Lawrence's Department Store on the back sat at the bus stop. There were three women she knew there, maids going home. She nodded to them but didn't sit down with them. The rain had stopped and the westering sun was visible behind the oak trees at the end of the street. She shifted her pocketbook to a more comfortable position on her arm.

"Hard day, Clarissa?" one of the women said.

She shook her head.

"This my tile-floor lady's day," another said. "I'm tired. Don't do nothing at that house but mop and wax, wax and mop, and then the children come in from school and ruin half of it."

"You get paid for it, don't you?" Clarissa said. "Dollar and a quarter an hour and bus fare nowadays too. It's a heap better than it used to be."

"Well, excuse me, Mrs. Johnson," the woman said. "I forget that some folks think they were born to work."

"All folks were," Clarissa said. "It's mighty few escape it."

"Don't argue, ladies," the first woman said.

The third woman, a thin scarecrow of a woman with her head lost under a huge pink hat, suddenly stood up and looked down the road. "Yonder comes Tinny Bynum," she said. "I'll get us a ride home." She stepped into the gutter and started waving her handbag as a gray rattletrap of a

Ford came down the road. "Hi, Tinny," she hollered. "Going home? Going home, Tinny? Give us a ride, boy."

Clarissa watched her in disgust. Mable Wright, half-witted and always had been, but she'd work forever because she didn't have the sense to ask for her dollar and a quarter an hour or even for them to put in for her social security. So there she was making a spectacle of herself on the public street and giving them all the name of halfwit. The car stopped and the other women stood up.

"Going home, Clarissa?" Tinny said.

He was Kate and Ben Bynum's boy, a good boy, worked at the supermarket. For a moment Clarissa wavered and almost got in the familiar old Ford to go home. Then she shook her head and moved over and sat down on the bench. "Got to go downtown," she said. "Thank you kindly, Tinny."

The old car went away down the street trailing exhaust smoke. In a few moments the bus going out of town drew up and stopped with a hissing of airbrakes. The doors opened, an old lady and two teenage girls got off, the doors shut and the bus went away. Clarissa waited for the second bus for downtown.

She put her twenty cents in the box and went automatically, from years of long habit, to the back of the bus. Lots of them didn't anymore, but she was too old to change. It didn't mean anything to her anyway. The dollar and a quarter an hour did. That counted. It bought something decent to eat on Sunday and something decent to wear during the week. It helped everybody for them to dress better. She'd felt real good last year when she'd gone by the Negro high school just as it was letting out and seen all the young folks in skirts and sweaters and slacks and loafers just like at the white high school across town. Yes, she was too late to change, but she knew some of it was good, just the same. Not good enough or soon enough for her own. But for their children and their children's children, maybe. A faint smile crossed her face. Hers probably wouldn't have been any good anyway. Jackson would have been Jackson no matter what the Supreme Court did. He'd have been Jack-

251

son right on with all the civil rights in the world. So it was really her own poor judgment that had done her in and no use blaming anybody. There were white men about as useless as Jackson, too, and some fool woman a fool about them. Which was exactly why she was fixing to do what she was fixing to do.

She got off at the corner of Main by the five-and-dime store. The street was crowded with people waiting to catch the buses home. They all left from here and late in the afternoon it was always bedlam. A few years ago there used to be a lot of college students waiting to catch the bus out to the campus, too, but there weren't anymore. They all had automobiles nowadays. When she'd worked at the sorority house there hadn't been a car among the lot of them. None of the boys had one either. Of course there was the war, but for a long time after that they still didn't. Then it was like an epidemic—they broke out all over the campus. Didn't have anywhere to park them and they all had those little stickers saying where they could park. She didn't think they ever did park. They spent most of their time trying to run somebody down in the street.

She walked through the mass of humanity on the sidewalk, speaking occasionally to someone she knew, crossed at the streetlight and went down toward the courthouse.

It was a new building, a tall imposing structure of steel and concrete, the windows recessed so that it seemed a progression of square stone tombs without windows, until the sun caught one. She stood for a moment on the sidewalk looking up at it, fear in her because courthouse meant fear. Then she shrugged and went between the stone lions and up the steps and went inside.

Inside, surprisingly, it was light, the sun, even so far down now, striking whitely off the marble. She stood for a moment, trying to figure how the windows could be so inconspicuous from the outside and so light-giving from inside. There was no one in the empty corridor. She walked on down it, watching the sun on marble, to the door at the far end of the hall with its little green sign that said Sheriff.

She straightened her hat and put her purse firmly under her arm and went through the door.

Jimmy Lou Allbright looked up from covering her typewriter. "Hello," she said. "Clarissa, isn't it?"

"Yes'm," Clarissa said.

"Can I help you?"

"I need to speak to Mr. Gus Thurgood," Clarissa said.

"I don't suppose it'd wait till tomorrow," Jimmy Lou said. "He's just getting ready to—" She stopped, looking at Clarissa's face. "I'll tell him," she said, and got up and knocked on the door to the inner office.

"Come in," Gus said. "I thought you'd gone home."

She shut the door behind her, leaving Clarissa standing straight and silent behind the counter. "Clarissa Johnson's out there, Gus," she said. "Says she wants to see you. She looks a little grim and purposeful, so I thought maybe it was something important."

Gus looked puzzled. "I can't imagine what she could want," he said. "Neither of her kids has been into anything lately. And *she* never has been. I guess you better send her in." He sat down behind his desk. "I wonder—"

"Gus," Jimmy Lou said, "she used to work at that sorority house."

"Oh, my God," Gus said. "Well, send her on in and go on home."

Jimmy Lou laughed. "You don't give me much credit for curiosity, do you?" she said. She went through the door, leaving it open. "Go on in, Clarissa," she said. "Sheriff Thurgood can see you."

"Thank you," Clarissa said. She walked slowly past Jimmy Lou and into the office. Gus stood up and closed the door behind her. Jimmy Lou made a face at him behind Clarissa's back as the door closed.

"Sit down, right here," Gus said.

Clarissa hesitated, then took the chair across the desk from the sheriff. She put her pocketbook carefully on her knees and clasped both hands on top of it. "Yessir," she said.

"What can I do for you?" Gus said.

253

For a moment Clarissa was afraid she wasn't going to be able to say anything. She had never been in the sheriff's office before in her life and she was surprised to find it only a simple office where she'd been offered a chair. She stared across at Gus Thurgood, remembering that she'd heard a lot of good things about him from a lot of people. For a southern sheriff he was some sort of phenomenon, and she knew that. It was the only reason she'd been able to get up the nerve to come in here at all. Still, there was no denying she was frightened. Her voice seemed to have stopped permanently in her throat. It was like the time she'd gone to tell the bees about Jackson.

It had been a hot summer day when Dr. Frank Plowden had stopped her on the street downtown to tell her about Jackson. He'd done it about as well as anybody could do something like that. His being a doctor he was probably used to it. There was no messing around about it, no false stops and starts or ill-stated sympathy. He just said, "Clarissa, have you heard about Jackson?" She'd known, right then, she didn't have to hear the rest of it, though he said that pretty good too. She'd stopped walking and said, "No sir, I haven't heard nothing." And he said, "He was killed in a razor fight in Newcastle last week. I recognized the name."

She'd listened to what details he had and then she'd walked on down the street and caught her bus home. Neither of the children had been in the house when she got in and she'd gone back to the kitchen and had herself a glass of water. Then she'd just stood there, trying to believe it. Even though it was a thing she'd been expecting and knowing would probably happen one of these days it still didn't seem like it could have. A world without Jackson in it was as highly improbable to her as a world without work. Even gone, even so long gone, he lived with her, always had, always would. She'd stood there a long time in that kitchen and then she'd thought, I better go tell those bees. He don't live here, not really. But he *does* live here. He always lived here, in me. Those bees gonna know that. They gonna know somebody died.

254

She was proud of her bees. They were the only ones in the Negro section and they made good honey. She had her hive down behind the house at the edge of the lot where there was a cluster of bushes, snowballs and forsythia. In the late afternoon she often went down just to listen to the warm drowsy buzz of them around the white flowers. Now she went out the back door and walked slowly toward them, hearing them in imagination long before she'd reached the hive. She stopped and stood looking at it, the worn gray boards with just a few bees flying around them. And right then, like now in Gus Thurgood's office, she couldn't make her voice work. It just stopped there in her throat as though permanently. She reckoned she'd stood there a good thirty minutes before she'd been able to say it. And even then her voice had sounded strange to her, rusty, disused, and harsh, a white person's voice, not hers at all.

"Bees," she'd finally said, "there's somebody dead at our house. It's . . ." and after a long pause she added, "Jackson."

The bees had continued their soft droning and one flew past her to the forsythia. So she knew they'd heard and would stay. She had turned and started back toward the house before the other truth struck her and she'd had to go back and stand near the hive again. This time, though, her voice had come easier. "Bees," she'd said, "I reckon maybe it's Clarissa too."

Now, as then, she cleared her throat. "Sheriff Thurgood," she said, and it was just the same, the rusty, disused, harsh voice, but she knew she'd manage. He was watching her with a kindly look. "I have come," she went on, "to tell you what I know about that baby in the wall."

The faint look of perplexity went away from the sheriff's face. "I appreciate you coming in, Clarissa," he said. "You didn't have to."

"I know that," she said. "That you think that. But I did, too. Them girls' my babies."

"Yes," the sheriff said. "All right, Clarissa. Just take your time."

255

She tightened her grasp on the pocketbook. "Yessir," she said. "Well, I did it. I put that baby in that place."

The sheriff's face went perfectly blank. "*You* did? What do you mean?"

"I did it. It wasn't any of those girls. It was me . . . sir." She had said it now and she was surprised that it actually hadn't cost her anything. Not after she'd finally found her voice. It was like telling the bees that second time. Things about yourself are never too terrible to say. It's only the things about the ones you love.

Sheriff Thurgood sat very still, looking at her. "You mean it was *your* baby, Clarissa?"

"That right."

He continued to watch her and she noticed something behind the straight look on his face—a small gleam in his eyes. "Now just why, Clarissa, would you put a baby in the walls of a sorority house?" he said.

She was unprepared for the question and she just looked blankly at him, giving him the good old stupid stare, letting her eyes glaze over, shrugging finally, as though she hadn't understood what he said. The old technique, as good today as it had been on the edge of a cotton field a hundred years ago.

The gleam in his eyes increased. "I said, Clarissa, why on earth would you put a baby in the walls of the Delta House?"

She saw it wasn't going to work to play completely dumb with this one. "To hide it," she said.

The corners of his mouth twitched, and she realized the gleam was amusement. She looked down at her handbag.

"From whom, Clarissa?" he went on calmly.

She retreated back to the shrug.

He sighed and got up and walked over and stood looking out the window. Then he came back to the desk and picked up a pipe and spent a long time loading, tamping, lighting it. Clarissa watched him with patience. After a few moments they both realized they each had enough patience to outlast the other if they sat here till doomsday. Now the sheriff actually smiled. He sat back down and leaned back in his chair, puffing on the pipe.

Clarissa looked at him out of the corner of her eyes.

"It's a nice thing you're trying to do, Clarissa," he said. "Maybe nobody but me will ever know how nice."

She bridled then, in spite of knowing she shouldn't. "I ain't doing no nice thing, Sheriff Thurgood," she said. "I'm trying to keep out of trouble with the Law."

"Clarissa," Thurgood said, "you were a married woman. You had no reason on earth to put a baby in the walls of a house. Even if you had, I don't think you'd have put it there."

She shrugged. "I can tell you all about how I did it," she said.

He looked up at her then. "So?" he said.

"Yes. They were working up there, had been all summer, had the new bathroom just about put in. It was late and dark and night and everybody done gone to bed, so it was easy. I took a flashlight from the kitchen and I wrapped it up in a blanket. It was dead. You know that, Sheriff." She faltered for the first time. "You bound to know that," she said.

"I do know that," he said.

"Well . . . I want you to know that. Then I went up the stairs and I had to walk across a place where they hadn't finished the flooring in the hall." She paused and sighed. "I was afraid I might fall and go right down into the kitchen. Had me a bad picture of that. But I didn't. I got through the door into where they were just about through with that bathroom and I found the place where they still had it open there in the wall. It was just a little bitty ole hole, but it was a long way down into it, so I climbed up on one of the new fixtures they had laying there in the floor ready to put in, and I reached as far down and as far back as I could, and I put it in there, poor little thing. Then I got some scrap lumber and put in front of it so if anybody looked in there while they were plastering up that hole they wouldn't see nothing."

She stopped and the sheriff saw that she was crying. He

looked carefully away from her and she opened her pocketbook and took out a clean ironed handkerchief and wiped her cheeks and eyes, then put it back and closed the pocketbook with an audible snap of the clasp.

"Then I said a prayer," she said. "And I went back down to my kitchen and I grieved some. And then I went home. That's all. Thank you, sir."

"Clarissa," Gus said. He stopped, sighed, and thought, God damn it, I am in the wrong business. "Clarissa, I believe you. I believe you put the baby in there. But I don't for one minute believe it was your baby you put in there. Maybe you don't even know yourself whose it was. I am going to assume that. Do you know that? I am going to assume it. So now, if I assume that will you tell me that it was not your baby, but one you know about or found or heard about, and that you did what you did because you didn't know what else to do, and that you were trying to protect some girl you knew and loved?"

"It was mine," Clarissa said stubbornly.

"Clarissa, there are ways of finding out whether that's true or not."

Clarissa smiled. "You know better than that, Sheriff," she said. "My people ain't gonna tell you nothing about me they think I don't want told."

Gus Thurgood stopped himself just before saying the short obscene word in his mind. "Clarissa," he said, "I do not want to send you to jail."

"Don't know as I want to go," she said mildly.

Gus's mouth twitched again. "You're sure talking like it," he said. "Don't you know there's a possibility you could be tried for manslaughter?"

"I didn't kill nobody. It was dead. Never *was* alive, Sheriff. Never was that. Wasn't no whole complete baby yet. Six or seven months, maybe."

"I figured that, Clarissa, but you can't just go around disposing of bodies."

"I'm an old woman," Clarissa said.

"Who wants to throw herself on the mercy of the judge?" the sheriff said.

"Mayhap."

"Clarissa . . ."

"Yessir, I know. I'm black. That makes a difference."

"Yes, Clarissa, at this time in this town in this world it still makes a hell of a lot of difference. And you know it and I know it. Now why are you doing this?"

Clarissa looked straight at him. "I didn't want to," she said, "but, Sheriff, I figured and figured and I thought and I thought, and I never came to the point of seeing any way out of it. It was a thing I had to do right on. That's all."

And, well, dammit, Gus thought, we spend a lifetime trying to figure out how to cope with the evil in the world and we get to the point where we can live with it and endure even if we can't whip it, and then we find out that there is no damned defense, ever, against sheer goodness. And we know we've been had.

O.K., Gus, he thought. You're the sheriff. Do something. His pipe had gone out, so he spent another little while lighting it. That was the only thing he could think of to do.

"Don't be a prick," Jimmy Lou Allbright had said. *"Don't be a self-righteous prick."*

"Clarissa," he said, "they are going to hold a hearing tomorrow. Is that why you came in? Do you want to testify?"

He watched the cold terror come into her face, then go away again.

"Yessir, I guess so," she said.

"Without your testimony you know how the thing will go, don't you? It will be called misadventure and that will be the end of it."

She looked worried and puzzled then for the first time. He saw her sharp intake of breath. "You mean I done the wrong thing to help out?" she said.

He nodded slowly.

She watched him, puzzlement still on her face. "But Mr. Oscar," she said finally. "They said he was going to do something."

Gus shook his head. "He's not going to do anything," he said. "He's already got his land."

259

Clarissa's shoulders slumped. For the first time she let go her grip on the handbag and her hands went limp. They were good hands, worn and capable and long-fingered. There was nothing in them in the moment except resignation. "I meant to do right," she said. "Seems like a body can't ever do right without there's somebody standing in the way to get hurt. Seems like knowing what's right gets harder and harder along the way."

Ah, Clarissa, Gus thought, you have just stated the structure of the little squirrel cage my mind lives in. He didn't allow himself to think any further. He stood up and went to the window and said, with his back turned, "There was no secretary in here, Clarissa. Nobody took any of this down."

She didn't say anything, but he heard her sigh.

"Of course, if you want to testify I can't stop you," he said. "But you haven't been subpoenaed and if you want to come in here and tell me a cock-and-bull story just to try to protect somebody, that's your business. It happens quite often, you know. We get confessions that just ain't true on every crime that happens in this county."

He heard her get slowly to her feet. "You mean you don't believe me?"

"That's what I mean," he said quickly before she could say anything else. "I think you came in here trying to do a favor for some girl or girls you knew when they were young and that you were fond of. And I thank you. Now will you get the holy hell out of this office and go home?"

"Yessir," she said quietly, "but . . ." And he could feel the effort it was costing her because she was scared now, knowing how close she'd come to worse than she'd figured. "But . . . if it do turn out bad, if that hearing work out different, you call me. I'll come."

My God, he thought. I feel like I'm going to cry.

"Thank you, Mrs. Johnson," he said. "You've behaved like a public-spirited citizen. I will see you to the door."

You crazy fool woman, he thought. If you don't get out of this office I'm going to have to kick you out.

She moved across the room with dignity. She didn't hurry. She went through the door, head high, pocketbook

260

still held in both hands, nodded to Jimmy Lou, went out the door, and they could hear her footsteps going slowly down the corridor.

"What's the matter with you, Gus?" Jimmy Lou said.

"Will you do me something, J. L. Allbright?" Gus said.

"Most anything," Jimmy Lou said.

"Then do me this. The next time I get to bitching about the state of the world, the human race, and the human soul, remind me of that woman. Just say, Remember Clarissa Johnson. How about that?"

"O.K., Gus. I gather you don't want to talk about it."

He shook his head. "Go home, Allbright. We got a big day tomorrow."

"O.K., Gus," she said.

She watched him going back into his office, the strange look on his face giving way to contentment, if not peace. She loved him so terribly. It seemed a goddamned shame she had to like his wife.

The rain had stopped late in the afternoon and the sundown streets were lit with a steamy lazy late light. Edyth drove home with foreboding. She'd never had to do that in all her married life and she hated it. The last time she'd had this kind of foreboding had been when poor old Bob had obviously been going off his rocker. To think that now scared her to death.

Miley, who had been like the clichéd Gibraltar, had ceased to be that. The thing that scared her was the feeling that she should never have thought of him like that, that it hadn't been fair. Every person carries the seeds and sprouts of fear and insecurity, no matter how far along the road to maturity they or you might think they've come. To deny them this basic humanness, to use their strength to build on and to give you a cheater strength of your own just plain isn't fair. It isn't love. And she loved Miley so. It was just that she'd never before really understood that *he* needed *her*.

It wasn't all her fault that she'd never known that. He himself had created the image, shown himself to her and the world as strong, solid, sure. But *she* should have known. She should have looked under the rock for the sand, because it is always there. Only she never saw it. And now this was too much to handle, for her, or him, or love.

The traffic light at the corner turned red and she put on the brakes carefully because the street was still wet. Take driving. She still hated to do it, never had liked it, never would. Hell, if Miley hadn't made her she never would have learned to drive a car. She wasn't like Meredith, who drove like she breathed, or Martha, who had had to teach Frank how to drive, so she was always saying. Said he used to ride the brake. Well, so did she until Miley bitched her to death about it and she learned not to. Was Martha like Miley, too? Looking so strong and capable and having the fears inside just like everybody else? At any rate things hadn't worked out for her, capable and careful or not. Jesus, who could tell anything about anything. The light turned green. She accelerated carefully and a kid in an MG scratched off around her. Sorry, she said. I don't feel like dragging.

She discovered she was driving slower and slower as she got nearer home. Which is the craziest thing I can do, she thought. If I'm late he'll start in about where have I been, for God's sake. As if there's anywhere I could have been. Or wanted to be. Good, dear Lord.

She turned in the drive and saw that Miley was already there and cursed under her breath. She'd had to stay late to take care of the last appointment because she'd promised the girls they could leave early because they had dates. She'd had to. She simply couldn't say, My husband won't like it. Because everybody knew her husband, and they thought he was Gibraltar too.

At this moment, before she went in and they started in on each other, she understood the truth of it, knew that Miley loved her or he wouldn't care so damned bad, knew it was fear and unhappiness that made him attack her. But when she faced him, when he started in on her, she quit understanding and was hurt and defensive and put-upon and tired, just plain tired of being called the whore of the world. Because it's not like that, she thought. Even if it is in some measure true what he thinks, it still isn't like that. It doesn't make me worse than everybody else in the universe. I'm not that important. I was lonely and young and vulnerable and Miley was in the Pacific and I had an affair, yes, goddamn it, an affair, with a boy named Bob whom I can't even really remember anymore. It doesn't make me evil. But another part of her mind said, It does to Miley and therefore it is true.

She put the car in the garage and went in the back door.

He was sitting at the kitchen table and she could tell by the level in the bottle he'd already had two or three drinks. I won't have one, she thought, but she knew she would. She had to have one to get through it and of course all it would do would be to make her as belligerent as he was.

She kissed him on the cheek and he jerked away from her. "Where the hell have you been?" he said.

She sighed.

"Don't sigh at me," he said. "I asked you a question."

She took the bottle and poured herself a drink. "Fixing Faye Carol's dye job," she said. "That answer your question?"

"You're sure lapping up that bourbon," he said.

She drained the glass and poured herself another one. This time she put ice and water in it and sat down. "You want another one?" she said.

He handed the glass at her and she took it and fixed him another. He took it silently, looking at her as though there might be a mark on her somewhere that would confirm his suspicions.

I will be reasonable, she thought. "How was work today?"

"How do you think in this rain?" he said. "We had to paint over at the Clarence building. All day long, painting a lot of beige walls. Great."

"Sorry."

"Sure."

"Miley, please don't."

"Don't what?" he said.

She could feel herself getting mad and she fought it. "What would you like for supper?" she said.

"Whatever you think you can find time to fix," he said.

She finished the bourbon in the glass. "Oh, screw you," she said.

"Why not?" he said. "It's something you enjoy the hell out of doing."

She shut her eyes. "All right, all right, all right. I'm the whore of the world. Now will you just shut up and leave me alone?"

"You're doing all the talking," he said.

She got up and rummaged in the refrigerator and put some meat to thaw under the cold water tap in the sink.

Miley watched her. "Fix me another drink while you're up," he said.

She fixed it, and one for herself. The little warning bells were telling her this one was one too many, but she fixed it anyway.

"Were you this fond of your liquor back when you were in good old Delta sorority?" Miley said.

"I didn't have to be," she said.

"Oh, sure, everything is all my fault," he said.

"All this is," she said.

"No, it's not."

"O.K., it's mine. Now are you happy? Now will you hush? I've got to peel the potatoes."

He didn't answer her and she began to peel the potatoes, watching her hands making the motions automatically. She sliced them and put them on to cook. She put peas and butter and salt and pepper in another pan and set it on the back burner. She took a package of rolls out of the refrigerator and put them on a bread pan and into the oven ready to heat. She checked the meat under the faucet.

"Nothing bothers you, does it?" he said. "You can calmly go on fixing supper as though nothing in the world was the matter. You just don't care."

She set the table.

"Well, it's true, isn't it? Look at you. You just don't care."

264

She looked at him. "I almost think I don't," she said. "I think I'm too tired and too worn out with it to ever care anymore." To her horror she began to cry. She turned away from him and got a casserole out of the cabinet.

Behind her she heard him pour into his glass again. "You did it, didn't you?" he said.

She didn't even think about it, just walked across the room and hit him in the face. She'd never hit anybody in the face before in her life. She didn't slap, she doubled up her fist and hit like a man.

She saw the shock, surprise, then complete and utter anger on his face before he hit her. He didn't double his fist, just hit her with the flat of his hand, but it was good enough. It sent her all the way across the kitchen where she fetched up against the cabinet with a gash from the edge of it on her temple, feeling the raw edge where the enamel had come off her front teeth, the ringing in her ears, the sheer shock making everything something that happens in a dream. It would happen just this quick if somebody wanted to kill you, she thought. And you wouldn't be able to do anything about it at all. Then he was hitting her again. This time it was even less real and she thought, Maybe he really is going to kill me. The blows, after the first one, didn't seem to hurt anymore, there was only the panic, a panic as real and in the gut as the time Bob Allen had tried to drive them off the road. She could hear the water still running over the hamburger in the sink, and then she was crawling away from him toward the refrigerator. She opened her mouth to yell and he hit her again. Then he opened the door and went out and she began to cry.

She lay there for what seemed like a long time, crying, and then she got up, holding the wall, and went over to the sink and turned off the water. She looked at the package of hamburger, the pulpy mass showing through the cellophane wrapper. It didn't look like anything anybody would ever want to eat. But she took it out of the sink anyway and dumped it into a bowl and put in some oatmeal and eggs and milk and salt and pepper and garlic. Then she couldn't bring herself to mix it up. She just stood still, staring at what could be a meatloaf but wasn't yet. She heard a bubbling sound and realized it was the potatoes. She ran across the room and turned down the eye. They were all right and she felt thankful. She didn't believe she could have stood it if they had been burned. Her face felt wet and she put her hand up and felt the blood from the cut on her temple. She didn't feel anything about it, not even annoyance. She just went to the bathroom and washed it and put a Band-Aid on it. Just like when I cut my hand to keep away the elephants, she thought, and for the moment she felt all right. Not good, but all right. The numbness was gone. For a while there when she'd gotten up off the floor she'd thought, That is the end. She'd meant, she guessed, of everything—everything in the universe—no more stars. But now the act of putting on the Band-Aid told her it simply wasn't the end of everything, not even of anything. She washed her hands and went back to the kitchen and made the meatloaf.

The roof in the back of the shop had been leaking all day. Mary Alice had been trying for the past year to get Oscar Ridley to do something about it, but he put her off. He didn't have to fix it, where else was she going to locate a shop for college girls. It was the same with every tenant in the building. It housed a drugstore and a bookstore and Edyth's beauty parlor, and every one of them made their money from the campus a block away. None of them was going to move out and Oscar knew it. So when the roof leaked they put pans under it and cursed.

The spring line of blouses had come in today and Mary Alice had enjoyed unpacking them. In between cussing at the roof and the rain it had been pleasant to sort and stack the piles of soft silk and cotton and Dacron in the pale and happy shades of spring—pinks and blues and yellows, with prints of muted raspberry and lime and orange, white ones with bows and lace and intricate buttons, striped ones and madras ones, and a few of lavender and oatmeal beige. They were all on the shelves now, lending an air of gaiety to their corner of the shop.

Mary Alice was sitting down behind the cash register for

the first time since noon. She lit a cigarette. "Sit down, Sue, for God sakes," she said. "The worst is over. We can cart the rest of the boxes out tomorrow. Look, the sun's coming out. I've a good notion to call Lew to drive out and see how our lot looks after a slow steady rain like this."

Sue came and sat down by her. "You're expecting it to float away, maybe?"

"No. I just want to see it all wet. And I want Lew to go with me. He never seems to get out there."

"You better call him at the office," Sue said. "You know how he'll do. Decide there's just one more thing he can do and get too busy."

"I know," Mary Alice said. "Why do we all do that?"

Sue shrugged. "It's the human condition," she said.

"Inchworm, inchworm," Mary Alice said.

"What?"

"You know. We never stop and look at the marigolds."

"Oh, I don't know. We enjoyed those blouses today. That's a kind of looking at the marigolds."

"I guess so. Reach me an ashtray."

The bell tinkled and Lew came into the store. "Well, I'll be damned," Mary Alice said. "I was just fixing to call you to quit early so we could go out and take a look at our lot after this rain."

Lew came on to the back of the store. He looked embarrassed. "I guess my ESP's working," he said. "That was just what I had in mind."

"Go on," Sue said. "I'll close up."

"I hate to leave it on you, but all right," Mary Alice said. "Let me just put on my shoes."

They went out of the store together. "Leave your car here," Lew said. "We can pick it up on the way back in."

"All right," Mary Alice said. They started toward Lew's car and she started to go around to get under the wheel. It was an automatic action, and it occurred to her as she settled herself into the passenger side of the front seat that she couldn't remember the last time she'd sat there. They were always taking both cars and meeting somewhere after

267

work. She fastened her seat belt and leaned back. It felt surprisingly good *not* to be driving.

She kept her eyes closed during the first part of the drive, but when they turned off on the bypass that led out to the new country club estates she opened them and looked at Lew. He was watching the road, his eyes intent, the network of wrinkles around his eyes prominent in the late light. For the first time she noticed the slight sag at his jawline. It gave her a strange feeling of tenderness. She reached over and put her hand gently on his cheek. He smiled, leaned his cheek toward her, and kept driving.

How long has it been since I've really looked at him? she thought in wonder. That didn't happen overnight, but I've never seen it before. Maybe, she thought, it's just the light. Maybe it's the brightness of sun after no-sun all day long. But she knew it wasn't true. She just hadn't looked closely at him in a long, long time.

What happens? she thought. She remembered how she used to look at him when he came from camp, look at him as though she'd never get enough of looking. They'd sit across the table from each other in some roadside joint, the whiskey in a paper sack at their feet, hands clasped on the table top, and she'd just stare at him, at the way his ears grew against his head and the way his eyebrows grew and the way his mouth was shaped and the way his teeth looked when he smiled, tantalizing herself with not touching so that when they finally got away and were alone it made the touching all the more wonderful. And now he'd developed a completely new jawline and she hadn't even noticed it, hadn't seen it, and they lived in the same house and slept in the same bed, and there was no more camp or war to go away to, no memories to store up for the lonely days and nights. Somewhere along the way she had ceased to look.

"What's the matter, honey?" Lew said.

"Nothing. Why do you think that?"

"You're so quiet."

"Oh, it's just a quiet afternoon, I guess. I don't want to spoil it."

"Well, here it is," he said. He turned down the dirt road

and stopped the car near the little creek that even Oscar Ridley hadn't destroyed. They got out. There was a cut of chill in the air after the rain and Mary Alice pulled her sweater around her.

"You don't think Oscar's right about mosquitos?" she said.

"I don't care if he is," Lew said. "I want the creek. He isn't going to fill it in."

"I don't think he really wants to anyway," Mary Alice said. "They need it up toward the source for the golf course. He's just in such a habit of saying things like that he can't stop. Fill the creeks, cut the trees, bulldoze, scrape, and build. It's a little song he sings."

They walked over to a flat rock by the edge of the creek bank and sat down. The sun was going down, giving a mellow slanting light to the slope above them. Mary Alice squinted and looked toward the knoll. "Can you see it sitting up there?" she said.

"Yep," Lew said, "exactly. It's a lot of little white lines on blue paper."

"Oh, Lew."

"Sorry. That's the only way I visualize it. Maybe if they ever do us the mockup . . ."

Mary Alice smiled at him. "Do you really want this house, Lew?"

"I want it because you want it," he said.

"That's no answer."

"It's the only one I have."

"Then you don't really want it."

"Personally, in my heart, in my emotions, in my gut, no ma'm," he said. "I don't not want it either, however. It's just that I'm happy wherever we are. I don't really give a damn. I'll admit the scenery here is going to be nice. I'll like sitting on my terrace looking down at this creek with the sun setting behind it. Yes, that'll be nice, so maybe I do want it. But it's not the same thing for me that it is for you." He stopped and looked at her. "That's the first time you've asked me that," he said.

"I know it," she said, "and I'm ashamed of that. I got to

269

thinking about it, at Shari's the other night. How this house got to be a sort of symbol for me, as though it were the thing I was working for . . ."

She stopped, embarrassed, and he smiled encouragingly at her. "Well, anyway, what I finally thought was that it wasn't. I *like* to work. I need it and I want it."

"Didn't you know that?" he said.

"No, I don't think I did."

"I did," he said.

"You know more about me than I do you," she said. "Maybe I'm ashamed of that too. You see me better than I've seen you. For a long time."

"That's possible," he said carefully.

She turned her face away from him. "Do I have any wrinkles?" she said.

He laughed. "That sounds like a trap. That's a 'when did you stop beating your wife' question."

"No, it isn't," she said. "I want an honest answer. Do I?"

"A few, honey."

"Where?"

He laughed. "What is this? Dr. I.Q.? Well, let's see. There's one between your eyes. That's the only noticeable one and it was there when I met you, so it hasn't anything to do with age. Then there are a very, very few around your very, very nice eyes. There's a faint one across your throat, and when you're very tired two alongside your mouth. That's all."

"Does my jaw sag?"

"Only a very little on Sunday mornings after we've stayed out too late and drunk too much."

Mary Alice began to giggle. "I told you," she said. "You look at me better than I look at you."

Lew gave a sigh of relief. "Jesus," he said, "I thought you were trying to trap me into saying you were an old bag."

She laughed. "No, darling. I just wondered how well you looked at me."

He put his hand on her chin and turned her face toward him. "To tell you the truth," he said, "I know all that, but I *don't* ever really see it. What I see when I look at you is the face that used to look across those battered old tables in those honkytonks we used to go to. Same girl. Same face."

"Has it turned out that well?" she said.

"How well?"

"As well as we used to think across those tables from each other? Was it really all the things we felt and thought then? Has it been?"

"Honey, is this sorority house thing bugging you?"

"No, I don't think so. It's not that. Or is it? I don't know. You see, it makes you think of how we all were back then. You can't help it. You look a long way back and see what you made of what you had. And you know this is the one trip through. The ticket was stamped back there at the first tollgate, and at the end of the turnpike they'll take it back. So you wonder. Did you do well enough with it?"

"The end ain't in view, baby."

"Oh, yes, it is, Lew. It always is."

"We're fine," he said. "We are really very fine."

"It isn't that I don't love you and have always. But I've put so much time into that shop. And into Shari too. Too much, into both of them."

"No. It is you and the way you are. I have never felt deprived."

"Do you want to go to Dallas with me the next time I go to market?" she said.

"Honey, I would probably be very bored. We just don't have that kind of marriage. I know. I know what you're thinking. Some people do and we should have. But we are not that kind of people. We are not that intense or that singleminded in our passions. It does not bother me. It never has. I do not have to have you near every hour of the day to know you're mine."

"But some people—"

"Some people are not us. I am a happy man." He kissed her on the cheek. "At least I would be if you'd start thinking about when and where we're going to eat. I'm beginning to think about a drink and a dinner."

"We'll go." She stood up, brushing at her skirt. "Did you know they are having that hearing tomorrow?" she said.

"I heard so, yes. You're not planning on going, are you?"

"No, but I wish it were over."

"Well, it will be. And people can start forgetting it."

"They won't."

"Not for a while, no. But eventually. How many people really ever think about World War Two?"

"Where would you like to eat?" Mary Alice said.

"Oh, hell, let's go home where we can have a quiet knock and I'll throw some steaks on the grill. Shall we call Shari and Bill to come over?"

"No," Mary Alice said. "Let's don't ask them to come over. Let's just us have a quiet knock and throw some steaks on the grill."

They got back in the car and fastened their seat belts and drove a cautious fifty miles an hour home.

"I think I'll cook supper tonight," Syd said. *"I have one of those irresistible urges to do something tasty and fattening."*

"All right," Meredith said. "I'm amenable. Let's ask people."

"What people?"

"Any people. How about Kurt and Sandy?"

"It's late."

"I know, but they'll understand. Unless they've already started supper. I saw Sandy this morning. She looked like she could use a night out."

"You better call now," Syd said.

"Well, hurry and lock the front door before somebody comes in for a pair of shoes they've simply got to have for tonight."

"O.K." Syd went to the front of the empty store and switched on the window lights and locked up. He liked the store late in the afternoon when all the customers were gone. It had a displaced air that pleased him. There was something cozy about all the shelves and shelves of shoes, the faint leather smell in the air, the closed cash register. Maybe that was the secret, the closed cash register.

He could hear Meredith on the phone talking to Sandy. He watched her, the late light falling on her face. He felt sad—for no good reason—just sad. Only there is a good

272

reason, his mind informed him, and you know it. It is because it has crossed your mind—the doubt. There has been a place in Syd Green's far-too-human soul that has said, We were having an affair and there was the time I almost quit her, the hard times trying to convince Dad. The small doubt didn't shame him. It was a normal reaction for a man. Every husband with a stake in this thing had probably had it too. What shamed him was that his father didn't have any doubt, not even a small one. As far as Irving was concerned Meredith didn't even figure in the speculations.

In a way it was funny. He remembered Irving's impassioned speeches against shikses when he was trying to stop him from marrying Meredith. Well, when he'd given in he'd given in all the way. Meredith was as much his daughter as he, Syd, was his son. Maybe more so, because he'd had to learn to love Meredith. It hadn't been a foreordained fact.

He thought of the ceremony under the canopy and Meredith's low voice saying she wanted to become a Jew. As far as Irving was concerned she had become one. It was a matter of faith. It was like the Catholics and transubstantiation. They literally believed it. Without that literal belief there would be no Catholic religion, and because of it one had been going on several thousand chaotic and changing years. He knew he didn't have any faith, not that kind, not a belief in the impossible in static terms. His faith was in the imponderables, the empty spaces, the hopes and dreams and fantasies of the human soul. It did not include a true and emotional belief in transubstantiation of any kind. He was a rationalist. He'd always been rather proud of it, but in this moment, watching his wife put down the phone and smile at him, he had a sudden and intense desire not to be. For the first time in his life Syd Green knew what it was to long for God.

"They say, Great," Meredith said.

"So, good. What time?"

"Soon as we can all get home and shower off work," Meredith said. "Did your idiot father leave us his car again?"

273

Syd grinned. "Yep."

"We've got to stop driving it," Meredith said. "It's spoiling me."

"That's what he intends for it to do," Syd said.

They drove home through the twilight and while Meredith paid the maid and talked to the children he went out back and looked at his yard and wondered if it was warm enough to cook out. It wasn't, not if they ate late. He was proud of the back yard. He'd worked hard on it. There was a built-in barbecue grill and wooden tables and benches, a badminton court, and an old-fashioned swing hung between wooden uprights. That had been Meredith's idea. She said nobody had a swing anymore and she missed them. Her grandmother had had two, one on each end of her veranda. After they'd put it up he found he enjoyed it as much as she did. They'd sit out there at night in the summer, watching fireflies. He looked at his roses, just beginning to bud. It would soon be time to start the spraying routine. He always complained about the time roses took, but the truth was he enjoyed all the time he spent in his yard and garden. The complaining was only a way of propitiating the gods he didn't believe in. Like the Chinese. Meet my ugly unworthy daughter. Look at all the goddamned trouble the lousy roses cause.

He laughed abruptly, a snorting sound in the middle of his own silence. Maybe that's what they were all doing with the nagging little doubts. Doubting Meredith just a little might mean: Please God, don't clobber me with it *really* being her.

He looked toward the house. She'd turned on the kitchen light and he could hear the children talking to her. They were excited and happy that they were home for the day and that company was coming and they'd get ginger-ale cocktails. She passed in front of the open door and he saw her silhouetted against the light. His girl. There was still and always that little picture in his mind of the first time she'd come into his arms. Her head had been tilted just a little to one side so that her hair had fallen down across one cheek, she'd been flushed from the fire in that ratty old room he'd had, and she'd said, "Am I your girl?" What would life have been like if he hadn't said, "You're my girl." He didn't know, but he knew it wouldn't have been the life he wanted.

So would it really make any difference if it had been her, if she had panicked and been afraid to tell him and done a crazy thing? Yes, it would make a difference. But it wouldn't stop her being his girl right on, today, yesterday, and tomorrow. Maybe that was all the faith of Irving meant and was, a transubstantiation in truth. When love is there God is there also. She *is* my girl and I love her. Therefore nothing has, will, or can happen. Nothing did.

He went into the kitchen and kissed her to the delight of the children. They always liked it when he did. Then he kissed both of them. "What wonderful thing should I cook?" he said.

"Spaghetti, spaghetti," both children yelled.

"Yes," Meredith said, "with a peach and cheese salad and some good bread which we unfortunately haven't got because I forgot to stop at the store."

"I'll go get it," he said.

"No, I'll call Sandy to pick it up on the way out."

She went out to the phone and he began to peel onions. In a few minutes he began to sing. The kids liked that too.

There was a small store near the campus that stayed open late and Sandy had Kurt stop at the curb in front of it. She was in a hurry. They were already late because she'd had trouble getting hold of Clarissa to sit. The girl next door who usually sat for her had a date and so did Kurt's sister. The store where she always called Clarissa couldn't locate her at first, but just when she'd decided they'd have to call and beg off the phone rang and Clarissa said she'd come. Meredith had said they could bring the kids, but they both looked tired and she felt tired and she said she'd rather not.

Clarissa sounded tired too, but when Kurt came back with her she seemed her usual self, wry, ironic, and laced with a certain placid resignation.

"You get on," she said. "I'll put these younguns to bed. You need a night out, I 'spect."

275

There was no one in the little store except the man who owned it, his son, and two women she didn't know. She ran back and got the bread Meredith had said she wanted, then stopped and picked up a couple of cans of macadamia nuts for a present. She went up to the cash register with her purchases and turned her head toward the back where both the proprietor and his son were behind the meat case. The two men and the two women were watching her and just as she turned her head toward them the boy sniggered. It was a nasty furtive little sound and she felt herself flush. She was furious, not for the snigger so much as for the blush. She'd known, of course, that everybody in town was sniggering about all of them. But it hadn't happened where she could see and hear it before. She felt vulnerable, alone in the cramped store. She had an almost primitive feeling of panic for a moment as though these people might pick up a few cans and set upon her with appropriate twentieth-century stones. The tableau seemed to last forever, then the proprietor moved around the meat case and came toward the cash register and her sense of humor came back. It was, after all, amusing. Thank God.

"What's the matter?" Kurt said when she got back in the car.

"Nothing," she said. "I'll tell you when we get out there."

She told them, sitting in the living room over the first drink. It made both Kurt and Syd angry as she'd known it would, but she felt better after telling it. Meredith's house was cozy and there was a wood fire in the fireplace. It felt good after the rain and the after-rain chill. They could smell Syd's spaghetti sauce from the kitchen.

"I keep feeling like I ought to call Martha to come out," Meredith said.

"Why?" Syd said.

"Because she's the only one of us who hasn't got anybody," Meredith said. "Joan's got Dylan, and the rest of us have more than a plenty of family. But Martha just plain hasn't got anybody." She winked at Syd. "I know. You're

276

took with Miss Layne. But you've always liked Martha well enough. It wouldn't kill you to be nice to her."

"I didn't say don't ask her," Syd said. "But she do be a lot like the specter at the feast."

"I think she's better since this thing happened," Sandy said. "Don't ask me why. Maybe because it's given her something to think about besides Frank. Hell, you can't blame her for being put upon. There's not a one of us who'd be any different if our husband left us for a younger woman."

"Layne isn't all that much of a younger woman," Meredith said.

"Well, hell, any woman," Sandy said. "I'm quite sure I'd scream and yell and carry on about it."

"Well, that's just it," Kurt said. "Everybody would feel better if Martha *would* scream and yell and carry on. It's that damned self-righteous resignation that drives people nuts."

"Well, I'm going to call her," Meredith said. "Maybe she hasn't eaten yet. Can you hold the supper awhile, Syd?"

"Sure."

"All right." Meredith went to the phone in the hall.

"Sell a lot of shoes today, Syd?" Kurt said.

"Enough. How about insurance?"

"Enough."

"All God's chillun got shoes and insurance," Sandy said.

Meredith came back into the room. "She's coming," she said. "I must say it surprises me. She used to be peculiar about any spur of the moment thing."

"I told you, this thing has changed her," Sandy said. "Maybe it's not that at all, of course. It could just be time passing. You know, like when somebody dies. The day comes when you have to come back into the world."

"Yes, but she was peculiar about last-minute things back when she was still married to Frank."

"Well, that was just looking after good-old-Frank," Sandy said.

"Meow, baby," Kurt said.

Martha didn't know why she'd said yes. She kept doing

277

these things that weren't like her. Here for the third time in three days she'd been to see somebody. First Joan, then Sandy, now Meredith. It was setting a bad precedent. It was making her look lonely. It made it bad when she came back home, too. It was easier just to leave work and come to the empty apartment than it was to go out and have a good evening with somebody and then have to come back to the empty apartment. It wasn't that she was nervous about the lateness or the dark. The apartment house was on a well-lighted street where a lot of students lived. No matter how late it was, some of them were always up and around. It was just that it seemed so cold and empty.

"I will leave a light on tonight," she said. She never did that because it was a form of giving in to herself. She just left the hall light by the door on. But tonight she'd leave a lamp on in the living room. She just might leave the thermostat up in the bedroom, too. What the hell.

Martha stood for a moment outside Meredith's window, watching them through the glass. The fire looked warm and bright and cheerful and they were all sitting close to it drinking and eating nuts out of a silver dish. She felt cold and she knew she should go in before she caught cold, but she kept standing there, watching them. The scene reminded her of something and she felt that it was important she remember it. She pulled her coat around her and stood still and after a few moments it came to her.

It had been right after Joan Friday had told her she'd seen Layne and Frank together at the country club and she'd had that lunch with her. It hadn't been any great big surprise, not really. She knew there was a thing going on with Frank and Layne, but she hadn't paid any attention to it. She'd convinced herself long ago that the first premonition had been wrong. Frank had had lots of things about pretty girls. They didn't amount to anything. But if people like Joan Friday were going to be talking it around town it was time to do something about it. So she'd tried. It had always worked before, the subtle hints without having to come right out and say anything you could be called on later. Only Layne had acted as though she hadn't said

278

anything at all. Layne had used her own technique back on her. She hadn't realized that at first. She'd thought, Oh, it must just not be true.

Then the thing had happened. Right after that there'd been this party at the Carltons' and after dinner Frank had said he'd have Irish Sanka. The whole scene came back to her. She guessed it was because of the nuts. They'd been eating nuts out of a silver dish that night too. Layne had been sitting on a big pouf Cassie had, holding the silver dish in her hand, fingers dipping into it, carrying the little nuts to her mouth. When Frank had said that, she'd brought her hand down slowly, chewed once, gulped, and said, "What? What did you say?"

And Frank had said, "Irish Sanka," and Layne had started to laugh. She sounded as though she were going to have hysterics. She laughed so hard the little silver nut dish turned over and nuts rolled across the room. "Oh, hell," she'd said, gasping. "That is too damned much."

Martha had stared at her in disbelief, thinking, No, there isn't anything to it or she wouldn't take the chance of making fun of him to his face, and then she'd looked over and seen that Frank was laughing too.

She'd been mad then, really mad. She didn't let herself get mad often because something final usually came of it and she knew it. But she was mad now. She'd turned to Layne and said, "I fail to see what's so funny about that. He's got to operate tomorrow."

Then Layne had looked as though she was going to have a spasm. She was obviously trying to stop laughing and she couldn't. "I'm sorry, Martha," she said. "It's just so wonderful. It's the most beautifully pure form of coppering your bets I've ever heard. It's even better than my cousin and his swimming trunks."

"What cousin?" Frank said. He was still laughing too. She could have kicked him.

"Oh, hell, my cousin Ed," Layne said. "He and his wife had wanted a house with a swimming pool for years and finally they retired to Florida and got one. There were just the two of them and this huge house with a pool smack in

279

the middle. It was screened and walled and planted round with a high hedge and the lot was miles from anything or anybody. Every night he got out and swam the length of the pool six times for exercise. And he always wore his trunks to do it."

Everybody in the room was laughing now, Philip and Cassie and Layne and B.J. and J.D. and Frank. Oh, yes, Frank too.

He'd looked positively fatuous as though Layne had said something nice about him rather than making him look like an ass. Then he'd actually walked across the room and started picking up the nuts Layne had dropped and putting them back in the dish one by one.

"It's not that I'm your cousin Ed at all, honey," he'd said. "It's just that I want to get drunk, but I'm not interested in staying up for it."

Then he'd handed her the dish and their hands touched and they'd both quit laughing and stared at each other as though there wasn't anybody else in the room. A week after that she knew he'd slept with her.

She lifted the doorknocker and let it fall.

Meredith let her in. They all looked at her and for a moment she had the feeling she had had so often after she first found out about it, that everybody had just stopped talking about it when she walked in. Then she thought, Hell, they've been married for months and nobody gives a damn anymore, and came on into the room, and said, Hello everybody. Meredith got her a drink.

Joan made Dylan eat dinner at home. He was in a hurry to collect Miranda and go to an art movie they were showing on the campus, but she made him eat with her first. He sat across the table, looking impatient with her. She watched him all during the soup. After she served the roast beef she looked carefully down at her plate, then smiled up at him. It was one of those habits she'd gotten into with Bill because it had him halfway on her side before she said a word. It was amazing how many of the little gestures of everyday were like that, mannerisms that had worked with Bill. But they were too much a part of her for

280

her to change them now. Besides men were men. "How would you like to go to Europe this summer, darling?" she said.

Dylan put down his fork. "I thought you'd decided it was too expensive just now."

"Well, there was a nice little dividend from Neiman-Marcus this quarter," she said. "It just might make the difference."

He looked hesitant, then interested, then worried. She continued to smile brightly at him.

"I don't know," he said. "I'd put the whole idea out of my mind."

"Well, put it back, dear," she said, "Of course"—she paused—"I'd want you to pass everything this semester."

"Oh, sure," he said.

"Think of Paris in June or Rome in August. I wish I were young and about to see it all for the first time."

"You wouldn't come with me?"

"Heavens, no. What would a young man seeing Paris for the first time want with his mother hanging around? No. This would be for you."

He didn't look at her. After a long moment he said, "It's something I'll have to think about."

"Nonsense," she said. "Every boy your age wants some time in Europe." She laughed. "Wild oats. But for heaven's sake it's months before summer. I just wanted to let you know I've found the money after all."

"Yeah. Well, thanks," he said.

"There's pie for dessert," she said.

"I don't really think I want any," he said. "I'm running pretty late now."

"All right," she said. "I'll save it for a bedtime snack."

"Fine," he said. He folded his napkin and put it carefully beside his plate.

"Why don't you bring Miranda back with you for pie and coffee?" she said.

"I probably will," he said. "Bye, Mom. Good supper."

He kissed her on the cheek and went out the back door. She sat still, watching the candlelight on the table, hearing

281

the car start and go away down the hill. I don't know, Bill, she thought. You'd probably say I was being a mean hard woman. Maybe I am. But it's the way I am. You can't start being what you're not at my age. I don't want them to marry now. It's too soon and she isn't right. If he really wants to go to Europe and it makes him forget about her then I am right. So I'm not really doing anything. If it's love, a kind I know nothing about, then it won't matter and I'll still have done the best I can. Bill's ghost didn't say anything at all. It never did.

When J. D. Finch came in from the mill he was met at the door by all five children in a state of consternation.

"Mama's crying," they fought each other to tell him.

He stared at them. That was unusual enough on any day to cause consternation, not only to the kids but to him. But today, after the lunch together, it seemed incredible. He'd let her out of the car downtown about three and gone back to the mill. She'd said she'd take a taxi home, she wanted to do some shopping. She'd been in a great mood, tying her head up in an old scarf, laughing and waving to him as he drove off. The maid appeared in the door and told the kids to leave him alone. He looked at her over their heads and she shrugged. Then she herded the kids into the kitchen and he went on upstairs.

B.J. was sitting in front of her desk looking at something, and they were right, she was crying. He went across the room quickly thinking, What the hell? Then it occurred to him that it was probably something some idiot had said about this baby in the wall business, and he felt a rush of tenderness toward her. He went across the room quickly and stood behind her and put his hands on her shoulders.

She turned toward him. There were tears standing on her lashes and her eyes were a little red, but not much. She evidently hadn't been crying long.

"What's the matter, honey?" he said. "Some idiot's said something, I know it."

She looked up at him, then down at the calendar in front of her. "Oh, J.D.," she said, "I'm so glad you're home. I'm pregnant. My God, I'm pregnant."

282

He looked at her, a little annoyed, a little pleased, but still uncomprehending. He'd never known her to cry about being pregnant. Though, God knew they didn't need any more, and maybe she was feeling a little tired of the whole routine.

She saw his look of puzzlement. She'd quit crying now, but there was still a woebegone expression on her face. "Dammit," she said, "I should have known, but I never keep up good with the days. I just never have it straight when I'm supposed to start or anything, and today while I was downtown I stopped in Frank's to pick up a lab report I'd had done on my last routine checkup, and he came out of the office grinning like a possum and said, 'B.J., I'll swear to God, do you have so many you don't even notice it anymore when you get ready to have another one?' And I came home and counted up and of course I am."

He was still watching her with a worried expression.

"But don't you see?" she said. "The timing is absolutely horrible. Just as all these people get over thinking about this thing that's happened I'll start showing and everybody in Druid City will start thinking about the whole awful thing all over again."

He looked at her and all at once he felt a laugh start. He tried to hold it back, but she looked so dejected and comical with her hair sticking out in all directions and the betraying calendar in front of her. He started to laugh. She looked at him indignantly for one moment, ready to get mad, then she started to laugh too. They whooped and gasped and she got up and they clung to each other.

In the hallway the children all looked at each other and grinned. Then they turned around and went downstairs. They hadn't gotten there in time to hear any of the conversation because Sue had kept them in the kitchen and they'd had to wait till she went down for the wine before they could slip upstairs. But they'd heard the laughter and knew it was all right. Daddy had made Mama laugh and so obviously she wasn't crying anymore.

Sue appeared at the bottom of the stairs. "What you all up to?" she said. "Didn't I tell you to leave your Mama and

283

Daddy alone and let 'em get a little peace and quiet before dinner?"

"They're laughing," Timmy said.

Sue looked up the stairway. "So they are," she said. "Now get back in that room and look at the TV and let 'em laugh."

They all went into the den and sat down around the television set.

"Why do you reckon Mama was crying?" Jim said.

"It doesn't matter," Mary said. "She's laughing now. So it wasn't anything important."

"Maybe she had a headache," Bill said.

"I thought it might have been because I ruined her nail scissors," Liza said, "But I don't think she's found them yet. I hid them pretty good."

Timmy was staring at the television set. He was frowning and obviously thinking. The rest of them all looked at him. He could be depended on to figure out unusual and puzzling situations, particularly when they concerned grown-ups.

"Well," he said tentatively, "first she was gone downtown when we all got in from school. Then she went upstairs and sat at her desk and after a while she cried. Then when Daddy came they talked and ended up laughing and hugging each other." A small gleam came into his eyes. "I know," he said. "We're going to have another brother or sister."

They all looked at him, and then back at the television set.

"Is that all?" Mary said.

When Miley came home the house was dark. He'd spent a couple of hours hanging around Chuck's Beer Joint, playing the jukebox and watching the college kids. He hadn't enjoyed it. He was a middle-aged man, sleepy, tired, wanting to go home, hanging around a beer joint playing sad songs on a jukebox. He told Chuck good night and drove home.

The front door was unlocked. He was surprised she'd left it open. She was always afraid to be alone at home at night. He knew he'd left so quickly she couldn't be sure he had the key. The open door touched him as nothing else she could have done, but he hardened himself against the tenderness he felt. He didn't know what kind of reception he was going to get. He'd never hit her before. He hadn't meant to tonight. It had happened as though to somebody else, somebody he was watching on television. A man beating his wife . . . good God.

He went up the stairs in the faint light from the night light she had left on in the upstairs hall. The house was completely silent and he paused for a moment outside the bedroom door, wondering if he should get a blanket from the linen closet and sleep in the guest room. He'd never done that either. He braced himself and went into the bedroom.

He knew she was awake as soon as he came into the room, though she made her breathing regular. That hurt him, too. Maybe she was afraid. It shamed him to think Edyth could be afraid of him. But underneath the shame there was a hard core of unrepentance. Not because of what she had done, or even the possibilities of what she might have done, but for her indignation, her feeling of rightness, her bland assigning of the role of aggressor to him, of transgressed-against to herself.

He simply couldn't help the way he felt. There was a part of her, of womankind, that he saw as Eve in the garden, and he might as well face it. He was not civilized in the sense some men were. He could never as long as he lived feel unconcerned about his wife as a woman. He could not see her as a separate entity with rights and privileges exclusive of him. He did not see himself as a man with rights and privileges exclusive of her, either. They were not two people living in the same house. They were a unit. And while the fact of that unit kept a lot of the darkness out there away, it let other kinds in. That was the simple of it.

She hadn't moved. He went into the bathroom and undressed as quietly as he could just as though he thought she really was asleep. Then he came back into the room and got carefully into his side of the double bed. He couldn't

285

sleep. He knew he wasn't going to as soon as he closed his eyes and they banged open again. He lit a cigarette. The regular breathing continued and after a while he decided she really was asleep. His anger came back. He'd had the idea she was lying there as miserable as he was and here she was sleeping the sleep of the just.

"Well, sleep, dammit," he said.

She sat up and reached for the cigarettes and lit one. "I'm not asleep," she said. There was a mean edge to her voice, but he ignored it.

"It sounded like it to me," he said.

"You have a good time?" she said.

"Sure. I've been out with six different women," he said.

She drew on the cigarette and let the smoke out with a loud exhalation.

"I'm sorry I beat you up," he said, "but I still think I had every right to. You shouldn't have hit me."

"All right. I'm sorry too," she said. She didn't sound sorry to him. She sounded self-righteous.

He put out his cigarette and lit another one immediately. She was crying. She was trying to be quiet about it, but he could hear her. "What are you crying about?" he said.

"I can't stand what we're doing to each other. I just can't."

He didn't answer her and after a few moments he heard her draw a breath and go on. "There's something I've got to try to explain to you," she said, her voice almost a whisper. "I've thought and thought about it while you were gone tonight and I know I have to try to explain it. It may just make you madder. In fact, I think it will, but I've got to try. It's a thing I've never thought you'd understand because I've always thought you didn't know there was such a thing as weakness. But maybe you do, maybe I've been wrong thinking that. You see, the thing with Bob Allen. What you have to understand is that it was our weaknesses that made us . . . want . . . each other. There were the weak places inside him that were exactly like the weak places inside me and something in both of us recognized it and it made for a kind of love . . . You're being too quiet.

286

You are not understanding this, or I'm saying it wrong, or I just shouldn't say it at all. I don't know. But things can't be much worse than they are, so I have to try. You were so good and capable and strong, I always had the feeling you didn't really need me at all. You loved me, but you didn't need me. Don't you see that?"

He put his cigarette out in the ashtray and turned his back to her.

"All right," she said, "I'm wrong to try to say it. You simply don't or won't hear it the way I mean it. But you do love me. I know you do. So we have to keep trying. Some people, they marry those people with the weaknesses like their own and sometimes it all goes to hell and it's a mess. Other times the weaknesses go together to make a strongness and it's good. Other times one of them discovers they are strong after all and they run the other one. That can work all right too, if the other one never finds it out. With me and Bob there was this thing that happened when he tried to kill me . . . us. That's what he did, tried to kill us in an automobile. Not, I think, for any real reason, and that's another thing. Life is not a series of planned incidents. It just isn't. People do things that they haven't even thought about. People do things they don't mean to or want to. People wake up one morning feeling like somebody else entirely. You don't go around saying, I am not going to have this certain emotion. Emotion happens to you. And if that sounds primitive and superstitious, O.K. But anyway, he tried to kill us and when that happened it made him weaker and me stronger and we didn't have the same pattern inside anymore and it simply ended. What emotion there was just all went away."

She stopped. He was listening, but he wasn't going to help her. She lit another cigarette, even though her mouth was dry and she really didn't want it. "So you see," she went on, "you scare me. You make me feel all your emotion for me has just gone away. And I simply can't or won't believe that. Because we have more than emotion. We have more than just a mixing up of the strong and weak places. We have all these years of each other. We've taken the emotion and built something that's stronger and better and truer than the emotion, even though it couldn't exist without it. I just simply don't believe you can cut me out of your life. I couldn't cut you out of mine. I couldn't even if you did a thing like Bob Allen and tried to run me off the road in an automobile. It wouldn't change anything the way that did. I'd just die or not die wishing I hadn't failed you."

He didn't answer her and she thought, I'm not getting through to him, I'm making it all worse. It is truly better not to try to explain things. It does not work and I wish to God I could learn to keep my big mouth shut.

He lay still, turned away from her, rigid. Suddenly she knew she didn't care if he did hit her again, she had to touch him, had to try to let him know how she felt even if words simply would not, could not, do it. She got up and went around the bed and knelt down on the other side and put her arms around him and kissed him. She tried very hard to put everything she truly felt into the kiss and she thought desperately, if it is not there it is simply no use. There isn't any rhyme, reason, or God, and I'll just have to take that and go on the best I can with it.

He tried to pull away from her, but she held him, feeling him twisting away from her and praying a wordless prayer that meant only, Please, please, please.

Then his arms went around her and he kissed her back. "Oh, God, don't you see it's because I *do* love you," he said.

She came into the bed beside him, trying to hold him tight enough to be just one person with him, making another wordless prayer that meant, Yes, yes, yes.

Later she lay against him, smoking another cigarette, and he said, "You understand this doesn't really change anything. It means you're right about us. We can't ever let each other go. But it doesn't change the other, the fact that we feel differently about things, that we've got to feel our way."

"I know that," she said.

"I don't think it will ever be quite the same again. Not for me. I have to tell you that too."

288

"I know that," she said. "But I think it can be better. Better than now, maybe better than it ever was. It is just that we have to try harder. I don't think it's going to be easy, either. I know it isn't. I hate to be corny, but they've shut the gate on us, darling. And now we have to get out there and grub in the ground and labor and create."

They held each other very tightly and after awhile they went to sleep.

The movie had been Charlie Chaplin in City Lights. *They came away from it and got in the car and drove to the river to drink their bottle of wine.*

"I never used to like Chaplin," Miranda said. "Everybody thought Chaplin was the greatest and I couldn't see it. Then I saw a movie called *Children of Paradise*. Did you ever see that, Dylan?"

"No, I never saw it. They say—"

"Yes, they say it was absolutely great. And it was. Nowadays we have things like *La Dolce Vita*, but when *Children of Paradise* came out there wasn't anything like that at all. I talked to my mother once about what the other movies were then and they were all things like what we see on the late late show. So, God, what it must have been to the people who saw it then. Because it was great when I saw it. I saw it twice, once in the cut version and once again in full length. It ran four or five hours, full length. Well, anyway it went from this to that and people in it felt a little bit of everything and so do you. It was about a mime. And, my God, the last scene. He's trying to get to this woman and she's getting in her carriage to go. To go forever. It's a holiday and the streets are full of people and he's pushing and shoving and trying to get through them, and they turn and laugh and shout and push back. They're having fun, you see. It's a Mardi Gras sort of time. And he's desperate. Really desperate in the dictionary sense of the word. Do you know the dictionary sense of that word, Dylan?"

"No, Miranda."

"No, why should you? You've never been desperate. I guess I haven't either. I don't think you can be really desperate at our age, because there's always all those years out there. But it means at the point of committing reckless acts due to the complete and utter hopelessness of the situation. That's what it means."

"What's all this got to do with Chaplin, Miranda?"

She looked at him. "You're worried about something tonight, Dylan," she said. "You're so cross with me. When you're like that it's never me. It's something about yourself."

"Hmmph," he said.

"Yes, hmmph. Well, anyway after I saw that scene, which I never have forgotten—I can still see the dress the woman had on when she got into the carriage—well, anyway, I understood Chaplin. That's all."

"Did he get through the crowd?" Dylan said.

"Barrault? No. Of course not. There just comes the point when he quits shoving and pushing and trying to laugh back at the people who are holding him up and stands there while they mill around him. And the carriage drives away."

"You're very serious tonight, Miranda."

"Chaplin does that to me. Now that I understand him."

"I bet Pagliacci just tears you up," Dylan said.

She was hurt, but she tried not to let him know it. "Yeah, sure," she said. "Drop the cross one more time, buddy, and you're out of the parade."

He looked at her. "I'm sorry, Miranda," he said. "That was pretty nasty."

"Yes," Miranda said. "A girl can't go on laughing *all* the time."

"I know."

"What's the matter, Dylan?"

"Nothing. Oh, hell, why should I be an ass about it? Mother wants me to go to Europe this summer."

Miranda became very still and quiet. "Do you want to go?" she said after a while.

"I don't know," Dylan said. "I guess that's what bothers me."

Miranda looked down at her hands, clasped in her lap. "Well," she said finally, "I can understand that. I'd like to go to Europe myself. If my mother gave me the choice I guess it would be hard for me to make too."

Dylan looked at her intently. Then he smiled. He reached over and touched her cheek with the back of his hand. "You're sweet," he said. "Do you know that?"

"No, I'm not," she said. "Not really. But I try. Oh, not to be sweet, but not to hurt. You see, I know what it's like to be hurt."

"I guess everybody knows that, Miranda."

"Yes. That's what I mean."

"I want to make love to you, Miranda."

"All right."

"I want to, but it doesn't seem fair after what I've just told you about Europe."

"Oh, Dylan, what a thing to say. What's fair? I want you to make love to me too. That's about as fair as you can get."

He leaned over and kissed her gently on the cheek. "You see what I mean?" he said. "Sweet."

She smiled at him. "Say that again and I'm going to bust you right in the mouth," she said.

The phone rang, waking Frank Plowden at 2 A.M. He groaned and reached for it, but Layne had already answered it. He could hear her making soothing sounds and then settling back against the headboard and lighting a cigarette. He lay still, trying to wake up, wondering if he really had to wake up. She didn't sound concerned. He reached for his cigarettes and lit one, then poked her with his foot. She gave a stifled yelp, then went on, saying, "Oh, yes. That's exactly the right thing. Frank always says so. Now if you want me to wake him. Well, good. Yes. That'll be fine, I'm sure. I'll write it down right here where he'll see it first thing in the morning. Yes. Thank you. Thank you very much. Good night."

"That was old lady Clemmons," Frank said.

"Give the man a cigar," Layne said.

"What was it this time?"

"There's a man in her garden."

"I'm not awake yet," Frank said. "You're not making any

291

sense. What can I do about a man in her garden? Why didn't she call the police?"

"Well, there really *isn't* a man in her garden. That's just the point. She knows there isn't, but she feels like there is. She wanted to know if it would be all right to take a phenobarbital so she could quit thinking about him."

"Oh, good God," Frank said.

"I told her to take two," Layne said.

"Do you want to get arrested for practicing without a license?"

"Oh, I don't know. That's an interesting phrase there. Practicing without a license. Practicing without license. That's even better."

"Go back to sleep," Frank said.

"All right. She's coming into the office tomorrow. 'To have her pressure checked,' I believe she said. I better write that down." She switched on the lamp by the bed, scribbled on a pad, turned the light back off and flounced over onto her stomach. "Goodnight, Doctor."

"Goodnight, love."

He lay awake for a while, hearing her steady breathing, putting his hand out every once in a while to touch her, softly so as not to wake her, just small touches on her back, the bend of her knee, her buttocks. She smelled of her French perfume, not strongly, just enough to make him feel like sniffing after more. He wanted to put his face in her neck, but he knew if he did she'd wake up and turn toward him and she needed to sleep. She'd sounded tired on the phone.

"You play the red and the red comes up," he said softly. Then he turned on his side, put his arm around her, and tried to go back to sleep. He couldn't. There were odd and jagged little thoughts in his mind about the hearing tomorrow and after a while he gave in and listened to them because he knew by experience that was the only way he was ever going to get back to sleep.

There was the thought of Martha, Martha as she'd been in that long-ago summer, impressive, lovely, tall, gracious, capable, and certain. He had a picture of that Martha calmly walking down the hall of a sorority house and putting a dead baby in an airshaft. It was a rather ugly picture, but he had it, so he looked at it. She would have been quite capable of it if it had saved the situation. Martha always believed in doing that. But he was quite sure there hadn't been such a situation. He looked back, thought back, didn't see any possibility of it. He thought about Dixie Smith and the hiatus that had caused, thought that the baby hadn't been full-term, knew the possibility was there. Knew it was nonsense. She was capable of it, but not capable of getting herself into the mess in the first place. And that, Frank Plowden, is a silly thing to think, he told himself. You have been a practicing physician too long not to know that any grotesque accident can happen to anybody. But not to Martha, his mind said, so that he had to laugh at himself, because he still believed she was infallible even though he knew damned well she wasn't.

Another little picture, a dream he'd had once, the first one where Martha and his mother had been the same person in it. It was so obvious he wouldn't even let himself remember it until he dreamed it again and had to look at it.

The first dream he'd ever had about Layne. She'd been all got up like an airplane pilot, old style, helmet and goggles, ready to take off in a Camel and win World War I. Well, that one was obvious too. Sometimes his dreams made him think his unconscious must be a moron.

He thought about Janice for a moment, wondered if she'd ever become much of a person, knew that he really didn't care. It was an awful admission and it still gave him a great deal of guilt, but it was true. There had simply come a time when he had looked at her and known, his own daughter or not, his own flesh and blood or not, he didn't like her, knew that if she were somebody else's kid he'd pity them. The really weird thing was that he'd come to feel that way because she'd betrayed Martha to Layne. And he knew Layne felt the same way. It was all ridiculous. How could he blame Janice for doing what he'd done? He knew damned well how. Janice had hardly had any emotion about what she was doing. It had been about as cold-blooded as anything he'd ever seen in his life. After all, Martha was her mother. He snorted suddenly at his own rationalizations. Come on, Frank, he said. She was yours too.

So quit worrying it, he told himself. You have to get through that hearing tomorrow just like everybody else. Then it'll be over and you can forget about it.

He let himself think about the girl beside him, the way he used to think about her when she was far away across town and he was indulging himself with it—her face, her body, the husky way her voice went when she looked at him and talked just under audibility for anybody but him. Then he let himself know she was right here within touching distance and after that he went back to sleep.

"We've stayed out too late again," Sandy said.

The streets were empty as they drove through them with a late night emptiness and chill. Only the streetlights seemed alive.

"Oh, it was fun," Kurt said. "We even got Martha loosened up."

"So we did," Sandy said. "She actually made a couple of funnies. But I hate keeping Clarissa so late. I thought today, watching her go to the bus stop, that she was looking awfully old and tired."

"Maybe she went to sleep," Kurt said. "She knows she can."

"Yes, but she's one of those terribly conscientious people. She won't have. I've never known her to except on New Year's Eve when I insist on it."

The lights were on in the living room and kitchen. "See?" Sandy said when they turned into the drive.

Clarissa was sitting in the rocking chair in the living room, holding Kim across her knees, rocking gently, singing a half-song, half-story. In front of her the TV hummed a mandalaed test pattern.

Sandy ran lightly across the room. "He's sick," she whispered.

Clarissa shook her head. "Nothing the matter with him, Miss Sandy," she said. "You know I call you anything the matter. He just had a bad dream, that's all. I trying to get him back good to sleep."

He was asleep, small body limp in his striped pajamas, face flushed, a faint smile on it.

"I'm sorry about that TV," Clarissa said. "It went off while I was holding him and I didn't want to put him down. I think he's gone off good now, though. I'll get him down." She stood up carefully and went into the bedroom with Kim. Sandy switched off the TV.

"Why do I always assume they're sick?" she said.

"That is known, dear, as mother love."

She made a face at him.

Clarissa came back into the room. "Sleeping like an angel," she said.

"I'm sorry we're so late," Sandy said.

"Don't bother me none," Clarissa said. "Don't sleep when I'm home anyway." She went to the kitchen for her coat and pocketbook.

"Thank you, Clarissa," Sandy said. "You take good care of them."

Clarissa gave her a look of disgust. "What you 'spect me to do, honey? Have my boy friends over like some teenager?" She patted Sandy on the shoulder and went out with Kurt.

While Kurt drove Clarissa home, Sandy tiptoed into the bedroom and stood looking down at the children. She pulled up the covers and kissed them on the cheek. They made small sounds of disturbance and turned over and went on sleeping.

When Kurt came back she had two bottles of beer and some cheese and crackers out on the kitchen table.

"That's nice," he said.

"It's way too late for it, but I thought it might be fun."

"I bet you don't wake up at three o'clock this morning," Kurt said. "You'll be lucky to be asleep by then."

She smiled at him. "You know something," she said, "I think Clarissa really loves our children. Isn't that funny? Why should she?"

"Because she's watched them grow up and she's that kind of person," Kurt said.

"Yes," Sandy said. "I guess so. Love . . . what a funny thing it is. Nobody knows what it is and there are so many different kinds. And we all fight it. That's the part I simply don't understand."

"Sandy, love, it is almost three o'clock. Please don't get philosophical."

"Sorry. I'm having a bad spell of it lately."

"We're at an age for it."

"My God, what a nasty thought."

They laughed.

"We'd better go to bed," Kurt said. "We're never going to get up in the morning."

"I know." Sandy put the beer bottles in the closet and the cheese back in the refrigerator. She turned out the lights and they went down the hall toward the bedroom.

"You're that kind of person too," Kurt said as he started to undress.

"What kind of person? What *are* you talking about?"

"Somebody with a great capacity for love."

"Now *you're* getting philosophical," Sandy said.

"I know it. But it's one of those things. It's a talent, something you're born with. You have green eyes and an ability to dance and a great capacity for love. I don't know what it means, if anything. I'm just stating a fact."

"Does it show?" Sandy said.

"It shows," Kurt said. "It is why you are beautiful even though you don't have particularly good features."

"You're prejudiced," Sandy said.

"Admittedly."

"Go to sleep."

"I intend to," he said. He whacked her solidly on the buttocks, got into bed, turned over and was asleep before she got the light off.

She lay there in the darkness, smelling gardenias again, drifting finally into sleep where in a dream Bill Friday and Kurt were playing bowls in the old cemetery and Kurt said to her, "Look at old Bill. He's been asleep twenty years and came back just for today to play this game of bowls with me." She was sitting on the edge of a tombstone drinking something wonderfully delicious out of a shell that was iridescent and she said, "I knew you two would like each other." Then suddenly Clarissa was there saying, "There you go, always trying to change the world."

The baby got Shari Cross Adams up at four o'clock. She'd been hopeful he was going to make it through the night, he did sometimes lately. She crawled out of bed and went into the kitchen and took the bottle out of the refrigerator and put it on the stove. Then she went back and changed him and picked him up. Bill hadn't even moved. She made a face at him and went into the kitchen with the baby. He screwed his face up at the light and started to cry again. She made noises at him and jiggled him up and down and he stopped for a minute, hiccupped, then started in louder than ever. "You're a pig," she said, looking at him. "You're a small greedy pig and I love you." She kissed his red crying face and looked over her shoulder as though someone might be observing her in an indecent act.

She took the bottle out of the pan, saw it was too hot and ran cold water over it. The baby was howling now. Finally the milk tested out right and she went into the living room and sat down with him. The sudden silence when she put the bottle in his mouth always amused her. Just guk, and he'd stop, right in the middle of a new yell. She yawned and watched him pulling on the nipple.

All at once she thought about her mother and this crazy thing that had happened at the university. It gave her a weird feeling. She never could imagine her mother as a college girl, even though she knew perfectly well she had been. It was like looking at old photographs. You saw them, but you didn't believe them. This thing gave it all a different look too. It meant that not only had her mother been a college girl, but she'd been one just like she had, living with a bunch of other girls, all of them involved with men and sex and love—the whole bit.

Not that she didn't know her mother was an attractive sexy woman. She did know that, but in an abstract sort of way, like you know movie stars must be real people with real lives somewhere, but you can't quite grasp the reality of it.

She realized she was avoiding the real thought that bugged her. She pulled the bottle out of the baby's mouth and burped him. He watched her out of bright eyes until she gave it back to him. She grinned at him. He continued to eat solemnly.

"Yep," she said. "What's really bugging me, little one, is that your grandma might have done the deed. And of course I don't for one minute really believe she did it. Not Mother. But then, I can't imagine Mrs. Mackintosh or Mrs. Friday or B.J. or any of them doing it."

Still she said again to the baby, "Not Mother. That's just ridiculous."

A strange thought struck her and she sat still, looking down at the baby in her lap. "Will the day come, sweetie," she said, "when you make great and certain assumptions like that about *me* just because I'm your *mother*?"

The baby was almost through with his bottle now and his eyes began to close. He sucked slower and slower. She watched him in faint astonishment. Why I *am* your mother, she thought. I'm your *mother*. It scared her a little, and gave her a warm feeling, too.

The baby quit sucking and she stood up with him, holding him on her shoulder. He burped, his head lolled, and he was sound asleep again. She took him in and put him in bed. She looked at his round head on the white sheet and at the small fist tucked against his side.

"But that's an awful responsibility," she whispered.

The baby slept on.

"You have no idea, dear one, how vulnerable you have just made me feel."

Bill turned over, groaned, sat up and looked at her. "What are you doing?" he said. "Come on to bed."

She got into bed beside him. "Bill?" she said.

He mumbled at her.

She shook him. "Don't go back to sleep," she said. "I want to tell you something."

"In the morning."

"No. Now. Do you realize we're that baby's mother and father? And that he will be a person and everything we do will be something he remembers?"

"Gug," Bill said.

"Bill. It's scary."

But like his son he was already sound asleep.

The morning dawned clear and cool. The rain hadn't brought a cold front after all. Druid City rose early, looked out windows and doors, changed their mind about the clothes they were going to put on and what they were going to have for breakfast. Those who had a place to go went. The others stayed at home.

At ten o'clock Gus Thurgood and Jimmy Lou Allbright met Deputy Clancy Lenord, Deputy Jim Winston, and Dr. Frank Plowden in the corridor of the Druid County Court House. None of them had very much to say to each other.

"Judge Palmer managed to keep the hearing closed," Gus said, and there was a general sound of approval. There had been no way to keep people away from the courthouse so there was a general murmur in the air from the people who were standing around outside and the people in the corridors. Frank was glad Layne hadn't come with him after all. Just being a girl would have been enough to get her stared at this morning.

They filed into the judge's chambers and E. K. Edwards and the university police got up to meet them. A few moments later Miley Innes came in. They all sat down and looked uneasily at each other until the judge came in.

It went very quickly. Miley testified to finding the bones, E. K. Edwards testified to being called and calling the Law, Gus testified as to what he found and the deputies backed him up. Frank testified as to condition of said bones.

The judge asked a few questions in a mild voice, shuffled papers, scribbled on a pad and got up and left the room.

He came back, declared the incident a discovery of unidentified bones of infant, age unknown, cause of death

unknown, concealment of body by person or persons unknown . . .

It was over.

*At ten o'clock Edyth Innes was setting Mrs. Bentley Clay-
brook's hair.* She did it automatically, her eye on the clock,
her mind on Miley. Beneath the automatic and calm work
of her hands the other came back to her. Went away,
circled, stopped, went on.

*It was that hot night. It was ghastly. They had painted
that day and the smell was strong in all the hallways.
Nobody could sleep. Nobody did, all that summer. We used
to wear just our pants and that didn't help at all.*

*It was very late. It was after midnight. Something is
happening, I thought. Something will happen. Now. It was
a long time later when Clarissa went into the laundry room
and longer than that before she went up the stairs and
along that unfinished part of the floor. She went very
quietly, but I heard her. She went into that bathroom and
she seemed to stay forever, and then she went back downstairs again.*

*I lay there alone in that room, because we all had a room
to ourselves there being so few of us, and the fans from all
up and down the hall were making a noise, and it was so
hot, so damned hot.*

*I was thinking that Miley must never know about Bob, I
must never tell him because he'd never understand. I made
my life and the direction it took from that point. I was
wrong. I should have told him, not while he was overseas
like the selfish ones, but when he came back. Before he
married me. It would have saved a lot . . . wouldn't it? Or
would he just have left me then and we never have had a
chance at all? You just can't say. You just can't know. We
all of us do the best we can. We put the old things, the
things that didn't work, the things we don't want to look at,
in a hole in the wall. And we all hope we will be able to live
with it the day the walls come tumbling down.*

"You've done a very good job on my hair this morning,
Edyth," Mrs. Claybrook said.

She heard a car stop outside and knew it was Miley's. She

put Mrs. Claybrook under the dryer and went to the door. He had gotten out and was standing by the car. "It's over," he said quietly. "Person or persons unknown.

"Will you be going on to work now?" she said.

He nodded. "As soon as I can go home and get out of this suit."

She looked at him and crossed over to him and took a Kleenex from her pocket and wiped at his face. "You cut yourself shaving this morning," she said.

He looked at her, swiped at his face. Then he grinned. "What is it you're always saying?" he said. "It keeps the elephants away?"

She smiled at him. "And the stars way up there where they belong," she said.

"I'll see you at supper," Miley said.

"Is there anything special you'd like to have?"

"Try steak," he said. He got in the car and drove away.

She stood for a moment watching him till the car was out of sight. Then she went back in and took Janet Levy out from under the dryer and got ready to comb her out.

At ten o'clock Mary Alice took the receipts into her little cubbyhole of an office and sat down at the desk as though she were going to work on them. She drew the curtain over the door and told Sue to handle any customers. She sat there for a while, looking at the neat slips of paper and the lined pages of the ledger.

I will think about it once, she thought. Now. And not anymore. Not anymore because there isn't ever going to be another need.

It was after midnight. I know because it always got hotter after midnight. Suddenly it would be simply stifling, and the fans seemed to throw out hot air. Even if you'd managed to get to sleep before that you'd wake up. I heard something down in the kitchen. It scared me to death. Then I realized it was Clarissa. Nobody else would move around the kitchen that surely. I thought, Why is she still here? Isn't she going home tonight? And I thought, She knows somebody's in trouble or is going to need her, because she always knows. At some time or other she's helped us all.

301

I remember staring at my face in the bathroom mirror. It didn't look like my face at all. It was very strange and pale. I went on back to the bedroom and took off my pajamas because it was too hot. I thought, I am a married woman. I wonder what all the other girls would think if they knew that? I know what my mother would think. She'd disown me. She always had the idea I was too pretty for my own good.

Everybody in the house was awake except that stupid housemother. Isn't it strange how I realize that now? The next morning nobody came to breakfast. And for a whole week after that everybody was peculiar. I guess everybody heard Clarissa. She couldn't be quiet stepping over all those boards. And there was that feeling . . . something . . . Nobody went into that laundry room for a week.

I cried for a long time about Lew that night. I really thought he'd never come home from the war. And I was afraid, afraid my mother might be right and all he wanted was that. God, how she raised us to feel that way, as though that couldn't mean anything. At least Shari didn't have to start life with that handicap. I wonder if that old attitude has been there all the time, underneath, the real thing that has kept my marriage from being as close as it might have been. I don't know, can't know, but there's this one thing —I've been able to talk to Lew like I never have before. When we build the house I will not have to feel that it is some sort of end. It won't be the end of anything. Anymore than that dark night was. Nothing ever is.

After a while she picked up the slips and began to enter them in the ledger. She kept a very orderly set of books.

"Sleep in, this morning," J.D. had told B.J. So she was luxuriating in bed with a breakfast tray. She was feeling wonderful and lazy and contented like a horrible big cat on a cushion, and then she remembered the details. Just like that. Maybe because of the hearing. She realized it was ten o'clock, an improbable time for B.J. Finch to be in bed, and then it all just walked into her mind.

She'd gone out to the Coke machine about midnight. It

had jammed and she'd had to beat on it with a broom handle that they kept handy for that purpose. Then it had kept her nickel and she didn't have any more change. She'd knocked on Martha's door because Martha always had change and Martha had said, "My God, B.J., don't you ever go to bed?" and she'd said, "Your light was on." Martha had opened the door a crack, looking hateful, and handed her a dime.

She'd taken the Coke back to her room and drunk it and then it had gotten so awfully quiet. There were just the damned fans running and Clarissa messing around down in the kitchen. She'd thought, She must have stayed over tonight to fix pancakes or something fancy for breakfast. And next morning nobody had gone to breakfast. Nobody at all.

It had smelled terribly of paint and about an hour after she had the Coke she'd felt sick and had to go throw it up. It had made her furious because she never threw up, and then she'd started to cry. She'd stood there in the shower room crying, and she'd thought, I knew he didn't really care anything about me. He liked my tennis. Because maybe Joan Holmes would never know it, but she'd known about that. She'd seen him look at Joan one day and just known. So now here Joan was going to marry Bill Friday and that was the reason she was crying. Not because a tennis bum hadn't really loved her. What the hell. But because Joan Holmes was fixing to get married to Bill Friday, all smirks in a white dress.

She'd slept some then and been waked up, by somebody else crying. It wasn't unusual. There is always a lot of crying around a girl's dorm or sorority house. It's just the way it is. But it had made her panicky there in the dark. It had scared her knowing somebody else was awake and liable to stay that way, crying. It must have been daylight when she went back down to the shower room. The door to the laundry room was closed and it frightened her. She'd looked away from it and the lights in the hallway had seemed unreal and unnatural to her like the lights in a morgue. The paint smell got better with dawn and the fans started putting out a little cool air then. And Clarissa was *still moving around down in that kitchen when daylight came.*

Why were we all so sad then? she thought. Every one of us. That's why nobody came to breakfast on that Sunday morning. We were all sad and afraid and felt something . . . or knew something . . . and not one of us tried to help each other. We were all afraid of each other. Which isn't a pretty thing to think about the human race. Only Clarissa, she didn't feel that way. She was always there. Maybe that's why I want to be always there if the kids do happen to holler. Maybe that night will always be walled up in me somewhere in all its details and maybe the lonely places are the only things that make human beings of us all.

"Mother," Jim said from the doorway.

"What, love?"

"Aren't you *ever* going to get up?"

She laughed. "What do you want me to do?" she said.

He looked puzzled. "Why nothing," he said. "I just want you up."

She got out of bed and put the rest of her jam on a piece of toast and handed it to him. "Eat that," she said. "I'll go dress."

"Did you find your nail scissors?" he said.

"No. Are they missing?"

"Liza broke them."

"Oh, Jim, don't tattle."

"You'd find them anyway," he said. "They're in your powder box in the bathroom. It's not a very good place."

B.J. laughed. "Where would you have hidden them?" she said.

"I don't tattle," he said. He gave her a jam-smeared smile. "Well, I'll go now. I just wanted you to get up."

"Mission accomplished, sir," B.J. said. She went into the bathroom and ran the water for her bath.

The scissors had been lying on the lavatory, Martha remembered. Between the faucets, the scissors from the sewing kit they kept in the little upstairs living room. She'd looked at them for a long time, and then she'd taken them two doors down and put them back in the sewing kit.

Somebody had been crying somewhere. Somebody was always crying. What the hell was wrong with the human race? If she knew that maybe she'd know what was wrong with Frank. What made him do crazy things like fall for such odd women or act put upon about doing the very thing he wanted to do like going to med school? Or resist her when he knew he loved her? She was thirsty and annoyed because B.J. had taken her last dime for the Coke machine and it was dark in her room now. It was dark all up and down the hall inside the rooms. There were only the hall lights, like a hospital, and the bathroom lights. The light wasn't on in the laundry room like it should be. I'm not thinking good tonight, she thought. Frank's upset me again. He is going to come back to me, of course, so why does he do these things?

She went down the empty hall, her houseshoes quiet on the tile floor, and reached her hand inside the laundry room and flipped the light switch back up and shut the door. I could ask Clarissa for change, she thought. She is still up there in that kitchen like some ancient sibyl. But I don't want to ask her. I'll drink tap water. She'd gone back to her room and had some tap water and it had been uneasy on her stomach. Then her fan had quit. Just quit. It had seemed horribly unfair. It was so hot and the paint smell was so strong and she couldn't have a Coke. She began to think she could hear more than one person crying. It was a bad night for everybody, like the time she'd come in drunk from Frank's and found everybody in a mess and B.J. had kept saying, "But it's Tuesday. It's just Tuesday."

She must have dozed off because when she woke up she could hear somebody coming down the stairs from the unfinished part of the building, and she hadn't heard them go up. They came down very slowly and quietly and then they went on down the back stairs to the main floor. So it was Clarissa. She'd lain there till dawn before she went to sleep.

"Martha," the managing editor said.

"Yessir?"

"You want this story on the opening of the new country club?"

"All right," she said.

305

"There's another item concerning Mr. Ridley," he said. "He's taken a long-term lease on some of that university property down near the river. You might combine the stories."

"Yessir," she said.

"I didn't know that land could be leased," the editor said.

"Yes. I remember hearing there's some sort of loophole," Martha said. "In fact, I think the only land in town without a loophole is that land of Bill Friday's. After Joan and Dylan are both gone it reverts to the university for perpetuity," she said.

"Why do you suppose Bill did that?" the editor said.

"I don't know. Maybe he saw Oscar coming down the pike a long time ago," Martha said.

"Well, it's a nice thing to leave behind him," the editor said.

"He left poems too," Martha said. "What is that quote?"

"Have a child, plant a tree, write a book," the editor said.

"So he made it," Martha said.

"Well, do the story."

"Yessir."

He went away and she started hearing the presses again. She took out Janice's last letter, read it again, shrugged, and put paper in her machine. But nothing came. She just sat there, staring at the blank sheet of paper in front of her and after a while she realized she was thinking, "What did I do wrong?"

Joan hadn't gotten up when she'd heard Dylan and Miranda come in for pie and coffee the night before. She'd been awake, she'd heard the car come up the hill, heard them whispering and laughing in the kitchen. But she didn't get up, she didn't need to anymore. It had been very late and she was sleepy this morning because of it. She'd had to make an effort to be cheerful at breakfast. At ten o'clock she was still wishing she could go back to bed. Clara brought her a cup of coffee and she lay back on her chaise longue to drink it. It was a nice morning, cool and fair, just the way it had been the day the whole mess started. Well, at any rate it was going to be over soon. The speculations would go on, but then they always did. She had the beginnings of a headache, and she went to the medicine cabinet and got two aspirin. She stood in the bathroom washing them down with a glass of tap water and with the action all of it came back to her.

She'd been planning the wedding. That was what she did on the hot nights when she couldn't sleep well, laying out in her mind the kind of dress she wanted, the music, the flowers, the champagne punch, the cake with the little white ribbons with the silver charms for the bridesmaids. She started having the headache. It was the paint. That damned paint smell was driving all of them crazy. She looked in her purse, but the little tin box of aspirin was empty. She so seldom ever took an aspirin that she hadn't looked lately, and people borrowed them. The rooms up and down the hall were all dark and she didn't want to wake anybody. She could hear Clarissa downstairs but she didn't like to always and forever be asking Clarissa for something. Then she remembered the emergency kit. They'd got it together one weekend after somebody had tripped over some ·of the boards for the new addition and cut their leg. Everybody had put something in. There were bandages and iodine and Mary Alice had gotten some sulfa powder from Lew, and Martha had gotten some benzedrine and some seconal from some med student friend of Frank's. There were even a couple of phenobarbitals and two morphine tablets that one of Sandy's crazy friends had contributed. There was a bottle of aspirin, too. She'd gone down the hall to the bathroom and looked in the little box, but the bottle of aspirin was empty. She'd stood there looking at it and wondering if she dared take some of the stronger stuff. Then she'd heard somebody crying. She'd gone on back to her room and the headache got worse. She'd dozed off and come awake, more than once, and every time the sound of the fans seemed to be louder and the smell of the paint stronger. She was sweating, too. She'd had to get up and change her sheets. That was after she'd heard Clarissa go upstairs. The laundry room door had been shut, but the light was on. It was a *clean, small, lighted room, with shelves for the linen and baskets for the dirty clothes, and a sink and an ironing board and two straight chairs. It didn't have any windows.*

She hadn't slept really until almost daylight. She had been afraid. They had all been afraid. She knew that now. Nobody came to breakfast. Clarissa never did go home. A week later somebody had said that an awful lot of things seemed to be missing out of the emergency kit, but nobody ever said what they'd used. And after a while they forgot about it. The emergency kit had smelled of adhesive and very faintly of ether—she couldn't imagine why. Maybe some of the things had come out of some lab or office or something. It was funny too that she could remember smelling that when there had been so much paint.

Her head was aching worse now and she took another aspirin. She looked at her watch. It was eleven o'clock. She firmly closed her mind to memory, closed the door of her room behind her, and went to the kitchen for more coffee.

Clara looked at her. "You looking kind of peaked, Miss Joan."

"Just a headache," she said. "It'll be all right after I eat lunch."

She got her appointment calendar and looked at all the things she needed to do and had needed to do all week and had been neglecting due to this thing and to Dylan. She firmly made a list of phone calls to make and went to the hall phone. She called Meredith first.

"Hello, dear?" she said. "This is Joan. I guess we're all back to business as usual this morning. Have you made a decision about the new country club yet?"

From the front of the store Meredith could see across to the courthouse. There were a lot of people milling around but as nothing seemed to be happening some of them had started drifting away toward the drugstore across the street. She looked up at the curtained windows as though she could see something through them, but they were just windows. Syd came up and put his arm around her.

"It will go very quickly and be over," he said.

"Yes," Meredith said. "Nothing ever just stops still. It

goes right on from this to that, from yesterday to tomorrow. Sometimes it doesn't seem as though there's any today."

Syd frowned at her. "That sounds unlike you."

"I'm nervous," Meredith said. "I've been wanting to bite my fingernails all morning. I thought I'd gotten over that habit years ago. The only time I've done it since we've been married is when I went to the hospital to have Candace. It was so peculiar. Here I was a grown woman with a baby of my own at last and there I was biting my damned fingernails again." She laughed.

"What say I go out and bring us some coffee and doughnuts?" Syd said.

She looked at him. "You don't mind?"

"No," he said. "I don't mind."

She kissed him on the cheek and he went out and up the street toward the drugstore. She watched him, being watched by the people standing around in the street. Irving came to the front of the store. "He's a pretty good boy," he said quietly.

Meredith smiled at him. "I figured that out a long time ago, Irving," she said. "That's what you and I had to have a fight about."

"I'm glad I lost," Irving said. He went back to the back of the store and left her to wait for Syd.

She caught herself just before she put her hand to her mouth. It was so crazy. She never wanted to bite her nails anymore.

She'd been biting them that night. She'd bitten them right down to the quick. It was a bad night. Sinister. Too hot, too still. They'd needed a thunderstorm. They would have all been so happy for rain. She had sat on the edge of her bed, looking at the blackness outside the window, and she'd thought, If it should rain we would all be capable of dashing out in the middle of it and doing a dance of thanksgiving in our birthday suits. We all would give our souls for a little rain. She had prayed all night for the payphone to ring, but it never had. It hadn't rung for anybody that night . . . not once . . . and that was odd too. There was nearly always a call for somebody. In a way she was glad it hadn't rung. If it had and had been for someone else it would have been even worse than the waiting and waiting and no ring at all.

About midnight she heard B.J. go to the Coke machine and bang on it with the broom handle. Then it had gotten still again except for somebody crying and somebody whoopsing in the john once, and the shower running. And people walking up and down the hall. Somebody or other had walked up and down the hall all night long. Or maybe she only dreamed that, dreamed it in the half-waking, half-sleeping spells she'd had the whole night long. Dreamed that like the two real dreams she had had and never forgotten.

The first dream had been about her and Syd. They were sitting in front of the fireplace like Evelyn and Burke and it had been Irving offering Syd the drink in the silver glass and Syd taking it. She'd come up out of sleep with a shock. It had been like having a terrible nightmare, only the dream itself didn't seem to be really frightening at all. Our God is a jealous God, she'd said. And went back to sleep and had another dream that was much worse. In this one she had been hiding in a bush and seen Syd as Abraham with the knife poised over Isaac and she'd tried to yell at him, tried to say, There is a ram in the bush, take that, take that. But he had gone right on raising the knife and she'd screamed, and was awake again in the heat and the paint smell and the sounds of the fans running like the sound of an infernal machine. She had opened her door because she thought there might be some chance of a draft, but there wasn't. The light kept coming into the room and then a shadow crossed it and she looked out and saw Clarissa going by.

It had been so strange, like one of the Fates passing. She was walking so slow and she looked so sad. She thought, I'm afraid. Then she heard a door opened and shut and then steps going on up the stairs. After eternity Clarissa went back by the door again. She was hugging her elbows with her hands and she was crying. Somebody had been crying all night long.

It had taken a week for any of them to get that night out of their minds. It was like a hole in the universe. The black

310

Horsehead Nebula, that night. And they had all covered it up just as Clarissa had done. Well, maybe you had to with some things sometime. Maybe, too, there had to come the time to take them out and look at them before you could put them away again, maybe forever this time.

Syd came in with the coffee and they went behind the cash register and sat down together.

"The doughnuts are wonderful," she said. "Anything happen in the drugstore?"

"No, of course not."

"I was thinking about Sandy in that store last night."

"People don't snigger at somebody who looks capable of knocking them down," Syd said.

The phone rang. Meredith put down her coffee and picked it up. "Hello, Joan," she said.

Syd and Irving were both watching her and she winked at them. "Yes, I've thought about it," she said. "I'm not interested in joining." She waited a minute. "No, Joan. I don't want to be nasty, but I'm just not interested in being your token Jew." She saw Irving grin and look away from her. "But it is," she said. "If we join it kills two birds with one stone. To the entrance committee I'm not really a Jew, so they have an excuse, and at the same time they can point at Syd when anybody accuses them of having a restriction clause. No, thanks. No. It hasn't anything to do with being tired or upset this week. I decided all this a long time ago. About twenty years ago, in fact. Sandy?" She smiled. "Ask her." She waited again. "Of course no hard feelings. Of course we'll come to your dinner party next week." She looked up at Syd and winked. "No, I don't have a new car," she said. "You must have seen me driving Irving's. Isn't it beautiful? Goodbye."

She put down the phone and picked up her doughnut. "It doesn't look like anybody at all is going to buy any shoes this morning," she said.

"Do you want me to stay home today?" Kurt said.

"Do you want to?" Sandy said.

"Yes. I'll call in. You call the kid to take over for you.

311

We'll go back to sleep if you want and later we can drink coffee and read the paper and be disgustingly lazy."

Sandy got out of bed. "You just want to sleep late," she said, smiling at him. "I bet you don't want to keep me company at all."

"Ummm."

"I'll go get the kids off to school."

In the kitchen she fed them cornflakes and toast. "Have a bad dream last night, buster?" she asked Kim.

"I sure did," he said. He drowned his cornflakes with milk and looked at them. "It was about a bear."

"That's pretty bad," Sandy said. "But I gather Clarissa came to the rescue."

"Oh, sure. She sang songs."

"I think he just has bad dreams when Clarissa's here to get the songs," Mark said.

"She sings all sorts of things about Jesus," Kim said. "Then she sings other things about people riding on freight trains . . . things like that."

"No more bad dreams after the songs, huh?" Sandy said.

"No. Never after that," Kim said.

The songs against the dark, Sandy thought. We all have that. That night I had been in the library playing the Bolero and the Concerto for Left Hand. Sitting all by myself in one of those little cubicles wishing for something . . . I wasn't even sure what. Ravel to keep the bad dreams away. We all needed something that night. It wasn't a good time. It hadn't rained all week and it got sultrier and sultrier and nothing ever happened. Sometimes there was a little sheet lightning on the horizon, but it never built into thunderheads. They'd painted again, that third-floor hall. They kept saying they'd be through with the work soon, but they never seemed to get through. Just hammered and banged away and painted something else. I walked home from the library by myself and I didn't pass a single soul between there and the house. It was spooky. When I went in, that idiot, Mrs. Cowan, was sitting there at the desk and she said, "All the girls are in now, dear, would you help me lock up?" So I did. That was eerie too, me and that old lady

312

with the hairpins falling out of her hair walking around from door to door locking in the maidens, locking out who knew what.

We went in the kitchen and Clarissa was in there. She was sitting at the table drinking a cup of coffee and Mrs. Cowan said, "Aren't you going home tonight, Clarissa?" Sometimes she didn't when there was going to be a souffle for breakfast or when the weather was real bad. But there wasn't any reason for her staying that night. I could tell Mrs. Cowan was surprised to see her sitting there. "I 'spect I'll be staying," Clarissa said. Just that. And Mrs. Cowan said, "Well, if you decide to leave, lock the back door good." "Yessum," she said.

I went upstairs. Everybody was already in their rooms, some of the doors were shut and all the fans were on. The hall lights were burning down the length of emptiness; there was a light in the shower and in the laundry room. It looked dark up the stairs to the third floor because they were changing the fixtures up there and there wasn't a new one for the stairwell yet. I went over to the foot of the stairs and looked up. It reminded me of murder mysteries. What was that one? The Door? Then Martha came out into the hall in her bathrobe and said, "Sandy, what are you sneaking around here about?" "I wasn't sneaking," I said. "I just came in." She said, "Oh. It sure is hot, isn't it? Good night," and went back to her room. I walked on down to my room and got undressed. The paint smell was awful. It made all of us feel bad, especially on a heavy night like this. I kept thinking about Bill. I couldn't seem to help it. Joan had told us he wanted to marry her. I knew it was absolutely and exactly right, and I hated knowing it. I kept thinking all the time I was playing Ravel over in that library, What is wrong with me? Why do I fall in love with the most beautifully wrong person for me in the whole universe? How could I possibly fall in love with anybody who'd marry Joan Holmes? I wanted somebody to talk to so I put my slippers and robe on and went out in the hall and looked for lights under the doors. Meredith's was on and I knocked and went in and sat on the foot of her bed for a while. We

313

covered the weather and men. At that moment we both hated both of them. Then I went on back to my room. I. heard B.J. come out and beat the Coke machine. Then everything got quiet.

I don't know what woke me up. But I never woke up so quickly, before or since. I came up out of sleep like touching bottom after jumping into deep water. Rising straight up to the top, surfacing and gasping at finding air again. I was scared. *What time is it?* I said out loud and I scared myself saying it. My little alarm clock was ticking away on the dresser and I looked at it. The luminous dial said three o'clock. *What is it about three o'clock?* I felt nauseated. I got up and went to the window and leaned against the screen, but there wasn't a breath of air. The sky was dark and full of stars. Somebody was crying. Somebody was saying something just under audibility. I opened the door and looked down the hall. Nothing. Nobody. *I'm scared,* I thought, and I could feel my heart beating, banging away inside me like a damned cornered animal's. Something moved downstairs and it beat harder. Then I ran down there, all the way down the back stairs, almost tripping once, having to catch myself to keep from rolling all the way down. I turned my ankle, but I didn't even notice it then, not until the next day.

I went in the kitchen door and Clarissa was sitting there at the table, just as she had been hours ago. She turned and looked at me. "Clarissa, Clarissa," I whispered at her, "there is something terribly wrong." She shook her head at me and put her finger to her lips. Then she must have seen how really panicky I was. She stood up and came over to me and put her arms around me, rocking me back and forth like a baby. "It's all right, honey," she said. "Everything's all right. It's just a bad dream. You go on back upstairs now. Clarissa's down here, taking care of everything." I knew she was. I went back upstairs.

"Mama," Kim said. "Mama!"

"What, honey?" Sandy said.

"It's time to go."

"All right." She got up and automatically brushed hair,

314

found sweaters. She stood at the door, watching them to the corner. Then she went back to the kitchen and sat looking out at the new-washed grass.

I was so scared and so sick, but all the time I kept thinking, Clarissa is down there . . . in the kitchen . . . and somehow I'll get through this too. And I did, even if I can't stand to think about it, even now, after all these years. I got through it, just like I got through Bill betraying me. And I'll get through today too. But I wish, I really wish, Kurt had gone to work. I won't cry, though, she thought, and remembered how she had cried, but that finally she'd gone to sleep because Clarissa was going to do something and she didn't have to think anymore about tomorrow. *And I didn't beg,* she thought, a little proudly. *I never begged. Even though losing Bill when I needed him the most was the worst thing that ever happened . . . even worse than losing him the final time. Because I can still get that stab of useless love, for what is only white bleached bones, the both of you. Bare lovely bones where love was. Where love is. Because love was mine and I am still right here. Poor Sandy and Bill and little lost hope. The eternal footman was sniggering . . . even then.*

The day Joan buried Bill it had rained. She had stood there, watching the widow strew the flowers, saying to herself, *Oh, come on, Sandy. He has been dead for you for a long time, my girl. Don't go to pieces now. Don't keep weeping. They won't resurrect him.* But they had the baby. Yes, indeed. They had resurrected that.

And good God in your Manichaean hell and heaven, who knows what will happen tomorrow? Because something always happens to Sandy. Life is like that for her. No talisman against encounter . . . an epitaph for this lady, who if there is any sort of justice anywhere will lie quiet once they get her under and be spared anything at all the other side of stars and sex.

"Kurt?" she said.

He came into the kitchen, tying the sash on his bathrobe, looking sleepy.

315

"I was in love with Bill Friday," she said.

"Bill Friday?" He looked at her, shook his head and reached for the coffeepot. "Bill Friday?" he said again. "But how very strange. He was such an ordinary man. I always thought that—what an ordinary man for a poet." He laughed. "And how extraordinary for you to have loved such an ordinary man."

Sandy smiled. "Well, in a way that was just it. Women feel they can make something extraordinary out of the ordinary if they just try. It's the great feminine fallacy. Or maybe that isn't true at all. Maybe there really isn't any reason for anything. Things just happen, or don't happen. What the hell. But something else. Something you said last night. You said I had a great capacity for love. Everybody has, Kurt. Everybody. And for hate and fear and sorrow and rage and need. That's why this dragging up of the past has been hard on everybody. The capacity was there, for all of us. The special kinds of love and sorrow and fear. God help us, we all live in a fearsome place. We all need somebody down in the kitchen to tell us it was all a bad dream."

"You are in my kitchen," Kurt said.

"Yes," Sandy said. "How do you want your eggs?"

It took him till four in the morning to finish the sonnet. He typed it up and slept till eight and had breakfast with his mother. He met Miranda at nine o'clock at the College Inn.

"I am very sleepy, Dylan my love," Miranda said. "You are keeping me out much too late. I'm going to lose my youthful good looks."

"It is not bloody likely," Dylan said. "Drink your coffee. I've brought you a present."

"A present for breakfast? How perfectly wonderful," Miranda said. "Only I'm not alive yet. Another cup of coffee?"

"All right," Dylan said.

He watched her drinking it, then gave her the sonnet. She sat perfectly still reading it, her long hair hanging
316

across her face, her lips going soft, eyes blinking to keep the tears back. He didn't think it was much of a sonnet. It was nothing like as good as the worst of his father's. But it said what he wanted to say. It was something for Miranda. She would understand exactly why he'd written it. She read it:

> I wish that I could keep you in the garden
> Knowing full well you'd always seek the gate
> You'd leave the east of spring for the west of autumn
> The least of love for the highest form of hate
> You were not made for pale or partial passions
> I couldn't hold you with the snares I'd make
> If I try to make you faithful in my fashion
> I know full well you'd leave me for the snake.
>
> So, Miranda, I must say I love you
> Accept by saying it the turning sword
> Be thrust out in a world of sweat and metal
> To begat Cain and tie the silver cord
> So bring the apple, darling, on a platter
> The first bite's the hardest, after that, no matter.

She looked up at him. "I love you," she said.

It wasn't really hard to say at all he found out. "I love you, too," he said.

On the following Monday March had already come. The winds were warmer, the buttercups bloomed. Miley Innes supervised the laying of the cornerstone for the new Delta House. They didn't have a ceremony because everyone had decided it was in the best interests of all not to. So there was only him and the Negro straw-boss and three helpers. They got it in the ground and all stood around having a cigarette.

It was going to be a mild blue and gold day, Miley thought. They had plenty of time to get this building up before school started next September. He squinted up at the sky. He figured they would probably top out by, say, the twenty-eighth of August. He tossed his cigarette away and jacked up a trowel.

"O.K., boys," he said. "Let's build a wall."